Now professor emeritus, Harry Sturz was for many years Professor of Greek and Chairman of the Theology Department at Biola University in LaMirada, California. He became interested in early papyri and New Testament textual criticism while studying with E. C. Colwell at the School of Theology in Claremont, California. During this time he also participated in work on the *International Greek New Testament* project on Luke.

An ordained minister in the National Fellowship of Grace Brethren Churches, he received his graduate and post-graduate degrees from Grace Theological Seminary in Winona Lake, Indiana.

The Byzantine Text-Type
and
New Testament Textual Criticism

The Byzantine Text-Type
and
New Testament Textual Criticism

by Harry A. Sturz

THOMAS NELSON PUBLISHERS
Nashville • Camden • New York

Published in the United States in Nashville, Tennessee, by Thomas Nelson, Inc., Publishers and distributed in Canada by Lawson Falle, Ltd., Cambridge, Ontario.

Library of Congress Cataloging in Publication Data

Sturz, Harry A.
  The Byzantine text-type and New Testament textual criticism.
    Thesis (Th. D)—Grace Theological Seminary, 1967.
    Bibliography: p.
    Includes indexes.
    1. Bible. N.T.—Criticism, Textual.   I. Title.
BS2555.2.S78   1984   225.4'8   84-11479
ISBN 0-8407-4958-9

Printed in the United States of America

Contents

Preface

Widely different views are currently held on the history and usefulness of the type of text represented by the mass of the later manuscripts of the New Testament. Because of this, settling the question of the Byzantine text-type is essential for any student of the New Testament who seeks a means of evaluating external evidence for readings. The crucial nature of the problem is clear from the fact that the "history of the New Testament text" held by the critic largely determines whether he will set aside the testimony of the mass of the MSS or will take it into account in decision-making at places of variation. The "history of the text" he accepts and follows is unavoidably, even if unconsciously, an influential factor in his evaluation of evidence for readings.

His judgment regarding the value and usefulness of the Byzantine text may often make the difference in whether the textual student follows the reading printed in his edited Greek text or prefers a reading the editors have relegated to the critical apparatus. 1) If the critic holds that the Byzantine text represents a late, secondary and corrupt stage of the New Testament and that the Alexandrian text, e.g., best represents the original (Westcott and Hort *et al*), he quite naturally dismisses the Byzantine text from consideration and follows the reading(s) of the Alexandrian text. 2) However, if he holds that the Byzantine represents the "traditional" or original text most accurately, and that other texts are corruptions of it (Burgon *et al*),

9

he naturally gives the Byzantine supreme authority and the readings of the differing texts are relegated to the apparatus. 3) If, on the other hand, he believes that the "history of the text" is largely untraceable and that none of the text-types or MSS are capable of supplying any real external weight of attestation (Kilpatrick *et al*), his decision-making will rely chiefly upon internal (transcriptional, intrinsic and stylistic) evidence of readings. 4) However, if he believes that each of the main text-types (including the Byzantine) are equally old and relatively independent from each other, he will include the Byzantine testimony along with the others in order to determine external weight and spread of testimony.

The investigation lying behind the original dissertation on which this book is based was to see if there were valid reasons for making use of the Byzantine text-type as an early and independent witness to the text of the New Testament. The investigation having been made and with the conviction that such reasons exist, this treatment seeks to present a case for including the Byzantine text-type in the weighing of external evidence for various readings to the Greek text of the New Textament.

PART I

Current Attitudes Toward the Byzantine Text

CHAPTER I

Background

"Byzantine" refers to that type of text which characterizes the majority of the later Greek uncial, semi-uncial and minuscule manuscripts of the New Testament. It is also the type of text found in the Syriac Peshitta and Gothic versions and in the extant quotations of Church Fathers from Chrysostom on. This text derives its name from the provenance (origin) of most of its manuscripts: the Byzantine Empire. It has, in addition to "Byzantine," been called: "Antiochian," after the supposed place of its origin, and the "Lucian Recension," after its supposed editor. It is Semler's "Oriental," Bengel's "Asiatic," Griesbach's "Constantinopolitan," Westcott and Hort's "Syrian," and Burgon's "Traditional." Other designations of the same text include: von Soden and Merk's "K," standing for "Koine" or "Common" text, Lagrange's "A," and Kenyon's "Alpha." It is largely the text which lies behind the *Textus Receptus* and the *King James Version*. In this book the Byzantine text will be referred to more or less indiscriminately by the use of several of the above terms, especially those currently being used by writers in this area of study.[1]

---

[1]It should be noted that the early and later stages of the Byzantine text are sometimes distinguished by various authors. Westcott and Hort used the term "Constantinopolitan" when they wished to indicate a later "Syrian" text reading where an earlier and later stage might be discerned in the attestation of a passage. In these instances "Syrian" was reserved for the earlier stage. (For an example see Hort's "Notes on Select Readings," *The New Testament in the Original Greek*.)

The Byzantine text has had its ups and downs. Especially is this true with regard to what is generally thought of as its chief representative: the *Textus Receptus* (TR). Most textual students of the New Testament would agree that the TR was made from a few medieval Greek manuscripts, mostly Byzantine, of Von Soden's K^x strand. They would further concur that the TR, though it brought the students and translators of the New Testament infinitely closer to the originals than the Latin Vulgate, was far from the pure text of the original autographs. Indeed, it was "the text received by all" and therefore the text used by all.[2] However, the principal reason for this was probably the fact that it was the only text available to all.

Though voices began to be raised for revision of the TR early in the eighteenth century, its sway was not broken until the nineteenth century. Beginning with Karl Lachmann's bold exclusion of the late manuscripts in publishing his reconstruction of a fourth-century text, efforts continued through the collating and editing labors of Constantine Tischendorf. The climax came with the use of the genealogical argument, which, as applied by Westcott and Hort (WH) gave the *coup de grace* to the Received Text.[3] The text of WH then replaced that of the TR, and the reign of the Byzantine text came to an end. From a position of exclusive use, it fell to a place of almost complete disuse. To this day, at least as far as the West is concerned, it has become the least-used text.[4]

Though the scholarly world for the most part accepted the overthrow of the TR and along with it the rejection of the Byzantine text-type, nevertheless the agreement was not unanimous. From the

[2]Bruce M. Metzger, *Chapters in the History of New Testament Textual Criticism* (Grand Rapids: Wm. B. Eerdmans, 1963). See his chapter on "The Lucianic Recension of the Greek Bible," and especially pages 27:30 for a concise summary of the influence of the Antiochian Text outside the Greek Church.

[3]For a lucid summary of this transition period and the supplanting of the *TR*, see Ernest Cadman Colwell, *What is the Best New Testament?* (Chicago: The University of Chicago Press, 1952), pp. 16-39; or Kirsopp Lake, *The Text of the New Testament* (6th ed. rev. by Silva New), 13th impression; London: Rivingtons, 1959, pp. 62-73. For a fuller treatment see M. R. Vincent, *A History of the Textual Criticism of the New Testament* (New York: Macmillan Co., 1899), pp. 53-109.

[4]The Eastern Church has consistently resisted attempts to revise its text and versions away from the Byzantine norm. Cf. Robert P. Casey, "A Russian Orthodox View of New Testament Textual Criticism," *Theology*, LX. No. 440 (1957), 50-54.

first there was a reaction on the part of some Biblical scholars led by John William Burgon, Dean of Chichester. He sought to refute the theory of WH and to support the text which lay behind the TR, which he called the "Traditional" text.

Two clear-cut attitudes toward the Byzantine text have persisted since the days of WH and Burgon and are still current today. There are those who follow the theory of WH, and there are some who adopt John Burgon's defense of the Traditional text. These two theories espouse diametrically opposed methods when it comes to the use of the Byzantine text-type in the textual criticism of the New Testament. There seems to be no possibility of harmonizing or reconciling the two viewpoints. Not only are they mutually exclusive, but the adherents of each claim to base their theory on "the facts." For example, Kirsopp Lake concludes his remarks on the theory of WH by saying:

> The fact of the "Syrian" revision is merely the deduction which W.H. drew from the facts. If any one can draw any other deduction, well and good. But the facts will not be altered, and they prove that the later text is definitely an eclectic one, posterior in date, as shown by Patristic evidence, both to the Neutral and Western texts.[5]

If anyone thinks that the unyielding stand of Lake (1st edition, 1900, and the 6th edition, 1928) would have no adherents in more recent time, the following statement by Charles Stephens Conway Williams will indicate that the view is still strongly held:

> But whether we adopt the hypothesis of a definite revision or that of a gradual process of change in order to account for the existence of the α [i.e. alpha or Byzantine] text, the *fact* of the existence of such a text remains, and its character as a secondary text of relatively late origin must be taken to be one of the established results of criticism [italics by Williams].[6]

[5]Lake, p. 72.
[6]"Text of the New Testament," *Dictionary of the Bible*, ed. James Hastings (rev. ed., ed. F. C. Grant and H. H. Rowley; New York: Charles Scribner's Sons, 1963), p. 992.

In direct contrast, the attitude of a modern textual critic who follows in the line of Burgon may be seen in a statement by Edward Hills:

> . . . therefore the Byzantine text found in the vast majority of the Greek New Testament manuscripts is that true text. To reject this view is to act unreasonably. It is to fly in the face of the facts.
>
> Those, moreover, who reject this orthodox view of the New Testament text have rejected not merely the facts but also the promise of Christ always to preserve the true New Testament text and the doctrines of the divine inspiration and providential preservation of the Scripture implied in this promise.[7]

These two views are obviously irreconcilable, and it would be impossible for one working with the text to hold both at the same time. Both cannot be true; either one or the other may be correct, or they may both be in error. The writer feels that neither of these two groups is right in its theory of the Byzantine text. Furthermore, it is felt that each of them is over-confident in asserting that the theory he follows is based on established facts. This book seeks to show that the claims of both lack a solid foundation.

A third attitude toward the use of the Byzantine text involves what might be termed the *eclectic approach*. This is held by some, who, because of certain recent discoveries, feel that WH were too severe in their condemnation of the "Syrian" text. They are, therefore, willing to acknowledge that the Byzantine text has preserved early and in rare instances even original readings which somehow have not been retained in the other text-types or in the early uncials. Most of the critics in this category advocate an "eclectic" method of textual criticism. This method endeavors to have no favorite manuscript and no preferred type of text. Those using the method profess to be willing to consider various readings, from whatever source they may come. On the basis of internal criteria, judgment is made between the readings as to which is most likely the original. The eclectic approach, though quite objective in the sense of being will-

---

[7]John W. Burgon, *The Last Twelve Verses of the Gospel According to S. Mark* with an introduction by Edward F. Hills (h.p.: Sovereign Grace Book Club, 1959), pp. 65-66.

ing to consider all readings, is admittedly very subjective in that much depends on the personal element in the evaluation of the evidence. A concise statement of the method, together with a comment on some of its weaknesses, may be found in Robert M. Grant's *A Historical Introduction to the New Testament:*

> F. C. Grant has listed three basic principles of textual criticism which deserve further analysis. They are these:
> "1. No one type of text is infallible, or to be preferred by virtue of its generally superior authority.
> 2. Each reading must be examined on its merits, and preference must be given to those readings which are demonstrably in the style of the author under consideration.
> 3. Readings which explain other variants, but are not contrariwise to be explained by the others, merit our preference; but this is a very subtle process, involving intangible elements, and liable to subjective judgment on the part of the critic."

Robert Grant evaluates these principles by pointing out that

> All three principles, indeed contain a large measure of subjectivity. The first is more valuable negatively than positively; it means basically that all manuscripts and all types of manuscripts may contain errors. The second point introduces literary criticism . . . into textual study, and makes us raise the question whether an author always writes in what we may call his style. If not, the principle is not altogether persuasive. The third brings us in the direction of historical cricitism . . . and since it is admittedly subjective we need say no more than that the meaning of "explain" is clearer than the means by which the principle is to be employed.[8]

One of the most thoroughgoing and consistent defenders of the eclectic method is George Dunbar Kilpatrick of Oxford, England, editor of the second edition of the British and Foreign Bible Society's "Nestle Text."[9] Kilpatrick seems to be determined to have no favorite text in his application of this method. His stance may be

[8]New York: Harper & Row, 1963, pp. 48-49.
[9]Η ΚΑΙΝΗ ΔΙΑΘΗΚΗ (London: 1958).

clearly seen in part of the concluding statement of his article: "An Eclectic Study of the Text of Acts."

> The readings which have been examined . . . seem to admit of certain conclusions. We have not sought to decide for one or another kind of text as a whole but have tried to consider each reading on its merits. Where readings remain unclassified we have found that no one text has a monopoly of error or of truth. The same is true for kinds of variation. . . . No manuscript or type of text is uniformly right or wrong.
>
> This conclusion applies as much to the Byzantine text, represented by HLPS and many minuscules, as to the Western text and the Old Uncials. The outright condemnation of the Byzantine text by Westcott and Hort was one of the main errors in practice of their work.[10]

Kilpatrick, however, proves to be rather unique in his consistent application of the principle of playing no favorites. He treats readings of the Byzantine text on a plane with those of the other text-types. Other writers and textual scholars have given lip-service to a similar approach, but in practice they do not appear to carry out the theory or the method with consistency, especially with regard to the consideration of Byzantine readings.[11]

Therefore, for all practical purposes, because of the low esteem in which the text is still held by most critics, a Byzantine reading does not generally receive much consideration even under the eclectic method unless it happens to be attested by an early papyrus or unless it offers the only really acceptable reading among the available variants.

That this is not an overstatement may be seen by an examination of the comments made by the authors of recent works on textual criticism as they discuss the application of method or the eclectic approach in examples of specific passages. The allusions which are made concerning the relative merit of types of texts, and of the Byzantine type in particular, reveal the low opinion in which it is

[10]*Biblical and Patristic Studies*, ed. J. Neville Birdsall and Robert W. Thompson (New York: Herder, 1963), p. 76.

[11]On eclecticism see Bruce M. Metzger, *The Text of the New Testament, Its Transmission, Corruption, and Restoration* (New York: Oxford University Press, 1964), pp. 175-79; and J. Elliott, E. Epp, G. Fee and J. Ross in the bibliography.

still held by most New Testament scholars. Vincent Taylor, for example, simply ignores the Byzantine evidence in his "Notes on Select Readings."[12] J. Harold Greenlee concedes the possibility that

> in some instances the true reading has been lost from the mss. of the other text-types and is preserved only in the Byzantine text. For this reason Byzantine readings must not automatically be rejected without examination.

But, lest anyone gather that he is giving full weight to the K text or its readings, he hastens to add:

> At the same time, the general impression which is given by readings which are characteristically Byzantine is that they are inferior and not likely to be original.[13]

Moreover, Greenlee gives no example of such a preserved Byzantine reading in his section on the "Solution of Some New Testament Variants."[14] In fact, as the section is perused, one detects a rather deep-seated bias in favor of the Alexandrian text-type and against both the Byzantine and Western texts. Bruce Metzger, in his chapter on "The Lucianic Recension of the Greek Bible," concludes in part:

> The lesson to be drawn from such evidence, however, is that the general neglect of the Antiochian readings which has been so common among many textual critics is quite unjustified.[15]

One might gather from the tone of this conclusion that a much more extensive use of the Byzantine text is advocated by him. In his work on the *Text of the New Testament*, which was published after the above article, he does cite a few examples where the Byzantines have preserved the correct reading in his estimation (one of them distinctive).[16] But Metzger, while urging that Antiochian readings

[12]*The Text of the New Testament, A Short Introduction* (London: St. Martin's Press, 1961), pp. 76-107.
[13]*Introduction to New Testament Textual Criticism* (Grand Rapids: 1964), p. 91.
[14]*Ibid.*, pp. 114-34.
[15]*Chapters*, p. 39.
[16]Metzger, *The Text . . .* , pp. 238-239.

should not be neglected, apparently still considers the Byzantine text-type secondary and inferior. He says that "readings which are supported by only Koine or Byzantine witnesses (Hort's Syrian group) may be set aside as almost certainly secondary. . ."[17]

For an earlier description and recommendation of the eclectic method see the discussion by Leo Vaganay, who seeks to steer a middle course in the use of external as well as internal evidence.[18] Vaganay, however, also joins the prevailing attitude toward the TR saying: "today it seems this famous text is dead at last and, let us hope, forever" (p. 173).

The rise of the eclectic method with its increasing emphasis upon internal criteria coincided with and stemmed mainly from a disenchantment with certain major elements in the theory of WH.[19] In particular, it is generally agreed that the "Neutral" text of WH is a "will-of-the-wisp" and that even Vaticanus (B), its leading MS, is not "neutral" but shows definite signs of an edited text.[20] In connection with this, the distinction which WH made between the text of ℵ and B (i.e., their "Neutral" text) and what they termed their Alexandrian text is no longer felt to be tenable. Many textual critics add the further criticism that WH's almost complete dismissal of the Western text is unjustified, some even holding that the Western is closer to the original than the Alexandrian. For statements on these changes in attitude toward the theory of WH, see such writers as Sir Frederick G. Kenyon,[21] Vaganay,[22] and E. C. Colwell.[23] Colwell deals a devastating blow to the genealogical method as applied (or rather, as it was not applied) by WH. In his conclusion, he says in part:

[17]*Ibid.*, p. 212.

[18]*An Introduction to the Textual Criticism of the New Testament*, trans. B. V. Miller (St. Louis: B. Herder Book Co., 1937), pp. 91-95.

[19]See also J. K. Elliott, "The Greek Text of the Epistles to Timothy and Titus," *Studies and Documents*, vol. 36 (1968), pp. iii and 1-14, in which he faults WH and defends the eclectic method.

[20]This non-neutrality of the Egyptian text has been set forth by several writers and was extensively demonstrated by Hoskier in his *Codex B and Its Allies, A Study and an Indictment*, (London: Bernard Quariteis, 1914).

[21]*The Text of the Greek Bible* (London: Gerald Duckworth and Co., 1949), p. 171.

[22]*An Introduction*, pp. 180-181.

[23]"Genealogical Method: Its Achievements and Its Limitations," *Journal of Biblical Literature*, LXVI (1947), pp. 109-133.

No patching will preserve the theory of Westcott and Hort. Kirsopp Lake called it "a failure, though a splendid one" as long ago as 1904; and Ernest von Dobschutz felt that its vogue was over when he published his introduction (1925). But the crowd has not yet followed these pioneers . . .[24]

Werner Georg Kümmel, in a section where he discusses the present state of New Testament textual criticism, has occasion to say:

Other parts of Westcott-Hort's theory have proved a failure, above all (a) the exaggerated preference for B and the Neutral text, and (b) the general repudiation of the Western text.[25]

A fourth theory of the use of the Byzantine text-type is the one set forth by Hermann Freiherr von Soden in his *Die Schriften des Neuen Testaments*.[26] It allows a more or less equal status to the Byzantine text-type along with the Alexandrian and what he termed his Iota or "Jerusalem" type. Von Soden reasoned that the manuscripts which support these types of text are the remains of three recensions (edited revisions of the New Testament text) which were executed in different localities during the third and fourth centuries. The I or Iota group represents the recension of Eusebius and Pamphilus in Palestine, the H or Eta group represents the recension of Hesychius in Egypt, and the K or Kappa group represents the recension of Lucian in Antioch.

According to von Soden these three recensions go back to the lost archetype, the I-H-K text, used by Origen, but already corrupted in the second century by Marcion, in the case of the Pauline Epistles, and by Tatian, in the case of the Gospels and Acts. The discovery and elimination of these corruptions bring us to the original text.[27]

[24]*Ibid.*, p. 132.
[25]*Introduction to the New Testament*, trans. A. J. Mattill, Jr. and completely re-edited by Werner George Kummel, 14th revised ed. (New York: Abingdon Press, 1966), p. 383; *Journal of Bible and Religion*, XXX (1962), pp. 314-315. See article by Harold Hunter Oliver on "Present Trends in the Textual Criticism of the New Testament," particularly his remarks in regard to the genealogical method of WH and their attitude toward the Western text.
[26]I Teil: Untersuchungen, II Abteilung: Die Textformen, Göttingen, 1911.
[27]Metzger, *The Text*, p. 141.

Von Soden's theory has not had a general acceptance among English, German, or French critics, though some Spanish scholars seem to have found value in it.[28]

Later, Burnett Hillman Streeter was not persuaded by von Soden's theory of a relatively independent recension of the K text. Streeter, in his work on the Gospels,[29] made an advance on the theory of WH as he developed his own theory of "local texts." As for the origin of the Byzantine text, he retained the WH theory that it derived from a recension made at Antioch and was dependent on the other text-types. However, Streeter broadened the theory in order to include Old Antiochian readings. This made a third source in addition to the Alexandrian (combining Hort's Neutral and Alexandrian) and the Western text-types. The editors at Antioch obtained these Old Antiochian readings, not so much from old Greek manuscripts preserved in and around Antioch, as from early translations which had been made into Syriac. Therefore, according to Streeter, the Old Antiochian readings, which contributed to Lucian's revision, are found now in the Sinaitic and Curetonian Syriac.[30] Though Streeter acknowledges that "it is probable that some of the readings of the Lucianic text which do not appear in the Syriac were derived from the old text of Antioch,"[31] he does not place much weight on this, as is evident from his chart and his discussion. Streeter, along with the writers mentioned above, abandoned WH's idea of a "Neutral" text.[32] In addition, Streeter also questioned some of WH's criteria for internal evidence of readings;

[28]See the article by Kurt Aland: "The Present Position of New Testament Textual Criticism," *Studia Evangelica*, ed. K. Aland, F. L. Cross and others (Berlin: Akademie-Verlag, 1959), p. 721; Metzger's; "Recent Spanish Contributions to the Textual Criticism of the New Testament," *Chapters* . . . , pp. 136-141; and John R. Janeway, *An Investigation of the Textual Criticism of the New Testament Done by Spanish Scholars, with Special Relation to the Theories and Text of WH* (unpublished dissertation, University of Southern California, 1958), pp. 164-165, 320-325 and other scattered references.

[29]*The Four Gospels a Study of Origins, Treating of the Manuscript Tradition, Sources, Authorship, & Dates* (eighth impression; London: Macmillan and Co., 1953).

[30]See charts of his own and WH's theory (*The Four Gospels*, p. 26) which graphically illustrate this point. Note also his discussion of the revision by Lucian, especially pp. 112-119.

[31]*Ibid.*, p. 119.

[32]Cf. his section on the recension of Hesychius *Ibid.*, pp. 121-127.

he speaks, for example, of the "the fallacy of the shorter text."[33]

While WH's theory of a "Neutral" text and their attitude toward the Western text has been abandoned by many scholars, Hort's theory of the "Syrian" text still dominates the field. Moreover, those scholars who follow the "eclectic" approach (i.e., of choosing readings on the basis of internal criteria) usually feel free to reject the points of WH's theory that have been mentioned. At the same time, however, probably a majority of them continue to share WH's view that the Byzantine text is secondary in nature and dependent upon the Alexandrian and Western texts.

While those who follow WH in this matter characterize the "Syrian" as the worst and most useless text for help in recovering the original, the followers of Burgon, contrariwise, maintain that the Byzantine is the best text, the "traditional text," and the text which most closely represents the original.

Because of this clear-cut antithesis, and the irreconcilable nature of these two viewpoints, together with the fact that the theory of WH in regard to the Byzantine text seems to hold the predominant position in the western world, the approach of the next chapter will be to outline the theory of WH with regard to the K text. Following this, in Chapter 3, the rebuttal to WH by Burgon and Hills is reviewed. Chapter 4 indicates reasons for turning away from the position of Burgon and Hills. In Part 2 reasons are presented for believing that the Byzantine text-type, though it may not necessarily be considered the "best" or the "standard" text as is contended by Burgon's followers, nevertheless should not be set aside as insisted upon by the theory of WH. Part 2 seeks to show that the Byzantine text should be recognized as having an important and useful place in textual criticism because it is an independent witness to an early form of the New Testament text.

[33]*Ibid.*, p. 131 ff.

CHAPTER II

A Summary Of The Argument
That The Byzantine Text Is Secondary

There appears to be a near consensus among modern New Testament scholars that the Byzantine text is practically useless for help in recovering the original text. This position is based on a century-old theory of textual history which contended that the Syrian text was derived from "older" text-types.

Westcott and Hort discerned what they felt to be the best text of the New Testament in two fourth century manuscripts Sinaiticus (ℵ) and Vaticanus (B). This text they called "Neutral," arguing for its early existence[1] and also for its purity and pre-eminence.[2] WH also distinguished what they felt to be a "scholarly revision" of this pure text, which they called "Alexandrian." Though their "Alexandrian" text did not exist by itself in a pure state, they said it could be found in manuscripts CL 33 etc. Modern critics generally do not uphold WH's distinction between the "Neutral" and the "Alexandrian" texts, but tend to combine the manuscripts of the two into one group and refer to the complete collection of witnesses as representing the Alexandrian or Egyptian text-type. The early existence of this text is attested by quotations from Origen, the Egyptian versions, and more recently, by Egyptian papyri—particularly the Bodmer papyrus XV and XVI (p^{75}).

[1]*Introduction*, pp. 150-151.
[2]*Ibid.*, pp. 210-212.

Another text which was acknowledged to be early by WH and others is termed the "Western" text. Though this type of text is less homogeneous than the Alexandrian text, no one questions its early existence, for it is widely attested, having more and even earlier patristic attestation than the Egyptian. WH saw little value in the Western text. They felt that it was corrupt and untrustworthy, except in the case of certain omissions where they said it should be allowed a hearing and may even in rare instances actually represent the original.[3] Today opinions vary among critics. Many are willing to give a somewhat larger place to Western readings than did WH, and a few critics, following A. C. Clark, hold the conviction that the Western text-type more faithfully preserves the original than does the Alexandrian. In any case, the majority of textual critics still appear to agree that both the Alexandrian and the Western type-types originated earlier than did the Byzantine.

Following WH, three main arguments continue to be used in an effort to demonstrate that the Syrian (Byzantine) text was derived from the others. They are as follows:

(1) *Conflate Readings.* In the first place it is argued that the Syrian text must be late in its origin and edited in its nature because evidence seems to indicate that it was made from the other two types of text (i.e., the Alexandrian and the Western). The supposed proof for this lies in what WH called "conflate" readings.[4] WH listed eight instances of conflate readings, four from Mark and four from Luke.[5] These involve places of variation in the text of the New Testament where the witnesses to the various readings divide at least three ways. One variant is attested by Alexandrian witnesses, another by the Western witnesses, and the third reading appears to "conflate", or combine, the two shorter readings into one longer reading in the Syrian witnesses. The last of the eight examples, Luke 24:53, may be taken to illustrate the concept of conflation as set forth by WH, inasmuch as it exhibits rather neatly this threefold division. Here are the readings and attestation as given in the Nestle texts:

---

[3]WH called these "Western non-interpolations"; thereby they avoided saying that the "Neutral" had been interpolated.

[4]*Introduction*, pp. 93-107.

[5]For a list of the eight passages see Chapter VIII, p. 82.

εὐλογουυτες τον θεον	blessing God	p^{75}אBC*L pc sy^s
αἰνουτες τον θεον	praising God	D it
αἰνουυτες και εὐλογοῦντες τον θεον	praising and blessing God	AWϑ fam 1 fam 13 pl lat

Thus it appears, according to the argument, that the Syrian editor(s) had manuscripts of the Western text reading αἰνουυτες and also Alexandrian manuscripts reading εὐλογοῦντες, and since they did not wish to lose anything, they simply combined the two. The longer readings thus appear to demonstrate both a) the earlier date of the non-Byzantine texts and b) the method of the editor(s) that used them.

(2) *Silence of the Fathers.* The second line of evidence advanced by WH to argue that the Byzantine text is later and therefore dependent on the Alexandrian and the Western is patristic in nature: the silence of the Fathers. While there are quotations in the writings of the Fathers which are found supporting the Alexandrian text (especially Origen) and many of the early Fathers are found witnessing to the Western text, WH maintained that no church Father is to be found attesting the Byzantine text in quotations of Scripture before the time of Chrysostom, i.e. till the latter part of the fourth century. Therefore, because the text was not used or quoted by the early Fathers, the conclusion drawn is that it must not have been in existence in their time.[6]

(3) *Internal Evidence.* The third proof is taken from internal evidence of readings. WH contend that when the readings of the Syrian text-type are compared with those of the other text-types, they are found to be not only conflate but inferior in other matters involving content and style, thus indicating an editing process. This line of reasoning is set forth by Hort in the succeeding part of his *Introduction.*[7]

The conclusion drawn from this three-fold argument is that though the Syrian text predominates greatly in numbers of witnesses it should not be counted in evaluating evidence for readings, because it was formed from the other ancient texts. To use the Syr-

[6]See Hort's summary of this argument: *Introduction*, pp. 107-15.
[7]*Ibid.*, pp. 114-115.

ian text in weighing evidence for readings, therefore, would be unjustified because of its late origin and secondary nature.

WH maintain that a special proof of the lateness of the Syrian text
is its distinctive readings, i.e., readings which are peculiar to it, not
being found in the other textual traditions or quotations of the early
Fathers:

> Before the middle of the third century, at the very earliest, we
> have no historical signs of the existence of readings, conflate or
> other, that are marked as distinctively Syrian by the want of
> attestation from groups of documents which have preserved the
> other ancient forms of text. This is a fact of great significance,
> ascertained as it is exclusively by external evidence, and there-
> fore supplying an absolutely independent verification and ex-
> tension of the result already obtained by comparison of the
> internal character of readings as classified by conflation.[8]

This insistence upon the lateness of distinctively Syrian readings
is taken up again in the section having to do with the internal evidence of Syrian readings. Here Hort says that

> when distinctively Syrian [Byzantine] readings are minutely
> compared one after the other with the rival variants, their claim
> to be regarded as the original readings is found gradually to
> diminish, and at last to disappear. Often either the transcrip-
> tional or the intrinsic evidence is neutral or divided, and occa-
> sionally the two kinds of evidence appear to be in conflict. But
> there are, we believe, no instances where both are clearly in
> favor of the Syrian reading, and innumerable where both are
> clearly adverse to it.[9]

And, on page 117, Hort sums up this matter of the hypothetically
early existence and consequent possible usefulness of distinctively
Syrian readings:

> we are led to conclude that the hypothesis provisionally allowed
> [i.e., that where the Syrian text differs from all other extant

---

[8]*Introduction*, pp. 115-119.
[9]*Ibid.*, p. 116.

ancient texts, its authors may have copied some other equally ancient and perhaps purer text now otherwise lost] must now be definitely rejected, and to regard the Syrian text as not only partly but wholly derived from the other known ancient texts. *It follows that all distinctively Syrian readings may be set aside at once as certainly originating after the middle of the third century, and therefore,* as far as transmission is concerned, *corruptions of the apostolic text* [italics added].

Having determined that the distinctive readings of the Syrian text must be worthless, Hort reasons that the same data that led to this conclusion also lead to another which WH maintain is of equal or of even greater importance. This further conclusion has to do with the non-distinctive Syrian readings. "Non-distinctive readings" are those readings where the Byzantine text agrees either with the Alexandrian text or the Western text. According to the theory of WH, such an alignment must not be considered as lending any more weight of authority or originality to the reading. The reason given for this rejection of the K-text from consideration even when it agrees with an acknowledged ancient text, is the supposed derived and therefore secondary nature of the Syrian text:

> Accordingly a reading supported both by the documents belonging to the Syrian group and by those belonging to e.g., the Western group has no appreciably greater presumption in its favour than if it were supported by the Western group alone: the only accession is that of a lost Western MS not later in date than the time when the Syrian text was formed; and in almost all cases this fact would add nothing to our knowledge of the ancestry of the reading as furnished by the Non-Syrian documents attesting it.[10]

That this three-fold argument of WH, as to the conflate, edited, and consequently late and unusable nature of the Syrian text-type formed a "cord not easily broken" may be seen in the fact that it continues to be used by many critics. For one of the more vehement examples, consider Williams' statement in his article "Text of the New Testament":

[10]*Ibid.,* p. 118.

Here it is . . . that the original and epoch-making character of the work of WH is most conspicuous. The first proposition—and the one which strikes at the root of the claims of the TR—is this, that no *specifically "Syrian" reading occurs in the NT quotations of any Father before Chrysostom* [italics Williams']. In other words, wherever the Syrian family marks itself off from the others by a reading of its own, that reading cannot be shown to have been in existence before the latter part of the 4th century. The importance of this proposition is obvious, and it is noteworthy, as showing the value of Patristic evidence, that the proof of it rests wholly on the quotations found in the Fathers. The inevitable conclusion is that the Syrian text is a secondary text, formed (according to WH in Syria, and especially in Antioch) in the course of the 4th century. This secondary character is also established by an examination of representative Syrian readings . . . . As compared with the rival readings of other groups, they show the ordinary signs of editorial revision, such as the modification of harsh or strange phrases, assimilation of one version of an incident with another, greater literary smoothness, and the like. A special proof of secondariness is found in what WH call conflate readings. . . . The conclusion, therefore, is that the witnesses belonging to the Syrian family, although they predominate enormously in numbers, possess little intrinsic weight when opposed to witnesses of the other groups.[11]

Williams continues his conclusion and application further on in the same article and makes the additional claim that nothing has occurred since the days of WH to upset their judgment on the Syrian text:

It may be added that the course of discovery since the publication of WH's theory has furnished the best possible test of such a theory, that of wholly new and unforeseen witnesses, and that it has received therefrom much confirmation and no refutation. The discovery of the Siniatic Syriac, the fuller scrutiny of the versions, the testing of Patristic quotations . . . the papyrus and vellum fragments from Egypt and Sinai, the examination of more of the minuscle MSS, all these have brought additional support to readings of the β, γ, and δ families, for which the evidence previously available was sometimes very scanty, while

[11]*Dictionary of the Bible*, p. 991.

they have done nothing to carry back the date of the distinctively Syrian readings beyond the period assigned to them by WH, namely, the age of Chrysostom.[12]

One other recent writer may be cited to show that the basic line of argument for the theory of WH with regard to the Byzantine text is still very much entrenched. Bruce Metzger summarizes the general concensus of modern scholarship in this regard as he concludes his review of the WH theory:

> By way of retrospect and evaluation it may be said that scholars today generally agree that one of the chief contributions made by Westcott and Hort was their clear demonstration that the Syrian (or Byzantine) text is later than the other types of text. Three main types of evidence support this judgment: (1) the Syrian text contains combined or conflate readings which are clearly composed of elements current in earlier forms of text; (2) no ante-Nicene Father quotes a distinctively Syrian reading; and (3) when the Syrian readings are compared with the rival readings their claim to be regarded as original is found gradually to diminish, and at last to disappear.[13]

Those who follow Westcott and Hort in rejecting the Byzantine testimony often are also carried along by other elements of the WH theory. For the followers of WH, therefore, if one may give an oversimplified conclusion and summary, the true reading of the Greek New Testament (as far as external evidence is concerned) is to be found in the combination of the non-Syrian witnesses; or if these witnesses be divided, the reading is to be found in the Alexandrian text-type. If the Alexandrian text-type be divided, the true reading will be found where ℵ and B agree; or if they be divided, where B and at least one other witness read together. Occasionally, even B alone is followed; but in no case is the reading attested by the Byzantine bulk of manuscripts to be considered as worthy of following if it be the only support. Whereas WH gave little credence to Western readings (the exception being the "Western non-inter-

[12]*Ibid.*, pp. 991-992. Note the previous citation of Williams and his insistence that the "*fact*" of the α text's existence as a secondary text of late origin "must be taken to be one of the established results of criticism" (p. 15 above).

[13]*The Text*, p. 135.

polations," as WH called them), modern textual critics tend to give more consideration and weight to intrinsically probable Western readings—especially if the alternative Alexandrian reading is improbable in their opinion. Chapter 3 sets forth an opposite view of the Byzantine text.

CHAPTER III

A Summary Of The Argument That
The Byzantine Text Is Primary

In direct contrast to the theory of WH, which is based on a concept of textual history that derives the Byzantine text from other text-types, is the view that divine providence has preserved the Byzantine manuscripts as the best text. In this view, other texts or text-types are considered deviations and corruptions of the true text. While WH would say that the Byzantine text is the least useful text because it is secondary, John W. Burgon and Edward F. Hills would say that the Byzantine is the primary or basic text, the Traditional text, and is, therefore, the "norm" by which all other texts are to be judged. The basic premise of this view is that the agreement of a large majority of individual manuscripts constitutes the chief evidence for the true text because such plurality indicates the divinely preserved text.[1]

[1]John W. Burgon was the chief spokesman for this viewpoint in the days of WH. His works include: *The Last Twelve Verses of the Gospel According to Mark,* London: James Parker & Co., 1871; *The Revision Revised,* London: John Murray, 1883: *The Traditional Text of the Holy Gospels,* London: George Bell & Sons, 1896; and *The Causes of the Corruption of the Traditional Text of the Holy Gospels,* London: George Bell & Sons, 1896. The last two of these works were published posthumously (from Burgon's notes) by Edward Miller. More recently this view of the supreme value of the Byzantine Text is urged by Edward F. Hills in *The King James Version Defended! A Christian View of the New Testament Manuscripts,* The Christian Research Press, 1956; in his "Introduction" to a re-print of Burgon's *The Last Twelve Verses . . .* published by The Sovereign Grace Book Club, 1959, pp. 17-72; and in

In order to support this view at the outset preservation is intimately linked with "inspiration":

> If the doctrine of the divine inspiration of the Old and New Testament Scriptures is a true doctrine, the doctrine of the providential preservation of these Scriptures must also be a true doctrine. It must be that down through the centuries God has exercised a special, providential control over the copying of the Scriptures and the preservation and use of the original text have been available to God's people in every age. God must have done this, for if He gave the Scriptures to His Church by inspiration as the perfect and final revelation of His will, then it is obvious that He would not allow this revelation to disappear or undergo any alteration of its fundamental character.[2]

Hills seeks to bolster his argument by asserting that this has "always been held, either implicitly or explicitly, by all branches of the Christian Church."[3] He makes reference to a statement by Origen:

> Thus Origen in the third century was expressing the faith of all when he exclaimed to Africanus, "Are we to suppose that Providence which in the sacred Scriptures has ministered to the edification of all the churches of Christ, had no thought for those bought with a price, for whom Christ died!"[4]

Hills seeks to show that, contrary to the claims of WH and others, New Testament textual criticism is different from the textual criticism of ordinary books because of the unique origin and preservation of the New Testament documents. The concluding statement

[2]Edward Hills, *King James Version Defended*, p. 8.
[3]*Ibid.*, p. 8.
[4]*Ibid.*, p. 9.

Believing Bible Study, The Christian Research Press, 1967. David Otis Fuller has more recently edited two books dealing with the subject: *Which Bible*, Grand Rapids International Publications, 3rd ed., 1970; *True or False*, Grand Rapids International Publications, 1973. A further defense of the text of the majority of the MSS is made by Jakob van Bruggen in *The Ancient Text of the New Testament*, Winnipeg: Premier, 1976; and by Wilbur N. Pickering in *The Identity of the New Testament Text*, Nashville: Thomas Nelson Inc., 1977.

in his opening section having to do with "The Importance of Doctrine," is as follows:

> . . . if the doctrines of the *divine inspiration* and *providential preservation* of these Scriptures are true doctrines, then the textual criticism of the New Testament is different from that of the uninspired writings of antiquity. The textual criticism of any book must take into account the conditions under which the original manuscripts were written and also those under which the copies of these manuscripts were made and preserved. But if the doctrines of the divine inspiration and providential preservation of the Scriptures are true, then *THE ORIGINAL NEW TESTAMENT MANUSCRIPTS WERE WRITTEN UNDER SPECIAL CONDITIONS, UNDER THE INSPIRATION OF GOD, AND THE COPIES WERE MADE AND PRESERVED UNDER SPECIAL CONDITIONS, UNDER THE SINGULAR CARE AND PROVIDENCE OF GOD* [italics and caps by Hills].[5]

Hills concedes that the doctrine of providential preservation unlike inspiration was not explicitly stated in any creed until the seventeenth century,[6] but he maintains that it is not a seventeenth-century doctrine but rather the doctrine of the Scriptures and of Christ Himself.[7] As proof of this view he cites the two following passages to support divinely attested preservation of the Old Testament:

> Till heaven and earth pass away, one jot or one tittle shall in no wise pass from the law until all be fulfilled (Matthew 5:18). It is easier for heaven and earth to pass away, than one tittle of the law to fail (Luke 16:17).

Hills then turns his attention to Christ's teaching concerning the preservation of the New Testament:

> Christ also taught that the same divine providence which had preserved the Old Testament would preserve the New Testa-

[5]*Ibid.*, p. 9.
[6]*Ibid.*, p. 23.
[7]*Ibid.*, p. 24.

ment too. In the concluding verses of the Gospel of Matthew we find His "Great Commission" not only to the twelve apostles but also to His Church throughout all ages, "go ye therefore and teach all nations." Implied in this solemn charge is the promise that through the working of God's providence the Church will always be kept in possession of an infallible record of Christ's words and works. And similarly, in His discourses on the last things He assures His disciples that His promises not only shall certainly be fulfilled but also shall remain available for the comfort of His people during that troubled period which shall precede His second coming. In other words, that they shall be preserved until that time. "Heaven and earth shall pass away, but my words shall not pass away." (Matthew 24:35).[8]

Following this he again asserts that "the providential preservation of the Scriptures is also a necessary consequence of their divine inspiration."[9] He unites the two with language that appears to put them on the same level of precision.

The whole case for the primacy of the Byzantine text (as argued by Hills) is ultimately made to rest upon the providence of God. The remaining points that Hills makes as he traces his reconstruction of the history of the text are all colored by this same basic premise. He himself calls attention to this as he introduces his "axioms of consistently Christian Textual Criticism":

In working out a consistently Christian New Testament textual criticism special emphasis must be laid upon the doctrine of the providential preservation of Scripture, for *from this doctrine* can be deduced the main outlines of the history of the New Testament text [italics added].[10]

In pages 30 through 35 Hills enlarges on the following, which he terms "six axioms of consistently Christian textual criticism:"

(a) The purpose of the providential preservation of the New Testament is to preserve the infallibility of the inspired original text. (b) This providential preservation concentrated itself on

[8]*Ibid.*, p. 24.
[9]*Ibid.*, p. 24.
[10]*Ibid.*, p. 29.

the Greek New Testament text. (c) This providential preservation operated within the sphere of the Greek Church. (d) This providential preservation operated through the testimony of the Holy Spirit. (e) The text of the majority of the manuscripts is the providentially preserved and approved text. (f) The text of the majority of the manuscripts is the standard text.[11]

The conclusion, observed in the axioms (e) and (f), is that the text of the majority of the manuscripts equals the best representative of the original, and should be considered the standard text because it is the providentially preserved text. Therefore the Byzantine text (the text with the overwhelming number of manuscripts) should be the determining criteria in the weighing of evidence for readings because numbers do count. And, in contrast to WH, the Alexandrian manuscripts together with those of the Western text are to be treated as deviations or corruptions of the true text. Such early Alexandrian manuscripts exist today because they were rejected by the Church, which reorganized their inferiority, and therefore such manuscripts were not worn out with use as was the case with the early Byzantine manuscripts.[12]

While Burgon-Hills *et al* take as a basic premise: the best or true text is preserved where there are the greatest number of MSS, and such numerical superiority reveals the providence of God in preserving the inspired original in the Byzantine text-type; it is neither fair-minded nor honest to maintain that they did not understand the argument of WH, or that they appealed only to a theological argument in their reply. They examined the arguments of WH and found them wanting in several areas. They examined the "conflates." They, especially Burgon, researched quotations of the Fathers. They proffered a logical explanation, or a rational theory, for the history of the Text. Furthermore, Burgon and Hills have dealt with specific problems of variation in the text of the New Testament applying, in knowledgeable and extended fashion, all the categories of external, transcriptional, and intrinsic evidence.[13] However, they probably would not deny that the basic support for their view was theological—the providence of God. Chapter 4 seeks to examine and show the weakness of this viewpoint.

[11]*Ibid.*, p. 30.
[12]*Ibid.*, p. 43, 56.
[13]See above note 1 (Chapter III) for a list of their writings.

CHAPTER IV

An Examination Of The Argument That The Byzantine Text Is Primary

The Burgon-Hills argument rests on a theological and dogmatic basis which must be accepted and followed by faith. With no intention of belittling faith or of treating Scriptural doctrines irreverently, there are elements in Hills' argument with which orthodox Christians may disagree. Conservatives will agree that the Scriptures were given by verbal inspiration. Conservatives will also agree that by divine providence the Scriptures have been marvelously preserved. However, when it is insisted that "all orthodox Christians, all Christians who show due regard for the divine inspiration and providential preservation of Scripture, must agree with Burgon in this matter,"[1] there will be many such orthodox Christians who will not agree.

The chief weakness in the Burgon-Hills theory seems to be the foundation upon which the entire structure is built. To present preservation as a necessary corollary of inspiration, then to imply that preservation of the Scripture must be as faithful and precise as inspiration of the Scriptures, appears to be taking a position that is both unscriptural and impossible to demonstrate. Hills insists that

> . . . if the doctrine of the divine inspiration of the Old and New Testament Scriptures is a true doctrine the doctrine of the providential preservation of these Scriptures must also be a true doc-

[1]*Last Twelve Verses,* in Hills' introduction, p. 21.

trine. It must be that down through the centuries God has exercised a special providential control. . . . God must have done this. . .[2]

It should be pointed out that *providential preservation is not a necessary consequence of inspiration.* Preservation of the Word of God is promised in Scripture, and inspiration and preservation are related doctrines, but they are distinct from each other, and there is a danger in making one the necessary corollary of the other. The Scriptures do not do this. God, having given the perfect revelation by verbal inspiration, was under no special or logical obligation to see that man did not corrupt it. He created the first man perfect, but He was under no obligation to keep him perfect. Or to use another illustration, having created all things perfect, God was not obligated to see that the pristine perfection of the world was maintained. In His providence the world was allowed to suffer the Fall and to endure a defacement of its original condition. It may very well be that the Scriptures used to attest the promise to preserve God's Word do involve preservation. The point is that this is a different matter than insisting that God, because He inspired the Scriptures, is *ipso facto* obligated to preserve them; or, further, that He is obligated to preserve them in a particular way.

One danger of such a position is that the faith of some has been weakened when they have become aware of variant readings in the manuscripts precisely because they have confounded preservation with inspiration. Though both are biblical doctrines, the Scripture does not link them inexorably. Concerning inspiration, the Scriptures are very specific as to the direct working of the Holy Spirit. The Scriptures were "God-breathed" (II Timothy 3:16). "Holy men of God spake as they were borne along by the Holy Spirit" (II Peter 1:21). But while God promised that His Word would be preserved, "Heaven and earth shall pass away, but my words will not pass away" (Matthew 24:35), He did not stipulate in the Scriptures that He would keep Christian scribes from error or that the text-type with the most copies would be the best text. And even

[2]*King James Version Defended,* p. 8. See also the succeeding sentence, also bottom of page 24-25 where he speaks of the providential preservation of the Scriptures as a necessary consequence of their divine inspiration.

Hills is not willing to say that *all* the original words and *only* the original words are confined in the Byzantine Manuscripts. Hills, no doubt, holds to the verbal plenary view of inspiration, i.e. that every word in all the Scriptures was originally given by divine inspiration.

If providential preservation of the Scriptures is tied to inspiration, is placed on a level with inspiration, and is understood to mean that not one jot or tittle shall pass out of the Byzantine text-type, the theory is on shaky ground due to the fact that even the Byzantine text with its high degree of homogeneity is composite (i.e., there are strands within its homogeneity). Through the research of von Soden at least five principal strands have been identified, some of them with an array of subordinates, within the Byzantine text-type.[3] Even if it were agreed for the sake of argument that the Byzantine text were the best text—the text of God's special providential care—one who held an orthodox view of inspiration would still be unable to say that the preserved Byzantine text paralleled exactly and in every detail the verbally inspired original. One who followed the Byzantine text as the best text might claim this where the composite strands agree, but what will he say when K^1, K^i, and IK^a divide? And what will he say when disagreements of the later but more numerous K^x and K^r groups differ from the earlier K groups or between themselves in readings? In such cases, where does one locate the providentially preserved text? It is a mistake to put preservation on the same level of precision of operation as inspiration and then to limit preservation to *one* text-type.

Even if, due to internal disagreements, one text-type could not claim to preserve in every detail the verbally inspired autographs, this would disprove neither providential preservation nor inspiration. An attempt to disprove preservation or inspiration on the basis of variations in MSS could have weight only if these two doctrines have been artifically tied together and confined to one text-type. In such a case, variation within that text-type could be unsettling to belief in inspiration. Inspiration has to do with the very words which were originally God-breathed in the vocabulary and style of the original writers. Providence has to do with all that God has

---

[3]The main strands in von Soden's K̄OINH or Kappa text were labeled: K^1, K^i, IK^a, K^x, K^r; see also below pp. 43, 90-94.

allowed to come to pass in the preservation of that which was originally given by inspiration. Providence includes the preserving of the other types of text as well as the Byzantine.

Hills further seeks to strengthen his doctrine of preservation with an appeal to Jesus' promise: "Heaven and earth shall pass away but my words shall not pass away." But it is not demonstrated that this must be confined in meaning to the Byzantine manuscripts. It is doubtful that the Lord meant us to understand: "my words shall not pass away from the text having the most manuscripts," or "my words shall not pass away from the Byzantine text-type." Hills maintains that

> . . . down through the ages God's providential preservation of the New Testament has operated only through believers who have taken a supernatural view of that text and have applied to it standards of judgment which they do not apply to the text of other books. Whether Gregory, Basil, and Chrysostom belonged to this company of consistent believers would be hard, perhaps, to prove from their writings, but probably they did. Thus it is probably right to say that they were used by God as agents in the preservation of the New Testament text in a special sense in which Tregelles, Tischendorf, and Westcott and Hort were not used.[4]

One is tempted to ask: how can God's providence be limited only to men of the Byzantine area? For example, there is no question about the belief of Irenaeus,[5] Origen[6] and Augustine[7] in the inspiration of the Scriptures. But Irenaeus used a "corrupt" Western text, and Origen and Augustine are painfully aware of variants in their manuscripts. Athanasius certainly was orthodox, and he used a Greek text, yet it was Alexandrian and different from the text of

[4]*King James Version Defended*, pp. 26-27.

[5]See Hills' own quotations of Irenaeus, pg. 8, taken from Migne, *Patrological Cursus Completus*, Series Graeca, vol. 7, col. 805, col. 844.

[6]*The Ante-Nicene Fathers*, ed. A. Roberts and J. Donaldson (Grand Rapids: Wm. B. Eerdmans Publishing Co., 1951), IV, 371.

[7]*The Fathers of the Church, New Translation*, vol. 12, editorial director Roy Joseph Deferrari, *Saint Augustine, Letters*, vol. 1 (1-82), translated by Sister Wilfrid Parsons S. N. D., New York: Fathers of the Church, Ind., 1951, letter no. 82, pp. 392-394.

Antioch in the fourth century. These men were believers and took a supernatural view of the text of Scripture, yet, in God's providence, they used texts other than the Byzantine. Orthodox Christians who believe in inspiration and believe in divine providence can make mistakes in judgments about the text of Scripture. Irenaeus used the Western text, and Origen used the Alexandrian text; yet Hills himself cites Origen as pleading the providence of God in the preservation of Scripture.[8]

Every one of the six axioms of "consistently Christian New Testament textual criticism" that Hills sets forth, rests heavily upon the providential preservation of Scripture. As he himself says: "from this doctrine" he has "deduced the main outlines of the history of the New Testament text."[9] Under the first axiom, he again sets forth what he claims God must do:

> God must do more than merely preserve the inspired original New Testament text. He must preserve it in a public way. He must preserve it in such a manner that all the world may know where it is and what it is. God must preserve this text, not secretly, not hidden away . . . but openly before the eyes of all men through the continuous usage of His Church. No other manner of dealing with the sacred text would be in accordance with the purpose for which God gave it, which was that it might remain before His people forever as the guide of their footsteps and the ground of their faith.[10]

Again one must ask, where is the proof of this necessity upon God? Why must God do so? The answer is: "that all the world may know where it is and what it is." But this is a statement which appears to be refuted by history, because for about one thousand years the Western part of the church was largely ignorant of the Byzantine text, being shut up, for the most part, to the Latin Vulgate which differs in many respects from the Byzantine text.

Furthermore, the Bible itself reveals that there have been occasions when there has been a famine or dearth of the Word of God. One thinks, for example, of the days of Josiah (II Kings 22:8 ff.)

---

[8]*King James Version Defended*, p. 9, (quoted above p. 33).
[9]*Ibid.*, p. 29.
[10]*Ibid.*, pp. 30-31.

when apparently the Scriptures were reduced to one copy. Nevertheless, it still could be said that God's Word was preserved. The chief weakness of the Burgon-Hills position appears again in this foundational axiom. Hills fails to show why the sovereign God must act in a particular way. It is one thing to look at history and conjecture as to God's purpose. It is another to insist that God's purpose could only be that which is conjectured. To assert what of necessity lies upon God would seem to go too far when such necessity is not revealed in the Scriptures.

The further axioms continue to enlarge on this concept of providential preservation. The second deals with it on the basis of the Greek New Testament text; the third, on the basis of the Greek church. Under the third Hills says:

> Because God's providential preservation of the New Testament was concentrated on the Greek text, it follows that it operated within the sphere of the Greek-speaking Church, where Greek New Testament manuscripts were read and copied.[11]

He is still referring to the working of God in preservation through the Greek-speaking Church under his fourth axiom when he speaks of preservation operating "through the testimony of the Holy Spirit." He alludes to the guidance of the Holy Spirit in the formation of the canon and indicates that at a later time and in a similar manner the Holy Spirit led the Greek-speaking Church in the rejection of bad readings and in selecting of the true text.[12] But in this connection it should be remembered that Greek was written and spoken in Caesarea, Alexandria, and in Rome during the early period of the formation of the canon and afterwards. Moreover, all during this time and in these places Christians were copying and reading manuscripts in Greek. Since the testimony of the Holy Spirit did not operate through the Greek Church of the area of Antioch alone in the matter of identifying the canon, why should there be any necessity for Him to withhold such testimony with respect to the Greek text of other areas than Antioch?

Other difficulties come to mind. Irenaeus, Clement of Alexandria, Origen, Athanasius, Eusebius, and others used Greek texts

[11]*Ibid.*, p. 31.
[12]*Ibid.*, p. 33.

other than the Byzantine. According to Hills' concept of providential preservation, when they read "Heaven and earth shall pass away but my words shall not pass away" in their New Testaments, they had no right to apply such a promise to their own texts. Consider the New Testament of Athanasius which was Alexandrian in its text-type. Can anyone say that this great defender of the faith used a text which was not supported by God's providence?

The weakness of the basic argument becomes apparent in the last two axioms. Hills argues that "the text of the majority of the manuscripts is the providentially preserved and approved text." In the middle of the paragraph he says that

> . . . the errors of the scribes therefore, were corrected by the God-guided preferences of the Greek-speaking Church. . . .
>
> The New Testament text, therefore, which is found in the vast majority of the extant manuscripts is the providentially preserved and approved text, the text upon which almighty God, expressing Himself providentially in the usage of the Greek Church, has placed His divine sanction.[13]

Again it must be asked: If providential preservation is put on the same level with inspiration, how does it come about that the Byzantine text is composite, i.e., how could the text have differences within it? Furthermore, being composite, how is one to know what the providentially preserved reading is when K divides? Is it to be on the basis of numbers solely? That is, in a place of variation, is the original reading to be determined on the basis of the most manuscripts in its support by actual count? In such cases, where the K groups divide, the reading of the K^x group would always have to be followed since its manuscripts are the most numerous. But here a problem is raised because K^x is the group least known! It was for this reason that von Soden used the symbol "x" to designate it. It is the form of the Byzantine text of the Middle Ages and appears to have dominated from the tenth to the twelfth centuries. By the thirteenth century it was displaced by the K^r text which, though fewer in numbers, is the next most numerous group of K manuscripts and is characterized by lectionary apparatus which has been introduced into the text.

[13]*Ibid.*, p. 34.

In the last axiom it is seen that Hills does not really mean to restrict providential preservation as rigidly as it had appeared throughout his preceding pages. Here, in describing the Byzantine text, he used such expressions as the following:

> . . . it is the *best extant* text. . . . It represents the inspired original text very accurately, *more accurately than any other* New Testament text which survives from the manuscript period. . . . It is the text that should be followed *almost always* in preference to the non-Byzantine texts found in the minority of the Manuscripts [italics added].[14]

He is making room for some exceptions so that certain non-Byzantine readings may be included. There seems to be a fatal admission here. Providential preservation, then, has not operated on a level with inspiration and been confined to one text-type. If the chain of argument had been correct, there could be no deviation. God has been represented as giving equal concern and care to preservation as to inspiration. Preservation has been tied to the Greek Church and the majority of Greek manuscripts as its channel. If the doctrine of inspiration is verbal and plenary (every word in the autographs through all the scriptures), then providential preservation, as insisted upon by this argument, logically extends to every word within the majority numbers of the Byzantine manuscript tradition. Yet Hills, in his sixth axiom, seeks to evade this necessary conclusion to the basic premise.

That such an argument from providence may be speculative and beyond proof is illustrated in the context of the very quotation from Origen used by Hills (see above p. 33). Origen, in his reply to Africanus, is arguing on behalf of certain parts of the Septuagint, i.e., the History of Susanna and other apocryphal portions, as compared to the Hebrew canon which Africanus had alluded to. He sardonically observes:

> And, forsooth, when we notice such things, we are forthwith to reject as spurious the copies in use in our Churches, and enjoin the brotherhood to put away the sacred books current among them, and to coax the Jews, and persuade them to give us copies

[14]*Ibid.*, p. 35.

which shall be untampered with, and free from forgery! Are we to suppose that that *Providence* which in the sacred Scriptures has ministered to the edification of all the Churches of Christ, had no thought for those bought with a price, for whom Christ died; whom, although His Son, God who is love spared not, but gave Him up for us all, that with Him He might freely give us all things?

In all these cases consider whether it would not be well to remember the words, "Thou shalt not remove the ancient landmarks which thy fathers have set" [italics added].[15]

This appeal from providence by Origen is a plea to consider the Septuagint version, with its apocryphal additions, as more authoritative for the Church than the Hebrew Scriptures! It is essentially the same argument as that which undergirds the Burgon-Hills theory. How can one be sure that Hills' argument from providence in support of the Byzantine text has any more validity than Origen's in his support of the Septuagint!

There is no question but that the argument for the primacy of the Byzantine text is supported by sincere men of faith. However, as in the case of Origen, they appear at this point to use a biblical doctrine in an unjustified way. How can it be assumed that providence works only with numbers? In spite of the popular saying there are some who believe that "fifty million Frenchmen" can sometimes be wrong. And on the other side, it is quite unlikely that a biblical theologian would affirm e.g., that it was in spite of God's providence that Tischendorf appeared at the monastery of St. Catherine in the Sinai peninsula just in time to save the Sinaitic manuscript from destruction.

There is an unfortunate aspect concerning the manner in which Burgon and some of his followers have approached the defense of the Byzantine text, and with it the King James Version. It is that the orthodoxy and motives of those holding different views is sometimes called in question. One of the dangers in such an approach is that of the polarizing and hardening of positions; therefore, positive evidence for the quality and usefulness of the Byzantine text is shut out without a hearing. It is also unfortunate that there are some who, whenever it is suggested that the Byzantine text may have

[15]*The Ante-Nicene Fathers*, IV, 387.

some usefulness, immediately tend to prejudge and reject the position, identifying it with that of Burgon and his followers.

A variation or modification of the Burgon-Hills view discussed above has been put forth by Zane C. Hodges and Wilbur N. Pickering. Their theory of the text, rather than arguing from "providence," defends the superiority of the majority number of manuscripts on a mathematical principle that is based on the reasoning that "the copies nearest the autograph will normally have the largest number of descendents." According to this theory, in each place of variation, the original reading is the reading which has the largest number of manuscripts supporting it. Invariably, of course, this "largest number" will be made up of the MSS of the Byzantine text-type since it is the text with the greatest number of descendents.[16] To support the theory further it is suggested that there is no other explanation which accounts for the superior numbers of the Byzantine text. Hodges says

> The manuscript tradition of an ancient book will, under any but most exceptional conditions, multiply in a reasonably regular fashion with the result that the copies nearest the autograph will normally have the largest number of descendants. The further removed in the history of transmission a text becomes from its source the less time it has to leave behind a large family of offspring. Hence, in a large tradition where a pronounced unity is observed between, let us say, eighty per cent of the evidence, a very strong presumption is raised that this numerical preponderance is due to direct derivation from the very oldest sources. In the absence of any convincing contrary explanation, this presumption is raised to a very high level of probability indeed. Thus the Majority text, upon which the King James Version is based, has in reality the strongest claim possible to be regarded as an authentic representation of the original text. This claim is quite independent of any shifting concensus of scholarly judgment about its readings and is based on the objective reality of its dominance in the transmission history of the New Testament text. This dominance has not and—we venture to suggest—cannot be otherwise explained.[17]

[16]Note: an application of their principle may be found in *The Greek New Testament According to the Majority Text*, ed. by Zane C. Hodges and Arthur L. Farstad. Nashville: Thomas Nelson Publishers, 1982.

[17]"The Greek Text of the King James Version," *Bibliotheca Sacra*, 125:500 (October-December, 1968), 344, 345.

Pickering also believes that there is no other way of explaining the great numerical preponderance of the Byzantine manuscripts than that they represent the text that goes back to the autographs:

> I see no way of accounting for a 90% (or 80%) domination unless that text goes back to the Autographs. Hort saw the problem and invented a revision. Sturz seems not to have seen the problem. He demonstrates that the "Byzantine text-type" is early and independent of the "Western" and "Alexandrian text-types," and like von Soden wishes to treat them as three equal witnesses. But if the three "text-types" were equal, how ever could the so-called "Byzantine" gain an 80-90% preponderance?[18]

Despite these strong assertions there do appear to be other reasons, both historical and ethnological, which explain the great numerical preponderance of the later Greek manuscripts associated with the Byzantine area (empire) as compared with the sparse remains of Greek witnesses from the West and from Egypt.

There are at least three principle reasons why the Greek textual traditions of Alexandria and the geographical West have not been preserved in the numbers that are found in the Byzantine. In the first place as far as the West is concerned, Greek faded out in favor of the native langage—Latin. While there are some 5,000 Greek manuscripts of the New Testament, largely Byzantine, there are over 10,000 Latin manuscripts! A few Greek MSS associated with the Western text still exist. However, these Western MSS date from the 5th to the 9th century and are mostly Greek and Latin diglotts. It is thought that the Latin translation (or translations) of the New Testament Scriptures was produced and circulated in the West by the last half of the second or beginning of the third century.[19] The peculiar strength of the Western text's testimony lies chiefly in its versional and Patristic support. In addition to the volume of the Latin versional testimony mentioned above, it should be added that most of the earliest Fathers who have left writings of textual significance are associated with the West. If the reasoning of Hodges and Pickering were valid, then why are not the most numerous and therefore the most accurate Greek manuscript copies of the *Epistle*

[18]*The Identity of the New Testament Text,* revised ed. p. 118.
[19]Metzger, *The Early Versions of the New Testament,* pp. 287-289.

to the Romans found in and associated with the West? The West was the possessor of the original and it was in Rome that the earliest copying of that letter must have taken place. But there are no more "Western" copies of Romans than there are of the other Epistles!

Secondly with regard to the MSS associated with the text of Alexandria and Egypt, their multiplication in that locale—together with Greek speaking Christianity itself—was cut off in Egypt with the Moslem conquest and capture of Alexandria in A.D. 642. Four years earlier the same fate had befallen the Christian centers in Palestine, including Caesarea. Having come under Moslem domination, it is not surprising that the MSS from these locales are comparatively sparse. The chief uncials and the papyri representing the Alexandria-Egyptian area are for the most part older than the eighth century (contrast the Byzantine) and antedate the Moslem "shut-off."

In the third place, and on the other side of the question, with regard to the multitude of MSS associated with the Byzantine area: a) in contrast with the West, Greek was the native or primary language therefore Greek MSS would naturally multiply; and b) the Byzantine area was not overwhelmed by the Moslems till the mid-fifteenth century with the fall of Constantinople in 1453. Because of this there was no "cut-off" of manuscript reproduction prior to that time. For these reasons, together with the first and second given above, it seems natural and to be expected that the Greek witnesses of this area should far out-number those of the other locales.

Therefore we conclude that the superior numbers of the Byzantine text do not necessarily guarantee its "originality" or greater kinship with the autographs.

The following section seeks to present reasons why the Byzantine text-type should no longer be ignored but be used in textual criticism. It supports a position which contrasts with the principal viewpoints surveyed in the preceding part. It differs from the WH contention that the Byzantine text should not be used because it is secondary and it differs with the Burgon-Hills view, which would use only the Byzantine text because it is primary. The view supported here is that the Byzantine has a place of usefulness as an independent text-type. This part of the book is divided into two sections which take up two main reasons supporting the thesis that the Byzantine text should be granted independent status. Briefly stated, they are: 1) Its readings are old. 2) Its text is unedited in the Westcott and Hort sense. If these reasons can be substantiated, such a circumstance would call for a re-evaluation of the usefulness of the Syrian text.

PART II

Reasons For Considering That
The Byzantine Text Is Independent

Section A

Byzantine Readings Are Old

CHAPTER V

Distinctively Byzantine Readings Are Found In Early Papyri

Though not every old reading is original, a reading must be old to be considered as possibly original. One of the principal reasons given by WH for considering the Syrian text unusable was the supposed late origin of its readings. In their opinion, readings which agreed with neither the Western nor the Alexandrian text-types and were not attested by early Fathers but were found exclusively in the Byzantine and other late manuscripts must be late in their formation. "Distinctively" Syrian readings must be late readings and on this account should be discarded automatically[1] (compare with p. 28 above). Although the reasoning of WH seemed sound at the time they wrote, discoveries since then have undermined the confident appraisal that characteristically Syrian readings are necessarily late.

Beginning with the second edition of Hort's introductory volume in 1896, various writers have called attention to Byzantine readings which have found support in early witnesses discovered since the time of WH. Francis Crawford Burkitt, an enthusiastic supporter of WH who wrote the "Additional Notes" in the second edition of the *Introduction*,[2] has noted that the (then) recently discovered Sinaitic Syriac, though often supporting the Alexandrian text, occa-

[1]See above pp. 27-28.
[2]*Introduction*, pp. 325-330.

sionally agrees with the Syrian text in "distinctive" readings. Later, in an article on the newly discovered Chester Beatty Papyri, Burkitt comments on Byzantine agreements in these manuscripts,[3] as do C. C. Tarelli and others in *Journal of Theological Studies*,[4] Gunther Zuntz in 1946 in the Schweich Lectures on *The Text of the Epistles*,[5] and E. C. Colwell in 1961 in his article on "The Origin of Text-types of New Testament Manuscripts."[6] Bruce Metzger, in "The Lucianic Recension of the Greek Bible," gives a list of seven examples of papyrus-supported Byzantine readings.[7] In a footnote, he lists some sixteen other references of "distinctively" Byzantine readings which are also found in p^{66}.[8]

How are such agreements between early witnesses and the late Byzantine text to be explained? Does not such evidence tend to upset the theory of lateness of the K-Text? At first this possibility was not faced and the logical explanation (in the framework of the WH theory) was that the Byzantine editors had somehow used other sources in addition to the Western, Neutral, and Alexandrian types set forth by Hort. This was considered plausible in the case of the Sinaitic Syriac when the concept was first advanced by Burkitt and later picked up by Streeter.[9] But when the Chester Beatty Papyri appeared, such agreements became too much for the theory to hold. The brilliant scholar Burkitt was frankly puzzled about it. Though he did not wish to favor the Byzantine text in any degree, in his article "The Chester Beatty Papyri," while commenting on various features and alignments of the papyrus, he remarked on two

[3]"The Chester Beatty Papyri," *Journal of Theological Studies*, XXXIV (October 1933), 363-368.

[4]XL, 19-25: "Some Further Linguistic Aspects of the Chester Beatty Papyrus of the Gospel," 1942.

[5]The lectures were published in 1953, *The Text of the Epistles, a Disquisition upon the Corpus Paulum* (London: Oxford University Press).

[6]*Early Christian Origins*, ed. A. Wikgren (a Festschrift for H. R. Willoughby, Chicago: Quadrangle Books, 1961).

[7]*Chapters in the History of New Testament Textual Criticism*, p. 38.

[8]*Ibid.*

[9]Note: H. C. Hoskier used a similar explanation to account for phenomena in B and its related MSS. He claimed that they arose from influence of the early versions, especially the Egyptian versions acting upon the Greek text in Egypt. See *Codex B and Its Allies, A Study and an Indictment* (in two parts) (London: Bernard Quaritch, 1914). See footnote 30, p. 68 below.

instances where p^{45} agrees with the Byzantine reading. One of these is Mark 7:31 and the other is Luke 10:41,42. After listing the evidence for Mark 7:31, he says in part: "I have no particular affection for ς (the Received or Byzantine text), but I cannot believe it is here the actual villain of the piece."[10] And in his comment on the Luke passage he says:

> And certainly it is not the Byzantine text, but an earlier ancestor of it, that has produced mixture. p^{45}, written about A.D. 240, is too early to be influenced by the Byzantine text, so that when it agrees with it the cause must be earlier.[11]

The open bewilderment of this keen scholar who was losing confidence in the WH theory is revealed in the following:

> I do not know when or where Lk. 10:42a was reduced to "one thing is necessary," but it was obviously prior to A.D. 240. I regard this reading as a corruption of the original reading, as I do the addition of the "Longer Conclusion" to St. Mark; but both corruptions are to be found in texts that go back to something like A.D. 200. . . .
>
> I have, frankly, no constructional hypothesis to offer. But a textual theory which is to hold the field must be able to answer all objections. Above all, B and "the neutral text" are not synonymous. It is easier, from some points of view, to reconstruct the original than some halfway house like the "neutral" or the "Caesarean" text, that contains some corruptions but not all.[12]

Burkitt is sure of one thing, that in these instances the Byzantine text has not influenced the text of the papyrus, but he can not answer how the reading of the papyrus got into the Byzantine text.

Other writers began to draw further conclusions. In the article "Some Further Linguistic Aspects of the Chester Beatty Papyrus of the Gospels," Tarelli warns against the habit of taking for granted that certain readings, because they are in the late Byzantines but not in B or other earlier available manuscripts, are therefore to be construed as improvements.

[10]*JTS*, XXXIV (October 1933), 366.
[11]*Ibid.*
[12]*Ibid.*, p. 367.

Previous studies of the Chester Beatty papyrus p^{45} have suggested that it is at least unsafe to assume a late date for a reading which might be explained as an improvement. There are a number of other readings which are interesting from the same point of view.[13]

Amid his comments in this article is the following illustration drawn from a distinctively Byzantine, but now papyrus-supported, reading in John 11:19.

It is clear that the evidence of p^{45} changes the aspect of this problem. So long as we had no earlier manuscript than B, the notion of Alexandrian and Antiochian "improvements" had great plausibility. Thus in John 11:19 when προς την Μαρθαν και Μαριαν or προς Μαρθαν και Μαριαν was attested by BC*DLWX 33, and A and the vast majority of later manuscripts read προς τας περι Μαρθαν και Μαριαν it was arguable that the simpler reading was the original and the other an "improvement." The support of the longer reading by a manuscript a hundred years older than B reinforces the inherent improbability of such an emendation and confirms the likelihood that the passage was mutilated by copyists who did not understand the idiom, or feared that their readers would not understand it.[14]

Tarelli is pointing out that it is the Alexandrian and Western texts that contain the heavier editorial changes here. He concludes by saying that "it is difficult to feel any greater certainty about the habitual superiority of B in the Gospels."[15]

Colwell, in his article referred to above, makes this thought-provoking statement:

But the Bodmer John (p^{66}) is also a witness to the early existence of many of the readings found in the Alpha text-type (Hort's "Syrian"). Strangely enough to our previous ideas, the contemporary corrections in that papyrus frequently change an Alpha-type reading to a Beta-type reading (Hort's "Neutral"). This indicates that at this early period readings of both kinds were

[13]*JTS*, XLIII (1942), 19.
[14]*Ibid.*, p. 20. See also his remarks on John 11:29, same page.
[15]*Ibid.*, p. 25.

known, and the Beta-type were supplanting the Alpha-type—at least as far as this witness is concerned.[16]

Metzger, near the end of his article, makes the following statement:

> During the past decades several papyri have come to light which tend to increase one's uneasiness over Hort's reluctance to acknowledge the possibility that an ancient reading may have been preserved in the Antiochian text even though it be absent from all the great uncial manuscripts. Since the discovery of the Chester Beatty Papyri (particularly p^{45} and p^{46}) and the Bodmer Papyrus II (p^{66}), proof is available that occasionally the later Byzantine text preserves a reading that dates from the second or third century and for which there had been no other early witness. A few examples selected from a large number will serve to illustrate this changed situation in the textual evaluation of the New Testament. . . .[17]

After presenting a list of seven examples, Metzger continues:

> Though this list could be expanded, enough examples have been cited to suggest that some of the roots of the Antiochian text go back to a very early date, antedating Lucian by several generations. It does not follow, of course, that the Textus Receptus should be rehabilitated *en bloc*, or even that in the examples cited above the Antiochian text is necessarily the original text. The lesson to be drawn from such evidence, however, is that the general neglect of the Antiochian readings which has been so common among many textual critics is quite unjustified.[18]

Zuntz's remarks in this connection seem especially startling because they were made a decade before the Bodmer Papyri began to be published. Here is an extended citation from *The Text of the Epistles* taken from the close of his discussion of p^{46} and the Byzantine text:

> To sum up. A number of Byzantine readings, most of them genuine, which previously were discarded as "late," are anticipated

---

[16]"The Origin of Texttypes," pp. 130-131.
[17]"The Lucianic Recension," p. 38.
[18]*Ibid.*, pp. 38-39.

by p^{46}. Our inquiry has confirmed what was anyhow probable enough: the Byzantines did not hit upon these readings by conjecture or independent error. They reproduced an older tradition. The existence of this tradition was in several cases borne out by some versions or patristic quotations; but where such evidence is not forthcoming, the inference proved no less certain. How then—so one is tempted to go on asking—where no Chester Beatty papyrus happens to vouch for the early existence of a Byzantine reading? *Are all Byzantine readings ancient?* In the cognate case of the Homeric tradition G. Pasquali answers the same question in the affirmative; and, indeed, it seems to me unlikely that the Byzantine editors ever altered the text without manuscript evidence . . . [italics added].[19]

Zuntz makes clear, however, that he is not adopting the view of Burgon or of the superiority of the TR:

We are not going to resume the hopeless fight of Dean Burgon. The Byzantine is the latest text and it is both natural and evident that it contains the largest proportion of corruptions. Most of the specially Byzantine readings rule themselves out of court without ado. The chance that, even so, *they are far older than the manuscripts which attest them* is none the less great . . . [italics added].[20]

He concludes this statement by observing: "Even so, we are now warned not to discard the Byzantine evidence *en bloc.*"[21] In his next paragraph, Zuntz calls attention to one very important conclusion which was reached by the study of the papyri in their various alignments particularly with the late manuscripts of the Byzantine text:

The progress of our investigation will yield some criteria for the relevance of the late tradition. Already now we may book one result which is of paramount importance for our ideas about the tradition as a whole. The extant Old Uncials and their allies cannot be relied upon to furnish us with a complete picture of the textual material which the fourth and fifth centuries inher-

[19]*The Text of the Epistles*, p. 55.
[20]*The Text of the Epistles*, pp. 55-56.
[21]*Ibid.*

ited from earlier times and handed on to the Middle Ages. P^{46} has given us proof of that.[22]

The papyri have brought about a change in the thinking of others who had followed more or less in the train of WH; for example, J. R. Janeway traces the transition in the outlook of the Spanish textual and Biblical scholar Jose M. Bover. He notes that the testimony of the Chester Beatty Papyri had a profound influence on the work of Bover:

> But after the discovery of the Chester Beatty papyri and Hoskier's presentation of other ancient evidence, Bover began to challenge some passages where all the former critics were agreed. . . . He stated that this part of his task was incomplete and that he hoped to make a thorough revision.[23]

Surprisingly, the remarks of the above writers are based on conclusions drawn from a relatively small number of instances where early papyri were seen to attest "Byzantine" readings. Zuntz lists thirteen or fourteen examples of which five are distinctive. Metzger lists seven, says the list could be expanded, and then in a footnote gives sixteen references in John where "further examples of distinctively Byzantine readings . . . are also found in p^{66}."[24]

In the research for this book, it was felt that all the available early papyri should be surveyed in order to discover if other papyrus-supported Byzantine readings exist. The survey includes all kinds of alignments with the K-text where K is at the same time supported by an early papyrus. These various kinds of alignments are displayed in the appendix in Lists 1-5. Preceeding the lists is an explanation of the procedures followed in compiling them, including the defining and identification of Byzantine readings (see pp. 137-144).

List I (see pp. 145-159) displays some 150 distinctively Byzantine readings now found to have early Egyptian papyri supporting them. Distinctively Byzantine readings are readings which are supported by the bulk of the later manuscripts but which at the same time are

[22]*Ibid.*, p. 56.
[23]*An Investigation*, p. 363.
[24]*Chapters*, p. 38.

opposed (or not supported) by the principal manuscripts and witnesses to the Alexandrian and Western texts. It may be recalled that WH considered such "Distinctive Readings" a special proof of the editing and consequent lateness of the Syrian text (pp. 27-28 above). These 150 readings, in List 1, which by WH's criteria would be classified as "distinctively" Syrian, are now seen to antedate the time of Lucian. They are found in Egypt one hundred years before the time of Lucian. Several things should be observed concerning these "Distinctively" Byzantine readings found in the early papyri.

(1) These 150 readings are early. They go back to the second century, for they are supported by papyri which range from the third to the second century in date. That such readings must be early is almost universally admitted by textual critics, the exception being the few critics, such as Williams (cited above, pp. 15, 29, 30), who have chosen to ignore or deny their existence.

(2) These readings were not edited in the fourth century. A second and corollary conclusion is that these readings are not the result of a late recension. They could not have been so created for they were present in Egypt by the end of the second century. It is not surprising to find Beta-type (i.e., Alexandrian) readings in Egyptian papyri or even Western readings for that matter (for it has been known for some time that "Western" readings are both early and widespread). But it is startling from the standpoint of the WH theory to find that so-called "Byzantine" readings not only existed early but were present in Egypt before the end of the second century.

(3) The Old Uncials have not preserved a complete picture of the second century. The third observation which should be made in the light of these readings and other accumulating evidence is that it should now be realized and taken into account that the Old Uncials have not retained all of the second-century tradition, even though they have maintained from that period two distinct types of text. Zuntz (see p. 60 above) felt that p^{46} alone gave proof of this. The inadequacy of the "Old Uncials," to portray the second century textual picture, is underscored further when p^{45}, p^{66}, p^{72} and p^{75} are also seen to confirm the early and wide-spread existence of K readings which are neither Alexandrian nor Western.

WH, therefore, were mistaken in regard to their insistence that all the pre-Syrian evidence for readings was to be found in the Alexandrian, Neutral, and Western texts, i.e., that these three text-types and their chief witnesses preserved the complete second-century picture of the textual tradition on which the Syrian editor(s) built. Hort said that

> . . . before the middle of the third century, at the very earliest we have no historical signs of the existence of readings, conflate or other, that are marked as distinctively Syrian by the want of attestation from groups of documents which have preserved the other ancient forms of text. This is a fact of great significance, ascertained as it is exclusively by external evidence, and therefore supplying an absolutely independent verification and extension of the result already obtained by comparison of the internal character of readings as classified by conflation.[25]

The support of distinctive Byzantine readings by early Egyptian papyri has provided proof that WH were wrong at this point. The "fact" of such "great significance," in Hort's words, has now vanished into thin air in the presence of ancient papyri. E. C. Colwell (above, pp. 58-59) had made the important observation that in some instances one could see the process of editing going on in Egypt in the corrections of p^{66}. In some cases the correction was made from an Alpha type (Byzantine) to a Beta (Alexandrian) type. For examples of these found in List I notice John 7:39, where p^{66} corrects from the Byzantine to the Alexandrian text-type, also John 7:40 and 8:54, where p^{66} again corrects from the Byzantine to the combination of Alexandrian and Western type, and in John 12:9, where p^{66} corrects from the Koine either to a singular reading or to one which is very lightly attested. In other papyri, note Ephesians 2:12 for an instance where p^{46} corrects from the Byzantine to the Hesychian-Western form of text and in Hebrews 12:25 from the Byzantine to the Alexandrian form. Then, in Hebrews 11:4 papyrus p^{13*} and p^{46} read the distinctively Byzantine, but p^{13c} corrects away from the Byzantine to a reading which is supported by Clement of Alexandria. There are instances where the papyri correct the other way. In John 8:21 and 19:4, p^{66} corrects from the combination of Beta and Western to the Alpha or Byzantine type. In John 19:11 p^{66} can be seen correcting away from a singular or lightly supported reading to the Alpha text. Such phenomena attest that some editorial activity was going on in Egypt at the time that these papyri were copied. The main point here, however, is that Alpha-type readings existed early and were, in some instances, competing with the readings of the Alexandrian text which, however, eventually rejected them.

(4) The Byzantine text-type has preserved second-century tradition not preserved by the other text-types. These readings are evidence that the Byzantine text has preserved at least portions of the second-century tradition of the New Testament independently of the Egyptian and Western text-types. Until the discovery of these papyri, the Byzantine text had been the *sole repository* of these readings from the second century. In view of this circumstance, it would seem, at least in so far as papyri-supported distinctively Byzantine readings are concerned, the Byzantine text-type can no longer be ignored in textual decisions. This is not meant to suggest that the K readings should be considered original when they are papyri-supported. It does suggest, however, that because of their proven age, at least such papyri-supported readings ought to be put on an equal level with the readings of the Alexandrian and the Western texts for the applying of internal evidence of readings. But what of Byzantine readings not supported by early papyri?

(5) Lateness of other Byzantine readings now questionable. With so many distinctively Byzantine readings attested by early papyri, doubt is now cast over the "lateness" of other Antiochian readings. This doubt brings to mind two questions: 1) What about Byzantine readings which occur in parts of the New Testament where there are no papyri, as yet, to confirm them? 2) What about Byzantine readings in places where papyri exist but the papyri support other readings and not the Byzantine? Should distinctively Byzantine readings in such places be considered early also?

Zuntz faced the first question and answered in the affirmative for all Byzantine readings (cf. above, p. 60). In a rather striking way Zuntz's remarks have been vindicated in cases where more recently discovered papyri have supported Byzantine alignments in places where the Chester Beatty (which he used) did not exist. (See the list in those areas in Luke and John where p^{66} and p^{75} attest Byzantine readings where p^{45} is not extant, as well as the places in I and II

Peter and Jude where p^{72} supports the Byzantine reading.) As for the second problem (i.e., where the papyrus supports a reading other than the Byzantine), such passages as Luke 11:50, where p^{45} reads with B 33 69 but the Byzantine reading, had no *early* attestation until p^{75} was discovered. Another example is John 2:15, where p^{66} reads with the Alexandrian but p^{75} with the Byzantine. See also John 10:19; 10:31; 12:36; Hebrews 10:17 for additional instances where papyri published in later years have been found to attest a Byzantine reading where another than the Byzantine had formerly been supported by a papyrus.

Numerous distinctively Byzantine readings now proved early would seem to reverse the burden of proof. Instead of assuming that characteristically Byzantine readings are late, it may be more logical and more in accord with the facts to assume that they are early. The burden of proof now appears to rest on whoever claims that a Byzantine reading is late. Furthermore, making textual decisions on the basis of how three or four "old" uncials read should be abandoned because they do *not* give a complete picture of the second century traditions.

How do such agreements as those exhibited in List I occur? Various possibilities suggest themselves.

(1) One possibility is that the agreement of early papyri in these readings is accidental, i.e., the papyri happen to agree in given instances because of scribal blunders which accidentally brought the papyri into agreement with the Byzantine text-type. E. C. Colwell, in a paper "Scribal Habits in Early Papyri: A Study in the Corruption of the Text,"[26] presented the singular readings of the scribes of p^{45}, p^{66}, and p^{75}. He concluded that certain types of readings exist where the support of a particular papyrus might be called in question because its scribe was prone to certain errors. An agreement in such an instance might be an accidental agreement and would not therefore reflect any genealogical relationship. He questions the support of p^{45} in cases of a transposition of words or where there is the omission of a dispensable word, as well as the support of p^{66} for the omission of a short word. Colwell also questions the support of

---

[26]Read before the Soceity of Biblical Literature in annual meeting in New York, 1964. Published in 1969 as Chapter VIII, "Method in Evaluating Scribal Habits: A Study of P45, P66, P75 in *Studies in Methodology* pp. 106-124.

any papyrus for the addition or omission of the definite article, for the omission of the personal pronoun, and for a reading which involved a harmonization to the immediate context unless it happened to be characteristic of a group.

When List 1 is re-examined with these scribal habits in view, Colwell's criteria could apply in a number of places. But it seems to be an impossible matter to determine with certainty that an omission was accidental. For example, in many places p^{45} and p^{66} agree with a longer reading involving short or dispensable words. The same phenomenon which would call in question the attestation of the papyrus on accidental grounds is observed when it agrees with the Alexandrian or the Western text. If, in such cases of agreement with the Alexandrian text, the idiosyncrasies of the scribes were reckoned as causing an accidental agreement, the attestation should then have to be withdrawn from the Alexandrian and counted with the opposing Byzantine! Thus, as far as total effect is concerned, the instances would appear to "balance out." In fact, when it is recalled that the Alexandrian text-type tends to favor the shorter reading, the supposed propensity of these papyri-scribes to make omissions suggests that on the basis of accidental agreement they would more naturally and therefore in a higher percentage of such agreements tend to support the Alexandrian rather than the other, usually longer, types of text.

However, agreement is most likely accidental when it occurs between a couple or a small scattered number of mss—not when it is to a reading characteristic of a group (possible exception being a common itacism). No doubt some of the Byzantine supported readings may be questionable in accordance with this possibility of accidental agreement, but it is obvious that the same type of accidental agreement of a papyrus with the Alexandrina or the Western reading would have taken away support for a Byzantine-supported reading. Therefore, while it may be true that some of these in the list have papyrus support because of accidental agreement, one could hardly say that such agreement is the criterion which would account for the majority of them; and in any given case it would be difficult to prove that accidental agreement had taken place.

The tendency of early Egyptian papyri to omit in singular readings and to be somewhat less dependable in the addition or omission of the definite article may well be giving us an insight into some of the handling of the early text in Egypt.

(2) Another explanation for papyrus-supported K readings is that the Byzantine text originated in Egypt. However, this explanation hardly fits the circumstances. There are more differences than there are agreements with the papyri and K in places of variation. The papyri do not suggest that the Byzantine text-type equals a pre-Alexandrian or Egyptian type of text, nor do any of the papyri present a pre-Byzantine type of text as has been maintained with some show of validity with p^{45} in Mark for a portion of the "Caesarean" text.[27]

(3) Still another proposal is that these readings originated in Egypt at an early period and were later adopted by the Byzantine editors. To hold that early Egyptian readings, that is readings lost or deleted from the H text-type, were adopted by editors at Antioch is to endeavor to explain them in the framework of WH's theory of the origin of the Syrian text. This was Burkitt's explanation for the Sinaitic Syriac agreements, i.e., that the Byzantine editors took Old Antiochian readings out of the Syriac version(s). Streeter followed him in this.[28] Burkitt in 1933 wavered when it came to applying this explanation to p^{45} agreements (cf. above p. 57). However, almost 30 years later in 1961 Vincent Taylor endeavored to fit all the criteria into this framework:

> The Byzantine Text, or TR, gains a new interest if families additional to the Alexandrian and the Western are recognized. In this situation the Byzantine text is more inclusive than a combination of the β and δ texts. In addition to the use of these families its editors must have drawn upon Antiochian [i.e., Old Syriac] and Caesarean MSS, since presumably these are of earlier origin. In fact, p^{45} contains Byzantine readings which are earlier than c. A.D. 250, that is before the Byzantine text was compiled. In short, this text is more eclectic than we had supposed.[29]

In Taylor's mind there appears to be no other possible solution than to keep applying the WH theory of the dependence of Anti-

[27]See Metzger's "The Caesarean Text of the Gospels," *Chapters*, esp. pp. 60-67.
[28]*The Four Gospels*, pp. 115-116.
[29]*The Text of the New Testament*, p. 75.

ochian editors on outside sources. Since the theory is accepted as fact, the new data must be interpreted in line with the theory.

But it must be protested here that the papyri are supplying the very kind of evidence to prove the early existence of Byzantine readings that WH had contended were absent from the Fathers. If these second-century readings originated in Egypt, then how (in accordance with the WH Theory) did they get into the "fourth-century edition" of Antioch when at a very early time they had been excluded from the Alexandrian text-type? This question becomes even more difficult to answer when it is realized, as it now appears from the evidence supplied by p^{75}, that the Alexandrian text-type had been well established by the late second or early third century. If the Antiochians had sent to Alexandria for manuscripts by which to correct their text, no doubt they would have desired a copy of the best and most highly regarded current text. Surely they would not have settled for one or more of the aberrant papyrus manuscripts which were circulating privately.

Moreover, if to retain the theory of Westcott and Hort for the origin of the Syrian text, the date for the Antiochian editing be pushed back into the second century the theory becomes almost impossible to hold. It is unlikely that at such an early period Antioch, conscious of her history and the high quality of her own first manuscripts, would have had any high esteem for manuscripts or readings coming from the area of the "School of Alexandria," or from Caesarea for that matter.[30]

(4) It is possible that these readings originated early in Antioch

---

[30]On Burkitt and Streeter's idea of deriving Old Antiochian readings in K from sy[sc]: This now appears to be as unlikely as Hoskier's attempt to derive distinctive readings of B from the Coptic and Old Latin versions. Hoskier may have borrowed this idea from Burkitt in the first place. There appears to be no question as to the Egyptian character and locale of the Vatican MS; but Hoskier's "proofs" that B was influenced in its text form by the Coptic and Old Latin *versions* fall short of demonstration. In Hoskier's work *Codex B* . . . there are numerous instances where he cites B supported by one of the Coptic versions alone, and holds this as evidence that it was the Coptic version which influenced the text of B. In many of these places one of the papyri, either P[66] or P[75], can now be added to the same reading. This indicates that the Alexandrian recension goes back into the second century. It is more reasonable to assume that it was the Coptic versions which followed the Greek in these readings, and not vice versa; so also with the Syriac and Greek agreements at Antioch.

and found their way to Egypt and into early copies of manuscripts there. This seems more logical for the early period than the reverse, Antioch being the missionary church. Such readings were then preserved at Antioch in the Byzantine text but became buried with the papyri in Egypt because they were rejected by the Alexandrian editors.

(5) Another explanation is that these agreements set forth in List 1, indicate the independent preservation of wide-spread second-century readings. They were in Egypt as seen by their preservation in the papyri. They were also in Antioch as is seen by their preservation in the Byzantine text. However, at the present stage of knowledge, it is impossible to trace their origin.

(6) They represent independent preservation of original readings. Here agreements indicate nothing as to manuscript relationships, but they constitute widespread and early testimony to original readings.

Therefore, in seeking to account for papyrus-supported K readings: Categories 4 (the readings originated early in Antioch), 5 (they represent independent preservation of wide-spread readings of unknown origin), and 6 (independent preservation of original readings), these along with 1 (an occasional accidental agreement), may each account for some of the papyri agreements.

Explanation 2 (that the K-text originated in Egypt) appears impossible; and explanation 3 (that the readings originated early in Egypt and were adopted at a later date by K) though conceivable, seems to be the least logical of the possibilities. Of the six categories, 4-6 would seem to account for most of the agreements.

In view of the above, it is concluded that the papyri supply valid evidence that distinctively Byzantine readings were not created in the fourth century but were already in existence before the end of the second and that, because of this, Byzantine readings merit serious consideration.

CHAPTER VI

Byzantine-Western Alignments Go Back Into The Second Century Independently And Originate In The East—Not In The West

WH rejected nothing more vigorously than the thought that the Syrian text or Syrian manuscripts could add any weight of authority to the Western readings.[1] However, the Egyptian papyri focus attention on a thought-provoking phenomenon. They attest the early existence of readings in the Eastern part of the Roman empire in which the Byzantine and the properly (i.e. geographically) Western witnesses agree and at the same time are opposed by the Alexandrians. In the treatment of this type of alignment (along with other true Western alignments), Gunther Zuntz has made a contribution which has received neither the attention nor the credit which it rightfully deserves. The first item that makes Zuntz's findings significant is that in his penetrating analysis he found no instances in which any distinctively Western reading had ever affected the Eastern texts.

> There is, so far, not the slightest indication that any properly Western readings, that is, readings which originated with or in the course of, the separate Western tradition, ever affected the East. The one type of variants which could bear out this view, namely the latinisms, has no Eastern support. If then at least some also of the errors which are attested only by Western wit-

[1]See Hort's discussion on this in the *Introduction*, p. 118, also p. 28 of this book.

70

nesses had a wider circulation at an early time, one may well wonder why p^{46} supports, almost exclusively, genuine Western readings.

The rewriting of I Cor. 15:2 and the peculiar order of the clauses ib. i. 2, attested by Western and by the most ancient Eastern witnesses, point to some common source. There is nothing to suggest, and everything to discourage, the assumption that this source was in the West. These common errors indicate some contact, at a very early date, between the predecessors of both; their sporadic agreements in genuine readings are evidence that, from a pre-Western and pre-"Alexandrian" stage, p^{46} and its allies retain some original elements which were soon to vanish from the "Alexandrian" and from the Eastern tradition in general, while one or more of the three Western archetypes caused them to survive in the West.[2]

The implications of Zuntz's findings in connection with the thesis of this book seem obvious: If the readings in which the Byzantine text agrees with the Western text did not come from the West but originated in the East, then a crippling blow appears to have been dealt the WH theory. The contention of WH that such Syrian-Western alignments are not weighty evidence because the Syrian text was formed in part from Western manuscripts has actually been reversed by Zuntz. The reversal of the weight of the Byzantine testimony at these points is required, for such alignments of witnesses are not only weighty external evidence but they also show the K-text in each instance to be the preserver of a very early form of the text as it was known and used in the East before it was adopted by the West.

Zuntz's work was with p^{46}, the earliest of the Chester Beatty Papyri. His conclusions with respect to Western readings in non-Western witnesses are of such importance that they deserve to be quoted at length. He entitles them "Some Conclusions: General, on Western Readings," and goes on to say:

The material so far surveyed yields one paramount conclusion: *Western readings in non-Western witnesses are, generally, ancient*

[2]*Text of Epistles,* pp. 95-96; see also p. 143, 156-157, and pp. 254-255 for a discussion of this significant passage by Zuntz. See also the application of these findings in Zuntz' conclusion, pp. 282-283.

survivals. They are *not* in the relevant witnesses, *secondary intrusions* into a previously pure form [italics added].

This assertion is, I believe, capable of strict proof. We have assembled, from I Corinthians and Hebrews, more than seventy Western readings which recur in the "oldest Alexandrians" (most of them appear in p^{46}; many also in its allies; very few in the latter only). . . . Only nine out of these more than seventy are properly, and only, "Western", all the rest having some non-Western support which indeed may consist of anything from an occasional quotation by Origen (I Cor. iii.3) to the mass of Byzantine mss (the latter often reinforced by the Peshitta and other Eastern versions). Whence comes this striking preference, on the part of p^{46}, for W + and W- omega [WΩ = Zuntz' symbol for Western-Byzantine] readings? Whoever shares the widespread view that Western readings in non-Western witnesses, say in (so-called) "Caesarean" or Byzantine mss, were grafted upon a previously pure, say "Alexandrian" or "Caesarean" basis—an assumption which, for example, led Professor H. A. Sanders to consider the "lesser Alexandrians" as "purer" than their big brothers—must credit the scribe of p^{46}, or its ancestor, with prophetic insight: This person must have forseen which Western readings would be picked out, centuries later, by the editors (if any) or scribes of "Caesarean" or Byzantine mss. In his selection of Western readings he must have been guided by this amazing foresight, embracing those which were destined, after centuries of oblivion to reemerge in, perhaps, one single twelfth-century minuscule (as in I Cor. 1:22; 3:10; 14:14) or also to be received into the later standard text—and to reject those which were foreordained to wither in Western seclusion. Looking at the same facts from the other end, the later "Caesarean" and Byzantine editors or scribes who are supposed to have introduced a number of Western readings into their manuscripts must have had an unaccountable preference for those which, in centuries past, had been embodied into the Chester Beatty papyrus (which, at the time, slumbered in the Egyptian sands).

The evident inadmissibility of these assumptions enforces the obvious alternative: *these "Western" readings in the East are elements of a continuous tradition, from and before the time when p^{46} was written and down to the Middle Ages.* The intermediaries which handed them on, from the early to the late witnesses, are not preserved. Once again we are reminded how incomplete is the extant evidence prior to the tenth century [italics added].[3]

Zuntz continues with the following statement on Byzantine-Western alignments:

> Purely (i.e., distinctively) Byzantine readings, as we saw before *may* be ancient. We can now add: Byzantine readings which recur in Western witnesses *must* be ancient [Zuntz's italics]. They go back to the time before the Chester Beatty papyrus was written; the time before the emergence of separate Eastern and Western traditions; in short, they reach back deep into the second century.
>
> Were it not for the deserved authority of the admirable Griesbach [followed by WH], one might well wonder how the other view—namely that they were added later—could ever be held. Scholars apparently never paused to think of the historical implications. Could a Byzantine patriarch in the eighth or ninth century [or even of the 4th] be supposed to have sent envoys to some Greek monastery in Sicily or south Italy in order thence to procure some obsolete manuscripts and from them to intrude a number of Western readings into that sacred text which his authority made prevail among the Orthodox? Obviously the Byzantines retained Western readings which had been carried down to them by the main stream of the Eastern tradition. The opposing "Alexandrian" witnesses, in these instances, represent a backwater of that stream; they were bypassed by the main current even though theirs often was the correct reading. *This conclusion is enforced with regard to those variants which have now reappeared in the Chester Beatty papyrus but evidently applies to all of them* [italics added].[4]

Zuntz's findings display and underscore the fact that the Byzantine text furnishes an early and independent weight of evidence for readings where it and the Western text agree against the Alexandrian. The rationale for this statement may be briefly summarized: 1) The evidence now shows that in cases of Byzantine-

---

[3]*Text of the Epistles*, pp. 142, 150.
[4]*Ibid.*, pp. 150-151.

Western alignments there has been independent preservation of such readings by each text-type from deep in the second century. 2) Furthermore, such agreements did not result from an Eastern adoption of readings which originated in the West. The only thing that could prove an Eastern adoption of Western readings would be "latinisms" and/or errors proven to have arisen in the West and held in common with Eastern witnesses, and these are missing in such alignments. 3) The West got these readings from the East originally (i.e., their origin was in the East, not in the West) for: a) The readings were in the East at the earliest period as is attested by early Egyptian papyrus-Byzantine-Western agreements; b) common errors between early papyri and Western witnesses point to an Eastern source; c) common "genuine" readings (i.e., genuine in the sense of original, or worthy of being considered original) thus attested also point to an Eastern source.

Reinforcing Zuntz's findings, List 2 (Appendix, pp. 160-174) sets forth approximately 170 of these papyri-Byzantine-Western alignments.[5]

In List 2 the corrections of p^{66} are of interest again. There are several occasions where p^{66*} agrees with the Byzantine-Western alignment, then corrects to the Alexandrian-WH type of text. (See John 10:22,26,28; 11:29,32; and 14:4 for examples of this type of correction.) In 14:14 p^{66*} reads with the Koine text together with the Western, and p^{66c} is to a singular reading; however, it seems to conflate in the direction of the Alexandrian text-type in adding τουτο. In addition to these there are several instances where p^{66*} reads with the Alexandrian text-type and WH but corrects to the Byzantine-Western combination. These are found in John 4:51; 7:52; 8:28; 11:54; 13:20,21,25. There is also a singular reading of p^{66*} in 13:24 which cannot be completely made out because the text is somewhat obscure at this point, but it is not exactly the same as the Alexandrian; however, the correction (p^{66c}) is to the Koine-

---

[5]The collation is more or less complete up through the latter part of I Cor. Following this point the tabulation is more scattered, and readings were accumulated less systematically. The collations are not quite as thorough for this list in p66 and p75 as they are for p45 and p46 (up through the I Cor. portion mentioned above), because the apparatus of Kenyon in the texts of the Chester Beatty papyri gave additional help in furnishing leads for the agreements of p45 and p46.

Western alignment. On seven occasions in this list the writer of p^{66} corrects from a Byzantine-Western alignment to an Alexandrian; and in another seven instances he corrects from an Alexandrian type reading to a Western-Byzantine type.

Therefore, these papyrus-Byzantine-Western alignments opposed by the Alexandrian text-type reveal readings which were well nigh universally known in the second century. But though they were eliminated from the Alexandrian text-type, they have been preserved independently in the Byzantine and in the Western traditions.

Hort strenuously resisted the notion that there could be any increased weight of attestation for a Western reading when it was supported by the Syrian text. His stance was a natural result of theorizing that the Byzantine text was in part dependent upon the Western text. However, these papyrus-Byzantine-Western alignments appear to demonstrate that in such Western-Byzantine combinations the Byzantine witnesses add the weight of an independently preserved type of text. These alignments are much more significant for New Testament Textual Criticism than a mere increased attestation of one additional MS for a "Western" reading. Such alignments do not prove that these readings (with or without papyrus support) are necessarily original. However, it should be realized and taken into account that such alignments in a reading immediately introduce the two factors of age and increased weight of attestation: 1) The reading is old for, originating in the East, it has been preserved separately in East and West from deep in the second century; and 2) the reading is heavily attested by external evidence for in each such instance it has the weight of two independent and widely separated traditions behind it.

Additional Note:

Why has there been so little acknowledgement of the significant findings set forth by Gunther Zuntz? There appear to be at least two reasons why Zuntz's findings, at this point, have not been given wider publicity: the first is that his development of the evidence and the conclusions he draws are difficult to follow for one not thoroughly acquainted with New Testament text criticism (NTTC). The second reason that Zuntz's conclusions have not been widely and enthusiastically acclaimed (though they constitute a "breakthrough") is that his findings deal a devastating blow to WH's basic theory of the history of the text, i.e. they destroy the supposed partial dependence of the K-text on Western sources.

If this dependence in K-Western alignments must be reversed as Zuntz demonstrates, then one half of the support for Hort's basic theory of conflation collapses immediately! But, not only does the WH theory fail at this point, it is changed into the opposite! This is more than the "general consensus of scholarship" can concede. It is an intolerable thought and too revolutionary to acknowledge that the Antiochian text may have been the source rather than the recipient of the common material in such Byzantine-Western alignments. There is a "dead-weight" of traditional antipathy toward the Byzantine text that just cannot allow itself to believe that the K-text is able to furnish any really valuable evidence for New Testament text criticism. This inherited antipathy has created a giant drag against progress in textual matters.

CHAPTER VII

The Silence Of The Fathers Is Explainable And Therefore Is Not A Proof Of Lateness

Someone might object to the study taken up in this book by saying, "There is no point in even opening the question of the usefulness of the Byzantine text because its secondary nature has been established by the absence of Patristic evidence." It is true that WH felt this to be one of their strongest and most convincing arguments. Patristic silence, i.e., the apparent failure of the earlier Fathers to use the Syrian text in their quotations of the Scriptures up to the time of Chrysostom, was taken as irrefutable proof of the non-existence of that type of text.[1]

Sir Frederic G. Kenyon has clearly indicated the vital importance of the patristic evidence to the WH theory:

> It is on this crucial point of the controversy that the patristic evidence becomes of decisive value. Hort, as we have seen, appeals to it as showing that the Traditional Text is characterised by many readings which cannot be traced back farther than the fourth century—readings which, moreover, have in his eyes the appearance of a secondary character, as derived from pre-existent readings which are found in the other groups of

[1]*Introduction*, pp. 112-115; cf. also p. 117. Indeed, it was this part of the WH argument that their followers (e.g., Lake, Williams, etc.) insisted undergirded the *"fact"* of the secondary nature of the Koine text. For the emphasis which these writers put upon this part of WH's argument, the statements of those which have been mentioned above may be recalled. See pp. 15, 29, 30 of this book.

authorities. Here is a plain issue. If it can be shown that the readings which Hort calls "Syrian" existed before the end of the fourth century, the key-stone would be knocked out of the fabric of his theory; and since he produced no statistics in proof of his assertion, his opponents were perfectly at liberty to challenge it.[2]

The preceeding pages present the kind of evidence that Kenyon said was needed. The papyri have now demonstrated "that the readings which Hort calls 'Syrian' existed before the end of the fourth century." Byzantine readings have now been proven to be in existence by the end of the second century! Since early papyri now support many "Syrian" readings, and thus demonstrate their early existence, the question naturally arises as to whether there may be a flaw in WH's argument from Patristic evidence. If Byzantine readings are early, wherein lies the flaw or weakness in Hort's argument? The following seeks to present an answer to this question.

In regard to the argument based on the silence of the Fathers, it should be observed first that, contrary to the statements of WH and their followers, quotations from early Fathers *have* been found in support of Byzantine readings. However, when such citations from early Fathers have previously been submitted, they have generally been disallowed as evidence for the early existence either of the Syrian text or of the reading in question. It was contended that the texts of the Fathers had been assimilated (changed or conformed) to the Byzantine norm by Byzantine scribes as they copied the manuscripts of the writings of the Fathers.[3] In the light of this it was further argued that the only place that the quotation of an early Father may be considered dependable is where it disagrees with the Koine.

No doubt some assimilation has taken place, and a few instances of such have been demonstrated.[4] However, in the second place, in List 1 (distinctively Byzantine readings supported by papyri) there

---

[2]*Handbook to the Textual Criticism of the New Testament* (2nd ed.; Grand Rapids: Wm. B. Eerdmans Publishing Co., 1912), p. 321.

[3]*Introduction*, Hort, pp. 110-111.

[4]See Streeter's discussion of "The Fathers and the Standard Text," *The Four Gospels*, pp. 45-47, in which he gives two examples of assimilation taken from the Latin tradition in the cases of Cyprian and Pelagius, whose citations had been assimilated from the Old Latin to a Vulgate form. He also cites an instance in the

are some Byzantine readings which, before the discovery of the papyri, had been attested by ante-Nicene Patristic support. It should be recognized in these readings which are proven early by the papyri, such Patristic support appears to be authentic (i.e., non-assimilated). Instances in the list where Byantine readings have early Fathers for their support are as follows: 1) Luke 10:21, Clement; 2) Luke 12:5, Tertullian; 3) Luke 12:22, Clement; 4) Luke 12:31, Clement and Marcion; and 5) John 2:24, Origen. Origen also attests 6) John 4:31; and 7) John 13:26. In the Epistles, example of patristic support may be found as follows: 8) Romans 10:14, Clement; 9) I Cor. 4:11, Clement and Origen; 10) I Cor. 5:10, Origen; 11) I Cor. 7:5, Origen; 12) I Cor. 7:7, Origen; 13) I Cor. 9:7, Origen; 14) I Cor. 9:21, Origen; 15) Eph. 2:12, (Origen) and Tertullian; 16) Phil. 1:14, Marcion; 17) Heb. 11:32, Clement; 18) I Pet. 2:5, Clement and Origen.

In spite of the preceding, it must be admitted that by and large, at least as far as critical apparatuses are concerned, the testimony of Ante-Nicene Fathers is quite light for the Koine text. It may also be admitted that Chrysostom is the earliest church Father whose writings contain substantial Antiochian citation. However, with these matters as a background, there are several additional observations which should be made in connection with the argument that the silence of the early Fathers in attesting the Antiochian text is proof of its non-existence:

Benedictine edition of the Fathers where the text of Origen has obviously been assimilated in a quotation from Matt. 26:3-5.

However, M. Jacob Suggs warns that "it is possible to make too much of this aspect of the problem." He is not maintaining that there was *no* such "correcting" on the part of the scribes. He is suggesting that this problem has been exaggerated. Suggs goes on to say: "While modern standards of reproduction were not in effect in the manuscript period, it would be untrue to say that verbal accuracy was not an aim of the ancient scribe—particularly of the trained copyist. There is little evidence of systematic revision of New Testament citations except in translated works, and this is paralleled by the practice of modern translators of theological works in quoting Biblical passages in a familiar version rather than supplying a fresh translation. Even medieval commentaries, which incorporate comments of early Fathers under *lemmata* of a later text, are less than thorough in revising the earlier forms to fit their own." ("The Use of Patristic Evidence in the Search for a Primitive New Testament Text," *New Testament Studies*, IV, No. 2 (January, 1958), 140.)

In the first place it is an argument from silence. It is astonishing to read the statements of some of these men—the emphatic way in which they talk about "the facts" when the foundational argument is one from silence.

In the second place it is an argument from the silence of Fathers in non-Syrian locales. One of the chief values in the literary remains of a Father is their use as an aid to establishing the text-type of his locale. His date and place of residence are known. Because of this, his Scripture citations shed light on the kind of text used in his time and area, and he thus helps to identify the text-type of the area. Irenaeus lived in Gaul and used a Western text; Origen is one of the chief supporters for the Alexandrian and Caesarean texts, and this is natural for he lived in both of those areas. It is therefore asking too much to expect Irenaeus and Origen to be of help in identifying the local text-types used by them (Irenaeus in Gaul and Origen in Alexandria and Caesarea) and at the same time expect them to be witnesses to the type of text which was used (or which was not used) at Antioch. For example, while Irenaeus is a second century father and Origen a third, the fact that Irenaeus' quotations do not support the form of text used later by Origen in Egypt cannot be used as proof that the Alexandrian text-type did not exist at a period earlier than Origen. But it is this same argument that is the mainstay of WH's theory! Compare the fact that Origen is the first real user of the Alexandrian text-type (Clement who preceded him tends to support Western readings) yet we do not limit the age of the H text to the date of Origen. Apparently, the testimony of the early papyri has made the argument from Patristic silence demonstrably invalid.

In the third place, this argument from the silence of the Fathers is an argument from silence as far as Antioch is concerned. Supporters of the WH theory point out that Chrysostom (who flourished in the last half of the fourth century) is the earliest Father to use the Byzantine text. However, they customarily neglect to mention that there are no earlier Antiochian Fathers than Chrysostom whose literary remains are extensive enough so that their New Testament quotations may be analyzed as to the type of text they support. The silence-of-the-Fathers argument has been asked to bear more weight than it is able to sustain. How can Fathers of other areas using other local text-types be expected to witness to the Antiochian text? And how could it be expected that the Antiochian text (i.e., the early form of it) can be attested by Fathers who have left little or no writings?

The argument from silence cuts both ways. Obviously one should not argue *for* the early existence of the Antiochian text from the lack of Scripture quotations in the Fathers. However, it is equally plain that its non-existence should not be argued from such silence either.

Finally, it should be pointed out that the papyri-supported Byzantine readings together with geographically-Western and Byzantine alignments actually amount to a more reliable testimony concerning the early existence of these readings than could possibly be rendered by quotations contained in late copies of works by early Fathers. Such data point up the invalidity of WH's argument from Patristic silence, and would appear to remove the main support for their theory.

CHAPTER VIII

The "Conflate" Or Longer Readings
Are Not A Proof Of Lateness

"Conflate" readings have been put forth as one of the main lines of evidence supporting WH's "demonstration that the Syrian text is later than the other types."[1] Hort presented eight examples of conflation, four in Mark: 6:33; 8:26; 9:38,49; and four in Luke: 9:10; 11:54; 12:18; 24:53.[2] Hort felt these readings were concrete evidence for what he considered the procedure or practice of the Syrian editors. These "conflations" led to the conclusion that the changes in the text had been mainly in one direction, i.e., the direction of conflation and fulness on the part of the Syrian text. Hort concludes that the conflations prove two things: 1) that the Syrian readings are always later in date than those of the other text-types and 2) that those who created these readings used manuscripts of Alexandrian and Western types to do so.

> Hence it is certain not only that the δ [Syrian] readings were always posterior in date to the α [Alexandrian] and the β [Western] readings in variations illustrating the relation between these three groups by means of conflation, but also that the scribes or editors who originated these δ readings made use in one way or another of one or more documents containing these

---

[1]Metzger, *The Text*, p. 135 (cf. pg. 30 above).

[2]Introduction, pp. 93-104. Cf. above page 26 in this book for a summary of Hort's last example.

α readings, and one or more documents containing these β readings . . .[3]

Having drawn these two conclusions, a third was built upon them: Since the Syrian editors used the Alexandrian and Western manuscripts in making "conflates," they must have also used them freely elsewhere in the editing of their texts.

But the proved actual use of documents of the α and β classes in the conflate readings renders their use elsewhere a *vera causa* in the Newtonian sense.[4]

Burgon acidly denounced the "conflations" of WH because they did not all fit the classification of conflation, and because they were too few in number to sustain such a far-reaching theory. Sarcastically, he suggested that the reason so few were set forth by WH was because no more could be found.

Of these, after 30 years of laborious research, Dr. Westcott and he flatter themselves that they have succeeded in detecting eight.[5]

Examining the conflates of WH in a lengthy note, Burgon sought to show that the Western and Alexandrian texts had abridged the "Traditional text."[6]

Some of Burgon's criticisms may have validity, but this book does not take the position that the longer or "conflate" readings are necessarily the original readings; some of them indeed may be the result of scribal activity. However, the evidence available now shows that such readings are neither a result or proof of late editing, but actually go back into the second century. If this is true even for some conflate and longer readings, then it should be apparent that the procedure of using a few examples of long or conflate readings in order to prove a late and dependent editing process for the whole text is invalid.

[3]*Introduction*, p. 106.

[4]*Ibid.*, p. 107. Cf. also Para. 187, pp. 134-135 of Hort's *Introduction* for the supposed propensity of the "authors of the Syrian text" to change in the direction of interpolations and additions for "lucidity and completeness."

[5]*The Revision Revised*, p. 258.

[6]*Ibid.*, pp. 258-265.

1. Some Byzantine "Conflates" and "longer readings" are now demonstrably early. Though longer readings similar to WH's example of "conflation" in the Syrian text are not very common, others than the eight listed by WH do exist. There are at least two in List 1 which might be thus classified. In John 10:19 the division of manuscripts attesting the various readings is as clear cut in regard to text-types as WH's Luke 24:53 example:[7]

σχισμα ουν	D 1241 r[1] sy[s]	Western
σχισμα παλιν	אBLWX 33 WH	Alexandrian
σχισμα ουν παλιν	ΑΓΔΘΛΠΨ pl	Byzantine

In John 10:31 there is another clear-cut division: This time four types of texts are involved in the breakdown of readings (with yet a fifth reading supported by sy[p]).

εβαστασαν	Caesarean
εβαστασαν ουν	Western
εβαστασαν παλιν	Alexandrian
εβαστασαν ουν παλιν	Byzantine

Examples such as these two might have bolstered the WH theory of conflation further and provided some answer to Burgon's accusation if they had been brought forward in his time. Today, however, they cannot help the theory of WH, for in each one the so-called "conflated" reading is supported by early papyri. In the John 10:19 passage, while p^{45} and p^{75} support the Alexandrian reading, p^{66}, the earliest papyrus, reads σχισμα ουν παλιν. In John 10:31 the "conflate" reading is supported by p^{66}, and the shortest one, εβαστασαν, is papyrus-attested as well, being supported by p^{45}. If p^{75} supports any of these, it would appear to be the Alexandrian εβαστασαν παλιν.

While it may be true that conflation has taken place in one or more of these instances, it is not logical to continue to hold that such readings are a proof of lateness. These readings were in existence before the end of the second century—before the earliest manuscripts we possess. Though these "conflate" readings were unsupported by early patristic evidence, their early existence had been accurately attested all the while by the Byzantine text.

2. Conflation is not limited to the Byzantine text as WH infer. Longer or conflate readings are not found in the Byzantine text alone. Examples may be found even in manuscripts and families

[7]See pp. 25-26 above.

outside of the Byzantine text. In John 5:15 the attestation of readings reveals a "conflation" in W. W is considered to have an Alexandrian text in this portion of John. (See fuller attestation in List 4).

ανηγγειλεν	P⁶⁶P⁷⁵B *pl* K
απηγγειλεν	DKUΔ *al*
ειπεν	אCL *pc* bo WH
ανηγγειλεν και ειπεν αυτοις	W

In John 5:37 (List 1) manuscript D may be seen as an apparent combination of the other two. αυτος is read by the Byzantine bulk, to which p^{66} is now added; εκεινος is read by the Alexandrians and p^{75}; while εκεινος αυτος is read by D.

In John 11:41 (not in the Lists) there is an example of what might be called a conflation in a Family Π reading:

ανω	P⁶⁶P⁷⁵ ABCDEGHSWΘΨΩ *pl*
εις τον ουρανον	sa
εις τον ουρανον ανω	KΠ 265 489 1346* Fam Π*rell*

Colossians 3:17 reveals an example of what WH would call a conflation if it were found in the Syrian text; however, in this instance it is found in א:

κυριου ιησου	B *pl* Byz
ιησου χριστου	ACDᵍʳFᵍʳGᵍʳ
κυριου	L
κυριου ιησου χριστου	א vgᶜ (C1) Ant

3. Conflations are even found in B and in the Beta Text-type. Near the close of their discussion of conflate readings in the Syrian text WH say

> To the best of our belief the relations thus provisionally traced are never inverted. We do not know of any places where the α group [Alexandrian] supports readings apparently conflate from the readings of the β and δ [Western and Syrian] groups respectively, or where the β group of documents supports readings apparently conflate from the readings of the α and δ groups [Alexandrian and Syrian] respectively.[8]

[8]*Introduction*, p. 106. Contrary to WH's claim, there are places where the Alexandrian text apparently conflates from the readings of the Byzantine and Western groups (i.e., the pattern is as clear-cut as any of the examples of Syrian conflation). If D is allowed to speak for the Western text in the Gospels there is a clear-cut case in John 5:37 (List I) where D conflates from the readings of WH's α and δ groups respectively.

E. C. Colwell points out that "Codex Vaticanus lacks the conflate readings of the 'Syrian text,' but it has conflate readings of its own."[9] In a footnote Colwell calls attention to several instances where Vaticanus is involved in what might be termed "conflate readings." One of these examples is quite significant because it involves not only Vaticanus but other important members of the Beta (or Alexandrian) text-type as well. In Mark 1:28:

ευθυς   ADEFGHKMSUVY ΓΔΠΣΦΩ 22 157
                          1071 1241 *pl* p f g^2 *l* vg sy$^{ph^1}$

παντάχου   W 579 b e q geo^1 aeth
ευθυς παντάχου   ℵ^c BCL Fam 13 543 837 892
omit   ℵ* Θ Fam 1 28 33 249 474 517 565 700
                          c ff sy^s bp geo^2 arm

Here indeed is an instance of that phenomenon of which WH wrote when they said they did "not know of any places where the α group supports readings apparently conflate from the readings of the β and δ groups respectively.[10]

Another passage, Luke 10:41, 42 (List 4), is one of those discussed by Burkitt in his article on "The Chester Beatty Papyri." Burkitt rejected the originality of the Syrian reading. Neither did he intimate in his comments that B or C^2 and L and ℵ in the readings they support had conflated. Instead of "conflation" of the B-text Burkitt speaks of the reduction of the text followed by Byzantine witnesses saying: "I do not know when or where Lk. 10:42a was *reduced* to 'one thing is necessary,' but it was obviously prior to A.D. 240" [italics added].[11] In the minds of the supporters of the WH theory, when the Byzantine text is longer, there is a "conflation," but when the Byzantine text is shorter, then it is termed a "reduction" or abridgement. A different view of this verse is taken by a more recent scholar, Aelred Baker, in an article "One Thing Necessary."[12] He holds that the Byzantine preserves the original reading. He traces the history of the citation of this verse in the

[9]"Genealogical Method," p. 117.

[10]It may be noted in passing that neither WH, the two Nestle (the 26th ed. does note), nor the UBS texts give any indication that the Alexandrian text conflates, or even that there is a variation in the text at this point involving a shorter reading; they simply adopt the conflate reading silently.

[11]"The Chester Beatty Papyri," p. 52.

[12]*Catholic Biblical Quarterly*, XVII (April, 1965) 127-137. Cf. also G. D. Kilpatrick's, "The Greek New Testament of Today and the Textus Receptus," in *The*

course of modern textual criticism and translation and shows that
there has been a reaction in modern times away from the reading
favored by WH to the shorter one read all along by the Byzantine
and supported now by two papyri, p^{45} and p^{75}.

Another instance of conflation involving B and some other manuscripts is found in John 7:39 (List 1), where WH follow the shortest
reading and give no acknowledgement of the straying of B even
though they have a note on this verse in their "Selected Readings."[13] In Philippians 1:14 (List 1), the Alexandrian manuscripts
support the longer reading. Though it may not be a "conflate" in
the strictest sense of the word, it parallels some of those WH classified as conflate in the case of the Syrian text.

One more passage (not in Lists), Colossians 1:12, may be noted at
this point.

τω ικανωσαντι	P[46]אACD[c]EKLP *pl* WH
τω καλεσαντι	D*FG *pc* d e f m
τω καλεσαντι και ικανωσαντι	B

Again WH make no acknowledgement of B's conflation but quietly
forsake it as far as their text is concerned.

If, for example, WH's principles were applied to these passages,
referred to above, in which the divisions are rather clearly set forth,
then the textual critic would have to acknowledge that because one
text represented by B and some of its followers conflates the two
other texts, therefore the text of B must be later in origin, and the
other two texts must be earlier than B. But WH could not make
such application of their principles, for that would make the Syrian
text earlier than the text of B!

These longer readings which contain in one reading the material
found in more than one other text-type may be conflates in some
instances and in others they may be readings which have been ab-
breviated in the other texts or manuscripts. With examples of "conflation" in both the Syrian and in the Alexandrian text-types,[14]
however, there appears to be no grounds for arguing that the longer

[13]*Introduction* (Appendix), p. 82.
[14]Some of the Syrian conflates are attested by papyri but none of the conflations
seen thus far in the Beta text-type have papyrus support.

New Testament in Historical and Contemporary Perspective, eds. Anderson and Barclay, Chapt. 8, p. 192. See also G. Fee, "One Thing Is Needful," Luke 10:42 in
bibliography, for argument to return to WH reading.

reading was late in its origin. Conflation may have taken place; but it would appear that if it did, it took place early—during the second century. The evidence indicates that the presence of a longer reading is not therefore to be taken automatically as a sign of lateness. It should be recognized also that where a segment of a supposed conflation in the Antiochian text is found in Western witnesses, this segment originated in the East not in the West (cf. discussion above based on findings of Zuntz, pp. 70-76).

4. Natural conflation did not take place in certain places in K. It should also be noted that there are places where conflation according to the habit and tendency of the scribes (as described by WH) would have been very easy to show itself but was passed up by the editors of the Syrian text. See for example such passages as Mark 5:42 (List 1), where in the alternative readings from the shorter Byzantine εξεστησαν ("they were astonished") may be found εξεστησαν ευθυς ("immediately they were astonished") read by the Alexandrian and εξεστησαν παντες ("they all were astonished") read by the Western; however, neither one (to say nothing of both) is taken over into the Byzantine text in what would have been a natural and smooth-reading conflation: εξεστησαν ευθυς παντες ("immediately they all were astonished"). A passage such as John 5:37 (List 1) indicates that the Byzantines could resist conflation (or the longer reading) even though it might be followed by another text.

5. The greater proportion of longer papyrus-distinctive-Byzantine readings attests the early age of such "long" readings. It is well known that the Byzantine text generally has the longer reading. It is the "smoother," "fuller" text. In the manuals, "prefer the shorter reading" is one of the rules which is often found for judging between readings. The theory is that the scribes tended to add material to the text and that the shorter reading was therefore seen as the earlier and more likely original reading. However, the Byzantine text is occasionally shorter than the Alexandrian text. With this fact in mind, and in the light of the supposed propensity of the scribes to add, it was anticipated that in places where the distinctively Byzantine text was papyrus-supported, the preponderance of such places would involve shorter readings because the shorter K readings would surely be the earliest K readings.

Such a phenomenon, however, did not appear as may be seen by consulting the lists of readings and the tables and charts which tabulate the readings found in the first three lists.[15] Instead of finding (as was anticipated) the greater number of papyrus-confirmed variants in K where the Byzantine reading was the shortest, the greater proportion was of longer papyrus-supported Byzantine readings. This underscores the danger of making it a rule "to prefer the shorter reading" as more likely the earlier and/or original one. Actually, the length of a reading has nothing to do with its age: long readings are old and short readings are old. Both are attested by manuscript evidence that places them deep in the second century. The criteria for judging between them must be something other than their respective lengths. Since "long" readings are so early attested, and since such readings are not confined to K but also include H, WH's basic argument from conflation would appear to be disannulled. Kilpatrick on the basis of internal criteria questions the rule, "Prefer the shorter reading."[16]

[15]See appendix, pp. 145-187; for Tables and Charts, pp. 209-230.

[16]Kilpatrick, in his evaluation of the text behind the *TR*, includes a discussion on conflation, in which he examines variant readings eclectically, and finds that in many instances the longer reading should be preferred as the original reading. He concludes the discussion on homoeoteluton with the following observations:

> This list is . . . sufficient to show both how prevalent this kind of mistake is and how frequently the *Textus Receptus* and its allies preserve the original reading. Westcott and Hort of course rejected their evidence and chose the shorter text even when it clearly impaired the meaning as at Mark x. 7.
>
> It is worth considering how this came about. One of the canons of textual critics in modern times has been *lectio brevior potior*. . . . On the other hand if we substitute the maxim, 'the longer text, other things being equal, is preferable', have we any reason for thinking that this is more mistaken than the conventional *lectio brevior potior*? We are used to this last but the fact that it is traditional is no argument for its being true. Nonetheless, Westcott and Hort do not seem to have thought of challenging it.
>
> Let us consider the matter further. There are passages where reasons can be given for preferring the longer text and there are others where we can find reasons for preferring the shorter. There is a third category where there does not seem to be any reason for deciding one way or the other. How do we decide between longer and shorter texts in this third category? On reflection we do not seem able to find any reason for thinking that the maxim *lectio brevior potior* really holds good. We can only hope that a fuller acquaintance with the problems concerned will enable us increasingly to discern reasons in each instance why the longer or the shorter reading seems more probable.

Cited from Kilpatrick's essay: "The Greek New Testament Text of Today and the Textus Receptus," Chap. VIII in *The New Testament in Historical and Contemporary Perspective, Essays in Memory of G. H. Macgregor,* ed. by Anderson and Barclay (Oxford: Basil Blackwell, 1965), p. 196.

CHAPTER IX

The Composite Nature Of The Byzantine Text Attests Early Existence Of Its Readings Where Its Strands Unite

Westcott and Hort had argued that the composite testimony of the two manuscripts, א and B, carried back to an archetype of over 200 years earlier than themselves.

> An answer, in our opinion a true and sufficient answer, is thus found to the question how far the testimonies of א and B are independent of each other. Their independence can be carried back so far that their concordant testimony may be treated as equivalent to that of a MS older than א than and B themselves by at least two centuries, probably by a generation or two more.[1]

Their contention with regard to the early age of the text on the basis of the composite nature of its witnesses has been strikingly confirmed by the recent Bodmer papyrus, p^{75}. This papyrus also confirms the view that B best preserves the early Egyptian form of the text which both א and B represent.

As in the case of the Alexandrian text, the composite testimony of varied strands within the Byzantine text carries its existence back to a much earlier period than the age of its extant manuscripts. Von Soden detected five major strands in the Kappa text,[2] three of

[1]*Introduction*, pp. 223-224.

[2]At first Von Soden's conclusions were rejected. However, the validity of his groupings is now generally accepted. Streeter, early in his book, *The Four Gospels*,

which he considered early: K^1, K^i, and IK^a. Von Soden indicated that part of the proof of the early existence of the K text was that traces of K-readings occurred plentifully in early manuscripts mainly belonging to other text-types. He found traces of K, for example, in A, C, א and Ψ.[3] Von Soden further maintained that K^1 had influenced B as well as the others.[4] This last mentioned part of Von Soden's concept, i.e., that K readings had influenced manuscripts of the Hesychian (Alexandrian) type, is now reinforced by the research in the papyri which has found Byzantine readings in Egypt at an early date.[5]

To return to the matter of compositeness, Silva Lake, in her work *Family* II *and the Codex Alexandrinus,* made a thorough study of one of von Soden's groups, the IK^a group. In her study of II and Alexandrinus, she found that the ninth-century manuscript II, compared to the fifth-century manuscript A, actually preserves in a purer form the text which lies behind them both and which must go back to an earlier period. She assigned it to the early fifth century or before.

> In working on the manuscripts included in this study it became clear to me that von Soden's K^a text was a real entity, although he had confused the issue by grouping the Codex Alexandrinus with K and II. . . . the Codex Alexandrinus is connected with K, and II, and the cognate minuscules in a very different way from that in which they are related to each other. K, II, and a certain group of minuscules are a definite family. This family

[3]Kenyon, *The Text of the Greek Bible,* p. 179.
[4]Kenyon, *Handbook,* p. 365.
[5]This, however, has more to do with another though related matter, that is the early spread and element of "universality" in the K-text.

---

has a lengthy footnote, p. 34, in which he gives expression to his great disappointment with the work of von Soden. However, by the time Streeter comes to the close of his book, he makes the following observation in his second appendix:

> I may add that in the course of writing this book I have had to study the MS evidence given by von Soden in innumerable cases up and down the Gospels, and have found nothing to conflict with the results obtained above. Accordingly, though it may be a few of the less important of the 28 MSS which groups as I$^\pi$ ought not to be included, he has discovered a real group; and *fam.* 1424 must be treated as an important constituent of the Θ family. I have also found reason to accept his view that 544 (ε 337) is a true member of the same family. (Page 578).

and the Codex Alexandrinus had, at some point in their history, a common ancestor which differed very little from the text which is found today in Π, rather more from that of A. The reconstructed text of Family Π, therefore, represents a manuscript older than the Codex Alexandrinus and affords another witness to a text which must have existed in the early part of the fifth century, if not before.[6]

While Silva Lake traced the text of Π beyond the date of Alexandrinus to the early fifth or late fourth century, one may wonder if this estimate was not too conservative. As in the case of ℵ and B, Π and A have a degree of homogeneity and yet represent two strands within a composite group. If two hundred years proved a valid estimate for the text which lies behind ℵ and B, it would seem, on the basis of the same kind of grounds, reasonable to assume that the concordant testimony of Π and A would go beyond the age of A (copied in the fifth century) to the beginning of the fourth and perhaps deep into the third.

H. H. Oliver in a review of Jacob Geerlings' *Family Π in Luke*[7] comments in regard to the second appendix in Geerlings' work that

> . . . a collation of Codex A with Fam Π, confirms the earlier view of Lake that A and Π have a common archetype, a finding which causes scholars to push the date of the origin of the ecclesiastical text further back into the Byzantine period.[8]

Oliver's remark calls attention to the composite testimony of Π and A, which Geerlings shows to have been sustained in other Gospels in addition to Mark, and indicates that such testimony pushes back the date of the text-type.[9]

G. D. Kilpatrick illustrates the use of composite attestation to detect the early date of a reading. In an article entitled "Atticism and the Text of the Greek New Testament," he demonstrates the way that most intentional variations may be traced back into

[6]*Family Π*, page ix.

[7]J. Geerlings, *Family Π in Luke* (Studies and Documents XXII), Salt Lake City: University of Utah Press, 1962.

[8]*Journal of Biblical Literature*, 82 (1963), 221.

[9]See also Geerlings, *Family Π in John* (*Studies and Documents* XXIII), Salt Lake City: University of Utah, 1963.

the second century. In pages 128-131, he discusses the matter of the early rise of the variants and the cessation of their occurrence by about A.D. 200. During this presentation he makes an application of composite attestation in connection with the Alexandrian text to show the early existence of a particular reading:

> . . . at Mk. 1:21 εισελθων is present in some witnesses and absent from others. אCLΔ f13 28 565 837 892 Origen lack the word and our other witnesses have it. אCL 829 [sic] have the Alexandrian text. None of them is a descendant of another in part or whole. This means that probably the shorter text was in being in the Alexandrian tradition before A.D. 250. But Origen f13 28 565 represent the Caesarean type of text and Origen belongs to the first half of the third century A.D. So the meeting point of the Alexandrian and Caesarean traditions of the text will be before A.D. 200. Therefore this reading will belong to the second century.[10]

Thus, apart from attestation of early papyri, the composite testimony of the Alexandrian together with Caesarean witnesses leads to the conclusion that the shorter reading existed before the close of the second century. In like manner Kilpatrick finds evidence in the remaining (non-Alexandrian) witnesses that the alternative longer reading also existed very early. Kilpatrick detects this by separating the clusters of manuscripts that constitute von Soden's early Kappa groups (SVΩ = K¹, AKΠ = IKᵃ, and EFGH = Kⁱ). He reckons that these, together with the two Iᵀ manuscripts ΣΦ, make up a composite testimony that carries the reading back into the third century, while the additional testimony of the Western text when combined with the Kappa is considered sufficient to assure that the reading originated prior to A.D. 200:

> On the other hand the rest of our witnesses have the longer text. It is uniformly in the Latin manuscripts and this suggests that it was in this version by the third century. The Greek text behind the Latin would in these circumstances be older still. Let us take another group of witnesses. AYΠ may be presumed to have a fourth century ancestor, EFGH and SVΩ probably each have a

[10]Page 128. *Neutestamentliche Aufsatze*, Festschrift für Prof. Josef Schmid (Verlag Friedrich Pustet Regensburg), 1963.

sixth century ancestor, and there may have been a common ancestor to these two last groups in the fifth century. At this point the Purple Manuscripts are represented by ΣΦ, each of the sixth century, and their immediate ancestor may have been of the fifth century. We may deduce from this that as far as the evidence of the manuscripts AEFGHSVYΠΣΦΩ is concerned this reading may be deemed to be as old as the third century. If the evidence of A and its allies is combined with that of D and the Latin, it seems reasonable to suppose that the reading they all support was in being before A.D. 200.[11]

Kilpatrick is using the concordant testimony of manuscripts (for the most part more recent than the fourth century) to demonstrate the early dating of this reading. It is his conviction that the largest part of deliberately caused variants in the apparatus go back to the same time.

Our brief examination of the witnesses has suggested that both readings were in being before the beginning of the third century, although all these witnesses themselves are with one exception not older than the fourth century. This process can be repeated for many other variant readings for which we do not have explicit evidence of their existence before A.D. 200. If we take together the readings of which we may assume on explicit or inferential evidence that they existed before A.D. 200 we find that they form probably the largest part of the deliberate changes in the apparatus.[12]

To sum up the matter of compositeness: Though the Byzantine text is a highly homogeneous text, it is also composite; i.e., it is made up of distinguishable strands. Therefore, in places where the three earliest strands (K[1], K[i], and IK[a]) unite in their support, such a compositely attested reading is considered at least third-century in date. The agreement of yet another type of text would then carry the attestation of the reading back to the second century.

[11]"Atticism," p. 129.
[12]*Ibid.*

CHAPTER X

Summary Of Section A

In summing up Section A it seems reasonable to conclude that the readings of the Byzantine text are old because of seven basic findings: 1) many of its distinctive readings, formerly thought to be late, conflate, and edited, are attested by early papyri, and 2) it was discovered that Western-Byzantine agreements also go back to the second century. Such readings are early and widespread, but though they were rejected by the Alexandrian text, they have been preserved from deep in the second century by the separate Byzantine and Western traditions. Furthermore, these K-Western agreements (contrary to WH) have their origin in the East not in the West. 3) The silence of the Church Fathers in regard to K readings is explainable because a) it is not as absolute as has been maintained, and b) it has a logical explaination. Lack of Patristic support from non-Byzantine areas (i.e., from non-Byzantine Fathers) is invalid evidence for an argument that the Byzantine text did not exist at an early period. Even without such evidence and reasoning, however, WH's silence of the Fathers argument (the argument upon which their whole theory rested) has been strikingly offset by the discovery of Byzantine readings in the early papyri. 4) It was found that the longer or "conflate" readings are not a sign of lateness in the text; neither are such readings restricted to the Byzantine text. Some "conflates" have been found in the Western and even in the

95

Alexandrian text-type, including Vaticanus itself. The papyri reveal that longer and what have been called "conflate" readings were already in existence in the second century. 5) The composite nature of the Byzantine constitutes yet another line of evidence attesting the early existence of the K readings where the testimony of the various strands is united. Additional support from another text-type appears to insure the second-century existence of a reading with such attestation.

6) Others have called attention to the early age of K readings. To the above may be added a reminder that the idea of the ancient character of Byzantine readings, of course, is not new or original with this writer. The remarks of Zuntz, Tarreli, and Colwell as mentioned above, together with others, indicate that a number of New Testament scholars have been calling attention to the early age of Byzantine readings.

7) Deliberate changes in all the text-types appear to antedate A.D. 200. Kilpatrick notes with approval the statement of Vogels that, "as distinct from errors, most deliberate changes, if not all were made by A.D. 200,"[1] and he makes the point that "recent discoveries confirm this."[2] Later in the same article, Kilpatrick presses the point that there is "no difference in kind between readings which can be shown to have originated early and those whose date is uncertain."[3] In the same statement, he suggests that examination will show that all the categories of deliberate alteration, including harmonization, stylistic variation, and so forth, are present both in groups that can be shown to be ancient by evidence and also in others for which the evidence may not be available to prove their early date.[4]

Kilpatrick also raises the question as to whether there are any readings which can be demonstrated to be later than A.D. 200. He calls attention to some three examples of readings which originated in the thirteenth century and were discovered by E. W. Saunders. Kilpatrick then notes earlier examples of attempts to introduce changes into the text on the part of Origen and the very poor success with which they were met.

[1]"Atticism," p. 128.
[2]Ibid.
[3]Ibid., p. 129.
[4]Ibid.

These two examples of alteration to the text of the New Testament after A.D. 200 show how uncommon such changes were in the later period. We would probably get a fair picture of the proportion of change after this date to changes made before it if we were to compare the numbers of the changes demonstrably later to the number of changes demonstrably earlier. There can be no question that the earlier ones are far and away more in number.

Origen's treatment of Mt. 19:19 is significant in two other ways. First he was probably the most influential commentator of the Ancient Church and yet his conjecture at this point seems to have influenced only one manuscript of a local version of the New Testament. The Greek tradition is apparently quite unaffected by it. From the third century onward even an Origen could not effectively alter the text.

This brings us to the second significant point—his date. From the early third century onward the freedom to alter the text which had obtained earlier can no longer be practised. Tatian is the last author to make deliberate changes in the text of whom we have explicit information. Between Tatian and Origen Christian opinion had so changed that it was no longer possible to make changes in the text whether they were harmless or not.[5]

Kilpatrick finishes this aspect of his article by saying:

> . . . by the end of the second century A.D. Christian opinion had hardened against deliberate alteration of the text, however harmless the alteration might be. The change of opinion was connected not with the canonical status of the New Testament but with the reaction against the rehandling of the text by the second century heretics. This argument confirms the opinion of H. Vogels, mentioned above, that the vast majority of deliberate changes in the New Testament text were older than A.D. 200. In other words they came into being in the period A.D. 50-200.[6]

It is concluded, then, that the readings of the Byzantine text are old. They, like the readings of the other text-types, go back deep into the second century.

---

[5]"Atticism," p. 129-130.
[6]*Ibid.*, p. 131.

SECTION B

The Byzantine Text Is Unedited
In The WH Sense

CHAPTER XI

The Evidence In Section A

The heading of Section B stems from the realization that if the theory of WH as to the derivation of the Byzantine text is no longer supported by the data, then the Byzantine text should be considered an independent witness to the text of the New Testament. It is not meant to suggest that the Byzantine text has undergone no editing. What is affirmed here is that the theory of a drastic and eclectic editing using Alexandrian and Western texts appears far less plausible now than it did in the days when the theory was promulgated by WH.

A striking instance of a modern textual critic whose views changed after the discovery of the Chester Beatty Papyri is found in the case of Jose M. Bover. John Raymond Janeway has a reference to the transition in the life and study of Bover after the Papyri came to his attention:

> There were two stages in Bover's critical study. The first, completed by 1930, was the study of the differences between the modern critical texts. The second stage began after the publication of the Chester Beatty papyri, and has never been completed. This is the investigation of the text accepted by all the former critics in the light of the new evidence. For Bover, this resulted in a reevaluation of the early Antiochian text. Thus, he set out to vindicate it as one which possessed the right to be heard in the debate over readings.[1]

[1]An Investigation, p. 534.

This writer agrees with Bover and feels that in the light of the new evidence the testimony of the Byzantine text has been neglected too long. If its readings are early and its text is unedited in the WH sense, it is not dependent upon the other text-types. If it is not derived from the other text-types, then its testimony ought to be given an objective hearing and due consideration in weighing evidence for readings.

The evidence in the preceding section indicates that the K readings were in existence long before the earliest date allowed by WH. Therefore, the Byzantine text appears unedited in the WH sense, because the data in the preceding section show that Byzantine readings are as early as those of any other text-type. Byzantine readings carry back into the second century, which is far earlier than the limits WH set for their theory and is therefore evidence against it.

The evidences in Section A for the early existence of K readings, in addition to upsetting the "time boundaries" set by WH, also cut away the main supports for their genealogical and patristic arguments. These arguments claimed that because of "conflates" found in it and because its distinctive readings were unsupported by quotations from early Fathers the Byzantine text must be both late in origin and edited in nature. These were the arguments upon which the theory of WH rested. However, as has been pointed out in the matter of conflation, some Byzantine "conflates" are attested by early papyri. Their proven early existence takes away the argument that longer (and/or conflate) readings constitute proof of lateness. In addidtion to this, "conflates" are found in other text-types than the Byzantine, including the Alexandrian with B and its allies. These two facts would seem to remove the WH argument resting on conflation.

As observed in the preceding section, the argument from patristic testimony is invalid because it is an argument from the silence of non-Byzantine Fathers and the silence of pre-Chrysostom Antiochian Fathers. Furthermore, it needs to be recognized that a second-century papyrus attesting a Byzantine reading constitutes much stronger evidence for the early existence of the reading than would the citation of a second-century Father, who might have used the very papyrus, yet whose quotation has been perserved to us in a fourth to an eleventh-century manuscript-copy of his writings. Therefore, evidence supporting the early date of K readings is also evidence against a WH-type editing of the K-text-type.

WH's third argument is from intrinsic evidence and is, therefore, subjective as defenders of the WH theory admit. For this reason less weight is usually attached to it. This argument is not avoided, however, and will be taken up below under a discussion of the style of the Byzantine text (pp. 107-114). The remainder of this section seeks to present further reasons for considering the Byzantine a non-dependent text—important in solving New Testament textual problems.

CHAPTER XII

The Significant Provenance Of The Byzantine Text-Type

Another item, the significant provenance (geographical origin) of the Antiochian text-type, raises further doubts about its dependence on Alexandria and the Western parts of the Empire. The theoretical dependence of the K-text becomes increasingly doubtful as the date of editing is pushed back to an early time, for the following question arises: "Why should the great apostolic and mission-minded church at Antioch send to Alexandria or any other center for Scripture copies by which to correct her own?" The Church at Antioch, conscious of her heritage and the excellence of her own first copies of the Scriptures, would have little reason to consider the resources of others superior. Antioch was the third city of the empire, a city with an independent and proud spirit; and something of this same independent spirit was part of its heritage as the "mother of all Gentile churches."[1]

[1] M. C. Tenney, *New Testament Survey* (Grand Rapids: Wm. B. Eerdmans, 1961), p. 253. Cf. Virginia Corwin, *St. Ignatius and Christianity in Antioch* (New Haven: Yale U. Press, 1960). See especially the second chapter on "Antioch and the Christians," where this author finds intimations suggesting that the church at Antioch did imbibe something of the proud and independent spirit of the city, pp. 31-51.

See also Glanville Downey, *A History of Antioch in Syria, from Seleucus to the Arab Conquest* (Princeton: Princeton U. Press, 1961); in which he not only traces the history of the city but also calls attention to the influence that the church at Antioch exerted over the whole area of Syria, p. 304 ff.

Antioch may well have been the prime source of the earliest copies of most of the New Testament Scriptures for newly established churches. It will be recalled that Antioch was the place where the first Gentile missions originated; it was the home base for the apostle Paul;[2] Luke may have been there;[3] Mark,[4] Barnabas and Silas, Paul's companions, were there;[5] Peter visited Antioch;[6] Matthew may have written his Gospel there.[7] Paul himself could have double-checked the local copies of his own epistles which were thus far possessed by the church at Antioch before he made his last journey from that place.

It should be remembered that the leadership of the Antiochian church was not characterized by illiteracy or a low level of education (see Acts 13:1), and therefore incapable of making good copies of "Scriptures." The first century generally was "literate to a remarkable degree."[8]

Furthermore, the apostles and other early Jewish members of the Antiochian church had the tradition of Israel's careful copying of the Scriptures as an example for their care. A high view of the New Testament writings as "Scripture" appears to have been held from the beginning by the church. This belief in "inspiration" was early. It is set forth in the canonical books themselves. Paul was conscious that he wrote "the commandments of the Lord" (I Cor. 14:37); and Peter included the writings of Paul with "the other Scriptures" (II Pet. 3:15, 16). Such high regard for apostolic writings would call for special care in their handling from the very beginning.

[2]Acts 12:25; 13:1-3; 15:30, 36 etc.

[3]A concise summary of arguments for Luke's association with Antioch is given by Wm. F. Arndt, *Bible Commentary The Gospel According To St. Luke* in his Introduction, especially pages 2-5.

[4]Acts 11:25; 13:5; 15:37.

[5]Acts 13:1-3; 15:32, 40.

[6]Galatians 2:11.

[7]See B. H. Streeter's discussion connecting Matthew with Antioch in *The Four Gospels, A Study of Origins*, pp. 500-523.

[8]Colin H. Roberts points out that "the world into which Christianity was born was, if not literary, literate to a remarkable degree; in the Near East in the first century of our era writing was an essential accompaniment of life at almost all levels to an extent without parallel in living memory. In the New Testament reading is not an unusual accomplishment . . . and reading may be assumed to have been as general in Palestine as, from the vast quantity of papyri of all kinds and descriptions, we know it to have been in up-country Egypt at this time." *Cambridge History of the Bible*, Vol. I p. 48.

When matters relating to the provenance of the Byzantine text are taken into consideration, they appear to further mitigate against the drastic editing called for by the theory of Westcott and Hort. If, because of the early existence of K readings, the date for a major editing of the Byzantine text must be pushed back before A.D.200, it is difficult to assume Antiochian dependence on other local texts for the improvement of her own. It might appear more logical to reason that if Antioch would send anywhere for copies of New Testament Scriptures in order to purify its own text, it would most likely send to Ephesus, Galatia, Colosse, Thessalonica, Philippi, Corinth, and Rome in order to acquire more perfect copies of the epistles originally sent to those locales.

Another reason for questioning Antioch's dependence upon manuscripts whose provenance was Alexandria is the difference of attitude toward Scripture and its interpretation which existed between the theological schools of the two cities. Beginning as early as Theophilus (died before 188) who, as an advocate of the literal interpretation of Scripture, is considered a forerunner of the "School of Antioch," Antioch developed a school of literal interpretation which was almost diametrically opposed to the "School of Alexandria" with its principles of allegorical interpretation. This makes it difficult to believe that Antioch would look to Alexandria for help in either the earliest period or later when the differences between the schools became even more marked.

CHAPTER XIII

The Koine Style Of The Byzantine Text-Type

An important consideration has to do with the style of the Byzantine text. This is a more subjective area of judgment, as Kirsopp Lake acknowledges.[1] However WH made internal evidence of readings their third main argument for the posteriority of Syrian to other readings.[2]

Hort's oft-quoted description of the characteristics of the Byzantine text is as follows:

> The qualities which the authors of the Syrian text seem to have most desired to impress on it are lucidity and completeness. They were evidently anxious to remove all stumbling-blocks out of the way of the ordinary reader, so far as this could be done without recourse to violent measures. . . . Both in matter and in diction the Syrian text is conspicuously a full text. It delights in pronouns, conjunctions, and expletives and supplied links of all kinds, as well as in more considerable additions. As distinguished from the bold vigour of the "Western" scribes, and the refined scholarship of the Alexandrians, the spirit of its own corrections is at once sensible and feeble. Entirely blameless on either literary or religious grounds as regards vulgarised or unworthy diction, yet shewing no marks of either critical or spir-

[1]*The Text*, p. 67.
[2]*Introduction*, pp. 115-119.

itual insight, it presents the New Testament in a form smooth
and attractive, but appreciably impoverished in sense and force,
more fitted for cursory perusal or recitation than for repeated
and diligent study.[3]

The Byzantine text does tend to be simple, lucid, full, unpretentious and plain in style. Much of WH's description is *a propos*.
However, it should be noted that their description of the "Syrian"
text, with few changes, could also be taken as an acceptable description of the Hellenistic Greek of the first century!

As is now known, the New Testament was written in the Koine or
"common" style of the day. This was not appreciated in the days of
Westcott and Hort as it has come to be since the work of Adolf
Deissmann, J. H. Moulton and A. T. Robertson. WH came to their
study of the New Testament with the background of an "Attic-
trained judgment."[4] This, no doubt, was a factor in their being
attracted to ℵ and B, the chief representatives of the Alexandrian
text-type. Where there is variation in the text, the Alexandrian
manuscripts often tend to favor the more brief, precise, and Attic-
like forms of expression.

Though Westcott and Hort resisted the connection of the "Neutral" text with any locale, they acknowledge that it may have been
"preserved" at Alexandria.

> That a purer text should be preserved at Alexandria than in any
> other church would not in itself be surprising. There, if any-
> where, it was to be anticipated that, owing to the proximity of
> an exact grammatical school, a more than usual watchfulness
> over the transcription of the writings of apostles and apostolic
> men would be suggested and kept alive . . .[5]

It now appears that the "exact grammatical school" may have done
more than "preserve" the text at Alexandria.

Kilpatrick notes several areas in which Atticism in the early period appears to have introduced changes into the text of the New
Testament. One involved the tendency to eliminate Semitisms:

[3]*Introduction*, pp. 134-135.
[4]Cf. J. N. Birdsall, "The New Testament" (Text), *The New Bible Dictionary*, ed.
J. D. Douglas (Grand Rapids: Wm. B. Eerdmans Publ. Co.), p. 1268.
[5]*Introduction*, p. 127.

One stylistic consideration can be quickly discerned. If we come to the New Testament from Classical Greek we soon perceive that among the distinctive features of the Greek Testament are idioms which, strictly speaking, are not Greek at all. No Greek of any period, left to himself, would say or write αποκριθεις ειπεν. In the same way "he answered and said" is not natural English. . . . Hence we are not surprised when we find that often where αποκριθεις ειπεν and the like occur in our Greek text there are variants designed to mitigate or remove this un-Greek expression. We may even suspect that sometimes the attempt to improve the language has been successful and that the more Greek expression is in our text and the original unGreek wording in our apparatus.

Let us take an example of this. At six places in our texts of Mark today (9:12,38; 10:20,29; 12:24; 14:29) εφη occurs and at each place in the apparatus there is a variant αποκριθεις ειπεν or its kin. εφη is a good Greek word of ancient lineage but it was going out of use in the first century. As we have seen αποκριθεις ειπεν is not a Greek expression at all. Have the scribes changed the good Greek εφη to the barbarous αποκριθεις ειπεν or the other way about? If we may assume that their intention was to improve the evangelist's Greek rather than to degrade it, then αποκριθεις ειπεν will be original.[6]

Besides distinguishing between what was Greek and what was not Greek, there was the temptation to improve or replace "poor" Greek with what was considered to be good Greek.[7] Kilpatrick illustrates by referring to the atticistic tendency to avoid the use of the "historic" present.

Sometimes Atticism involved mere change in spelling from a Hellenistic to an Attic form of the same word. Kilpatrick calls attention to the following Attic/Hellenistic spelling variants noted in the text of Revelation: ηρπάσθη/ηρπάγη, στηρισον/στήριζον, ερρηθη/ερρέθη, εσκοστωμενη/εσκοτισμένη. He then adds that "similar variations occur in the other New Testament books.[8]

A striking illustration of early Atticism involving the voice of a

---

[6]"Atticism," p. 126. Some passages in addition to those cited by Kilpatrick and involving apparent editorial deletion of αποκριθεις are: Mt. 24:2; 26:63; Mk. 5:9; 7:6; 8:28; 10:5; 11:29,33; 12:17; 13:2,5; 14:20; Lk. 5:22; 14:5; 20:34.

[7]Cf. Origen's complaint, p. 118 below.

[8]"Atticism," p. 126.

verb, which was apparently introduced in Alexandria, is found in the future forms of ζαω. In classical Greek writers the future active is used and the middle is condemned. In later and non-Attic writers, however, the middle form is found in popular use.[9] As Kilpatrick suggests, on this evidence we would expect the New Testament writers to use ζησομαι rather than ζησω.

> John uses the future of ζην six times . . . both active and middle forms occur in our manuscripts at each occurence as may be seen from the following table:

	Active	Middle
5:25	P[66,75]אBDW f[1]	ΓΔΛΨΑΠEGHSVΩΘMU f13
6:51	אDLWΘ	P[66]BCTΓΔΛEFGHSVΩΠMU fl,13
6:57	P[75]אBC[2]LTΠΘ f13	P[66]WΓΔΛEGHSVΩMY fl *l* 1561
6:58	P[75]אBCTLΔΛWEGSVΩNΘ fl	P[66]DHΓMU f13 *l* 1561
11:25	P[45]	[*rell*] (P[66,75]אABCDWΘ etc.)
14:19	P[75]BLX	P[66]אQWΓΔΛDAΠEGHSΩMUΘ fl,13

The evidence of $p^{45,66,75}$ makes it quite clear that the variation is older than A.D. 200.

As the variation came into being in the second century, the century of Atticism, it is more probable that the evangelist at the end of the first century used the non-Attic middle which was later corrected to the Attic active future. That the evangelist should go out of his way to introduce an Attic form into his Koine Greek which the second century scribes who were copying during the period of Atticism then changed to the Koine form seems most unlikely. We may accordingly regard the middle future as what the evangelist wrote and the active as an Atticist correction of the second century.[10]

Kilpatrick gives a breakdown of the principal manuscripts in a brief chart tabulating the number of times each supports the middle or the active form in the six passages examined. He then remarks:

> At once we notice the striking fact that p^{66} and A and its allies of the Byzantine text show up much better than the Egyptian witnesses especially p^{75}אBL. It would not surprise us that the influence of Atticism was strong at Alexandria.[11]

[9]See authority for this, *ibid.*, p. 132.
[10]*Ibid.*
[11]*Ibid.*, p. 133.

Following a number of other examples of the influence of Atticism on the text, Kilpatrick calls attention to its manifest tendency to delete pronouns:

> Manuscripts vary considerably over the pronouns, especially αυτος. At the same point in the text the pronoun will be present in some witnesses and absent in others. Two considerations are in favour of the text with the pronoun. First, the suffixed pronouns of Semitic idiom are much commoner than the pronouns are in Classical Greek. Secondly, Hellenistic Greek, less terse and more explicit than Classical Greek, makes more use of the pronouns than the older language does. If the pronouns are original in the text, then the return to Attic brevity would encourage scribes rigorously to cut down on the generous use of the pronouns that their texts displayed.[12]

By consulting Charts 3 and 4 (page 230), one sees that in the comparison of Byzantine and Byzantine-plus alignments the Byzantine text is observed to supply the pronoun almost one-third more often than it omits it. In fact the same may be said for most all of its additions in comparison with its omissions (see tables and charts 2-4). This, in accordance with what has been noticed above, indicates that in respect to Atticism, at least, the Byzantine text has resisted editing more successfully than has the Alexandrian. As a part of the conclusion to his article on "Atticism and the Text of the Greek New Testament," Kilpatrick makes another statement which is relevant to this study:

> . . . Westcott and Hort may have owed some of their partiality for אB to the fact that these manuscripts often display a brevity and an idiom which is akin to the classical Greek on which they were brought up. In particular this led to a serious underestimate of A and the Syrian text as they called it. We have however noticed several places where A or the Byzantine manuscript preserve a feature of the Koine where אB give us the Attic equivalent. . . . We must not draw from such an example the conclusion that A or the Byzantine witnesses are usually right, but we can conclude that they have a right to be heard and that at each point the text must be decided impartially on the merits of the readings involved.[13]

[12]*Ibid.*, p. 136.
[13]*Ibid.*

Non-biblical sources attest that there was such a simple and plain style of Greek writing and speaking stemming from the earliest New Testament times. Such sources as the non-biblical papyri and the Discourses of Epictetus, the Stoic philosopher, attest this style. In addition, there is a formal delineation of what the plain style ought to be, which has been dated at approximately the same time in which the New Testament was being written. Demetrius, *On Style*, names "the plain style" (του ισχνου καρακτηρος)[14] as one of four which he describes and discusses. Except for the allusion to compound words, the following parts of his treatment of this subject tend to remind one of descriptions of the Koine of the Hellenistic period and the kind of Greek supposed to characterize the New Testament:

> In the case of the plain style . . . the diction throughout should be current and familiar. The more familiar an expression is the homelier it is, while the unusual and metaphorical is elevated.
>
> Compound words should not be admitted (since they are appropriate to the opposite variety of style), nor yet newly-coined words, nor any other words which contribute to elevation. Above all, the style should be lucid. Now lucidity involves a number of things.
>
> First of all it involves the employment of current words, and next the words bound together. Writing which is wholly disjointed and unconnected is entirely lacking in clearness. . . .
>
> . . . this is the style which is compacted and (as it were) consolidated by the conjunctions. . . .
>
> Clear writings should also shun ambiguities and make use of the figure termed "epanalepsis." "Epanalepsis" is the repetition of the same particle in the course of a lengthy sentence; . . .
>
> For the sake of clearness the same word must often be used twice. Excessive terseness may give greater pleasure, but it fails in clearness. For as men who race past us are sometimes indistinctly seen, so also the meaning of a sentence may, owing to its hurried movement, be only imperfectly caught.
>
> These are a few remarks, where much could be said, on the subject of clearness. Clearness must be practiced most of all in the plain style.[15]

[14]The other three kinds of style treated by Demetrius are the "elevated" (μεγαλοπρετης), the "elegant" (γλαφυρος), and the "forcible" (δεινος).

[15]*Demetrius On Style*, with an English translation by W. Rhys Roberts, *The Loeb Classical Library* (Cambridge, Mass: Harvard U. Press, 1953), pp. 419-427.

In spite of the known existence of such a plain style as set forth by Demetrius and found in Epictetus, there were those in the early period of the Church and its writings who scoffed at the plain style and spoke contemptuously of it as it is found in the Scriptures. One of these was the pagan Celsus, who sought to refute the Christian faith in a literary attack penned sometime between A.D. 161-180. Origen indicates that Celsus ridiculed the Scriptures by holding them up to unfavorable comparison with the writings of the philosophers in places where there seemed to be some parallel:

> For he has quoted a considerable number of passages, chiefly from Plato, and has placed alongside of these such declarations of holy Scripture as are fitted to impress even the intelligent mind; subjoining the assertation, that "these things are stated much better among the Greeks (than in the Scriptures). . . ." Now we maintain, that if it is the object of the ambassadors of the truth to confer benefits upon the greatest possible number, and, so far as they can, to win over to its side . . . every one without exception—intelligent as well as simple—not Greeks only, but also Barbarians . . . it is manifest that they must adopt a style of address fitted to do good to all, and to gain over to them men of every sort. . . .
>
> I have made these remarks in reply to the charges which Celsus and others bring against the simplicity of the language of Scripture, which appears to be thrown into the shade by the splendour of polished discourse. For our prophets, and Jesus Himself, and His apostles, were careful to adopt a style of address which should not merely convey the truth, but which should be fitted to gain over the multitude. . . .[16]

In the light of some instances of observed Atticisms in manuscripts of the New Testament, which have been shown to have arisen before the end of the second century, it is tempting to speculate as to whether they may owe their rise (at least in part) to the reaction of Christian scholars to attacks on the grammar, style, and vocabulary of the new Testament writings.

The consideration of the matter of style and the tendency of the Alexandrians to exceed the other text-types in Atticising suggests

[16]*Origen Against Celsus*, Book VI, chapters 1 and 2, *Ante-Nicene Fathers*, Vol. IV, p. 573. For estimate of the date of Celsus' work, see same volume, p. 231.

that two "rules" of textual criticism be reconsidered: 1) "prefer the shorter reading," and 2) "prefer the more difficult reading." These two rules are "tailor-made" to favor the more Attistic and less Koine (plain) type of text. In view of the above, it would seem that in many instances reversing the rules would lead more directly to the original text, i.e., "where atticising is suspected, prefer the longer and/or or the simpler reading."

There are, no doubt, many occasions where the true or original text is shorter, and in many instances the true reading may be the more difficult reading. In the textual criticism of Classical texts the principles of the "shorter" and "more difficult reading" probably have greater validity and application. However, in view of the information now accumulating on the Alexandrian and Byzantine texts of the New Testament, it would seem that these two rules ought to be applied with much greater restraint. The reason for this is that the simple, full, lucid, yet unpretentious Byzantine reading may often be the unedited reading. Thus the style (or "internal evidence of readings") involved in Byzantine readings may often now be seen not so much to condemn as to commend them. This being true, WH's third main argument against the usefulness of the Byzantine text (the argument from internal evidence) is not only taken away, but actually in certain kinds of readings becomes evidence in its favor[17] (See note on p. 125).

---

[17]For further reading on matters relating to style, cf. other works by Kilpatrick and J. K. Elliott. "Phrynichus' Influence on the Textual Traditions of the NT," *Zeit NT Wiss* 63 (1-2, '72) 133-138, *The Greek Text of the Epistles to Timothy and Titus*, U. of Utah Press, 1968, pp. 1-12. See also J. M. Ross, "Some Unnoticed Points in the Text of the New Testament," *Novum Testamentum* 25 (1983) 59-72.

CHAPTER XIV

The Conservative Users

The Byzantine text may be unedited in the WH sense because its users appear conservative in their view of Scripture as compared with some of those who used the Alexandrian and Western texts.[1] A conservative attitude toward the handling of the sacred text existed very early among the Fathers generally. The attitude of the Antiochians toward Scripture seems to suggest that they were jealous in the care of it. It will be remembered that the school of Antioch was the school of "literal" interpretation, while the school in Alexandria championed the allegorical method. This is not to imply that the Alexandrian Christians had a low opinion of Scripture. Antioch, however, had a much narrower and more conservative view of the canon than Alexandria, if the views of Africanus and Origen in their exchange of letters can be taken as criteria of their respective schools. It will be recalled that Africanus took Origen to task for citing parts of the apocryphal books of the LXX as Scripture, and that Origen responded by defending the use of the LXX over against the Hebrew.[2]

Although the patristic evidence from Antioch is absent for the earliest period, the earliest Fathers from other areas of the Empire,

---

[1]Note: Not a reference to "conservative doctrine," i.e., in the sense of "Fundamentalism" or orthodoxy. Antioch is considered the place where Arius, as a student of Lucian, obtained the seeds of his heresy.

[2]ANF, Vol. IV, pp. 385-393.

whose writings have been preserved to us, were aware of and complained about changes which had been made in copies of the Scriptures in their areas. Furthermore, they themselves assigned various reasons for the corruptions in the text.

Dionysius, Bishop of Corinth, wrote an epistle (ca. A.D. 168-176) to the church at Rome (from which extracts are quoted by Eusebius). In one of the passages he spoke of the fact that the text of his own letters was tampered with—and not only so but some individuals had presumed to edit the "Lordly Scriptures as well."

> For when the brethren desired me to write epistles, I did so. And these the apostles of the devil have filled with tares, cutting out some things and adding others: for whom the woe is reserved. It is not marvelous, therefore, if some have set themselves to tamper with the Dominical [των κυριακων . . . γραφων] Scriptures as well, since they have also laid their designs against writings that do not class as such.[3]

Not much later than this, Irenaeus (fl. 178), in refuting the Valentinians, had occasion to remark on their change of the tense of a verb in the Scripture. He derides this impiety by pointing out that through such tampering they exalt themselves above the Apostles.

> . . . "No man knoweth the Son, but the Father; neither knoweth any man the Father, save the Son, and he to whom the Son was willed to reveal [Him]." Thus hath Matthew set it down, and Luke in like manner, and Mark the very same; for John omits this passage. They, however, who would be wiser than the apostles, write [the verse] in the following manner: "No man *knew* the Father, but the Son . . ." and they explain it as if the true God were known to none prior to our Lord's advent; and that God who was announced by the prophets, they allege not to be the Father of Christ (*Against Heresies,*[iv.6.1]).[4]

---

[3]Hugh Jackson Lawlor and J.E.L. Oulton (trans.), *Eusebius, Bishop of Caesarea, the Ecclesiastical History and the Martyrs of Palestine* (London: Society for Promoting Christian Knowledge, n.d.), IV. 23, p. 130.

[4]*ANF*, Vol. I, pp. 467-468. In passing, it may be of interest to note that Irenaeus, in his reference to Mark (in the above quotation), preserves an instance of assimilation (or harmonization) which was present in the text which he used, for this passage is not now found in extant manuscripts of Mark's Gospel.

Tertullian, the early North-African Father (c. 160-200) took up the Marcion and Valentinian heresies, dealing with them at length in his "Prescription Against Heretics." He discouraged the use of Scripture with heretics because they do not use, but only abuse, Scripture. There is therefore no common ground between them and the Christian. He said they abuse Scripture by the rejection of parts or through changing by diminishing or adding and also by false interpretation. He charged the Marcionites of being especially guilty of textual corruption and the Valentinians with using perverse interpretation, though "they also have added and taken away." He argues that the genuine text is in the hands of the catholic churches because their text is older than that of the heretics. He maintains that the late date of the changed manuscripts proves their forgery. Tertullian also claims that the authority of the churches supports the traditions of the Apostles. Truth must precede forgery and proceed straight from those by whom it is handed on.[5]

Near the end of the second century Clement of Alexandria (fl. 194) complained of those who tamper with (or metaphrase) the Gospels for their own sinister ends (Stromata, IV. 6), and he gave one specimen of their evil work in this regard.[6] Scrivener cites Tregelles as pertinently remarking that "Clement in the very act of censuring others, subjoins the close of Matt. v. 9 to v. 10, and elsewhere himself ventures on liberties no less extravagant . . ."[7] It must be pointed out, however, that there is an important difference. Clement's complaint is primarily concerned with the Gospels as transcribed records. As is well known, he himself does not customarily use percise or literal citation when he quotes or alludes to Scripture. But this is far different from the thing which he is condemning, namely tampering with the transcribed text! The point to be especially noted here, however, is that Clement who lived in Alexandria has knowledge of such liberties being taken with the text, which the Alexandrian scribes were supposed to be transcribing unchanged.

Origen's active ministry began with the opening of the third century. He was born about A.D. 185 and became teacher in the catechetical school at Alexandria while still in his teens. In his commentaries Origen frequently dealt with the problem of variant readings which appear in the manuscripts available to him. He used language in describing the state of the text which would seem strong if used of the present state of the text some seventeen centuries later. In one place he says:

> Had it not been for the diversities of copies in all the Gospels on other points—και ει μεν μη και περι αλλων πολλων δια-φωνια ην προς αλληλα των αντιγραφων—he should not have ventured to object to the authenticity of a certain passage (Matt. 19:19) on internal grounds: νυνι δε δηλοντι πολλη γεγονεν η των αντιγραφων διαφορα, ειτε απο ραθυμιας τινων γραφεων, ειτε απο τομης τινων μοχθηρας της δι-ορθωσεως των γραφουμενων, ειτε και απο των τα εαυτοις δοκουντα εν τη διορθωσει προστιθεντων η αφαιρουντων (Com. on Matt., Tom. iii. p. 671, *De la Rue*). "But now," saith he, "great in truth has become the diversity of copies, be it from the negligence of certain scribes, or from the evil daring of some who correct what is written, or from those who in correcting add or take away what they think fit."[8]

Origen seems to assign variants to one or another of three principal causes: 1) the negligence of some scribes, 2) correction with evil intent (i.e., to promote heresy), or 3) correction with a view to improving the text's grammar or content on the basis of conjectural additions or omissions ("what they think fit.").

Eusebius cites an anonymous work, purportedly against the heresy of Artemon,[9] which was written ca. 230 and sheds further light on the corruption of manuscripts by heretics.

> They have tampered with the divine Scriptures without fear; they have set aside the rule of the primitive faith; they have not known Christ. For they seek not for what the divine Scriptures declare, but laboriously set themselves to find a form of syllogism which may support their godlessness. And if one puts before them a text of divine Scripture, they try whether a conjunctive or disjunctive form of syllogism can be made out of it.

[8]Scrivener, *Introduction*, p. 265.
[9]Cf. Lawlor and Oulton's note Vol. II, p. 189.

And deserting the holy Scriptures of God, they pursue the study of geometry, since they *are of the earth and speak* and know not *him that cometh from above*. Thus, to study Euclid is for some of them a labour of love; Aristotle and Theophrastus are admired; aye, Galen in like manner by some is even worshiped. But that those who use to the full the arts of unbelievers to establish their heretical opinions, and *corrupt* the simple faith of the divine Scriptures with the craftiness of godless men—what need is there even to say that such are nowhere near the faith? Therefore they laid hands fearlessly on the divine Scriptures, saying that they had corrected them. And whosoever desires can find out that in saying this I do not falsely accuse them. For anyone who will collect their several copies together and compare them, one with another, will discover marked discrepancies. For instance, Asclepiades' copies do not agree with those of Theodotus and you may get possession of many of them, because their disciples have vied in copying their several corrections (as they call them), that is, disfigurements. And, again, those of Hermophilus are not in accordance with the first-named. Aye, and those of Apolloniades do not even agree among themselves. For you may compare the copies they made at an earlier date with those they again altered later, and find great divergence. Nor is it likely that they themselves are ignorant of the audacity of this offence. For either they do not believe that the divine Scriptures were spoken by the Holy Spirit, and, therefore, are unbelievers; or they consider themselves wiser than the Holy Spirit, and what is that but devil possession? For they cannot deny that the audacious act is their own, since the copies have been written in their own hand; and since they received no such Scriptures from their instructors, they are unable to show any copies whence they transcribed them. But some of them disdained even to falsify them, and absolutely denied the law and the prophets. Thus under the cover of a lawless and impious teaching they have sunk down to the lowest depths of perdition.[10]

This lengthy but interesting quotation contains several things which are related to the subject at hand. 1) The high view of Scripture and its inspiration is inescapable. 2) Inspiration is made a test of faith. He calls "unbelievers" those who do not hold that the "di-

[10]*Ecc. Hist.* V. 28. 13-19, Lawlor & Oulton, pp. 173-174.

vine Scriptures were spoken by the Holy Spirit." Along with this is the implication that lack of such belief in inspiration could account for disrespectful freedom in tampering with the text. The presumption to emend the text in favor of their theories he calls demon possession. 3) That boldness in correcting is condemned in such strong terms suggests that at the time and locale of this writer, the orthodox did not exercise freedom in this direction. 4) The characteristic handwriting and perhaps certain other external features in manuscripts seem to have been the means to identify the scribe or scriptorium. 5) The comment concerning the inability of the heretics to show the source of their manuscript traditions seems to indicate that there was an accepted or common procedure making it possible to vouch for the ancestry of current or local copies. Evidently, in some areas some kind of access or appeal was commonly available in order to trace the source of the texts which were used by the orthodox in order that the background of questioned readings could be "double-checked." The heretics were unable to produce or indicate the parent manuscripts from whence they had derived the authority for the peculiar readings of their manuscripts. This was further proof that the "corrections" were actually their own personal innovations.

Note how these quotes, bridging the close of the second and the beginning of the third centuries, reflect an opposition to emendation of the Scriptures for any reason. Other citations could be made from the Fathers, but these are sufficient to show that they recognized the problem of early variation and, as far as the variant readings are concerned, they had definite ideas as to the causes that gave rise to them. While scribal blunders were recognized by them as one cause of variation, the strongest and most pointed statements, by the Fathers, are in connection with the changes introduced by heretics.[11] In addition to these, some of them also called attention to changes which were introduced by some who felt the need of "improving" the text either in the way of style, grammar, or doctrine. The main point in this chapter, however, is that these early Fathers (from the last half of the second century on) are voicing strong disapproval of any tampering with the text of Scripture.

[11]Note: Westcott & Hort's insistence that the text of the New Testament was not altered in any material respect from *doctrinal motives* was made in face of the fact that this was one of the primary reasons given by the early Fathers for changes in the text.

They thus appear to reflect the highly conservative attitude toward the text of Scripture which prevailed generally.

It is no doubt true that the scribes at Antioch polished and worked with their local text to some degree. This would be true especially in the early period if the locale of Antioch developed a diversity of local differences similar to the situation in second-century Alexandria as is reflected in the papyri from Egypt. It seems unlikely, however, that Antioch, so literal in the interpretation of the Scriptures, would undertake or sponsor such a radical re-working of the text as is condemned by the above writers or what is called for by the theory of WH.

This high regard for the Scriptures, on the part of the early Fathers, may have worked toward a more careful handling of the K-text than has generally been acknowledged. In fact, it is the conviction of some textual critics that the editing of the Byzantine text actually appears to have been less drastic than that which is found in the other main text-types. This, at least, became the considered opinion of Jose M. Bover. Bover, in making a special study of the codices which support each variant, came to the following conclusions concerning kinds of alterations which characterize the various text-types:

> The important or serious deviations are found in the Alexandrians and the Westerns, the slight ones in the Antiochians. . . . In profound modifications the Alexandrians and the Westerns are to be suspected, in additions principally the Westerns, in slight changes or retouches the Antiochians . . . BS [א]D manage the axe or the scalpel, the Antiochians, the file or varnish.[12]

Hoskier also raises the question as to which text is responsible for the greatest revising. His answer is that "the אB group should be given the palm. Otherwise we cannot explain the facts."[13]

---

[12]Jose M. Bover, "Un Caso Tipico de Critica Textual," *XV Semana Biblica Espanola* (Madrid: C.S.I.C., 1955), pp. 221-226. Translated by Janeway in *An Investigation*, p. 417.

[13]*Codex B*, p. iv. See his further statement on his conclusions in this regard pp. iv and v. Compare also C. C. Tarelli's remarks concerning the reduction "of the amount of that text [i.e., Byzantine] which can possibly be the result of an eclectic Antiochian recension and even suggest a doubt whether current theories as to its nature and origin furnish the best possible explanations. . . ." "Chester Beatty Papyri and the Caesarean Text," *JTS*, XL, January 1939, (compare above p. 58).

CHAPTER XV

The Silent History

History is completely silent with regard to any revision of the Byzantine text. The evidence now seems to indicate that deliberate changes which have been preserved in major groups of witnesses antedate the year 200. The church resisted changes in the text after this date.[1]

Johann Leonhard Hug had postulated three recensions in the third century: one by Origen in Palestine, one by Hesychius in Egypt, and another by Lucian at Antioch.[2] WH rejected certain aspects of Hug's theory (especially an Hesychian recension including אB, which they considered neutral) and reserved the full-fledged recension concept for the "Syrian" text, which they felt might have been created by Lucian. Von Soden, rejecting WH's "neutral" text, revived the three recension theory. He theorized that there had been a recension in Jerusalem by Eusebius and Pamphilius, another in Egypt by Hesychius, and the third in Antioch by Lucian. He dubbed these the I (*iota* for Jerusalem), H (*eta* for Hesychius), and K (*kappa* for the Koine or "common" text, Lucian's recension) which finally prevailed over all the others and became the Byzantine text.[3]

---

[1]Note: See Vogels and Kilpatrick above, pp. 94, 97.
[2]See Metzger, *The Text*, p. 123.
[3]*Ibid.*, p. 141.

In his article "The Lucianic Recension of the Greek Bible,"[4] Bruce Metzger gives some credence to the theory that the Byzantine text is derived from an editorial effort by Lucian of Antioch. However, when Metzger summarizes the evidence for Lucian's textual work, he appears to concede that the connection between it and the Byzantine text is somewhat nebulous. Because of the paucity of historical allusions, information on Lucian's recension is restricted to "the manuscripts *which have been thought to contain*" it [italics added].

> We are told nothing as to the amount of revision which he undertook in either Old or New Testament text, the nature of the manuscripts which he consulted, the relation of his work to the Hexapla, and other similar matters. For information bearing on such problems, we must turn to the manuscripts which have been thought to contain the Lucian recension.[5]

J. N. Birdsall, in an article "Texts and Versions; the New Testament," also seems to feel that there was some attempt at recensional activity in Antioch, but he says that "it is a curiosity of history that little direct evidence of this is to be found."[6]

Merrill M. Parvis makes a strong statement in regard to the historical record of a recension involving the Byzantine or any other text-types. In his article, "New Testament Text," he says:

> As far as is known, during the MS period no rigid control ever was exercised over the copying of MSS, nor was an official revision ever made in any great ecclesiastical center.[7]

By way of contrast, the well-known reaction which developed over the revision of the Old Latin text(s) by Jerome may be recalled. There are abundant and varied witnesses to the editing process which resulted in the Latin Vulgate.[8] But in the case of the Byzan-

---

[4]*Chapters*, pp. 1-41.

[5]*Chapters*, pp. 6-7.

[6]*The New Bible Dictionary*, ed. J. D. Douglas (Grand Rapids: Wm. B. Eerdmans Pub. Co., 1962), p. 1269.

[7]*The Interpreter's Dictionary of the Bible*, Vol. IV (New York: Abingdon Press, 1962), p. 599.

[8]Illustrative of this is the exchange of letters by Origen [Augustine] and Jerome concerning various aspects of Jerome's translation work.

tine text—silence. The lines of evidence referred to above would seem to require that any editing process, or recension which involved the Byzantine text, must be pushed back to a time similar to that which appears to be the probable date for the Alexandrian "recension;" that is, back before the year A.D 200, before the time that p^{66} and p^{75} were copied.

E. C. Colwell asserts that "the Greek Vulgate—The Byzantine or Alpha text-type—had in its origin no such single focus as the Latin had in Jerome."[9] It may well be that Lucian undertook such a project in the third or fourth century, but if he did, his "recension" of the New Testament does not seem to have taken hold any better than the changes by Origen mentioned above (pp. 96-97); that is, they did not affect the manuscripts of the Antiochian text-type. Furthermore, if the thesis of Vogels and Kilpatrick is correct in the restriction of most deliberate alteration of the Greek text to the period before A.D. 200, (cf. above pp. 92-97) then Lucian, who follows Origen in time (died c. 312), could hardly have been able to make the wide-ranging changes in the Antiochian text as is required by the theory of WH. Colwell calls attention to the fact that

> . . . different scholars exempt a specific text-type from a date-of-origin. Hort's assumption (now held to be invalid) that the Neutral text-type was an unedited preservation of the original placed its origin at the beginning. The counterblast of early twentieth-century champions of the Western text type claimed it to be primitive and unedited, hence as "original" in date as Hort's claim made the Neutral. Everyone has since the days of Hort admitted the existence of a date-of-origin for his Syrian text, also called the Byzantine text type or the Koine.
>
> The first action required by the new evidence is to split the fourth-century date for the origin of the text types in half and to push the halves apart.
>
> All the text types began earlier than we had assumed.[10]

This realization should now be taken into account in regard to the Byzantine as well as in regard to the other text-types.

While the Byzantine text has evolved in two or three forms and

[9]"The Origin of Text types," p. 137.
[10]Ibid., p. 130.

has gone through several stages (indicated by von Soden's Kappa groups), nevertheless it has maintained a high degree of homogeneity. It has not undergone an extensive cross-fertilization from the other text-types. Therefore in places of variation, when the majority of K groups agree in attesting a reading, it should be recognized that the Byzantine witnesses (in each such instance) are displaying the weight of an independent text-type whose witness carries all the way back into the second century.

It may seem incongruous to reject one argument from silence (testimony of the Fathers as used by WH), then turn right around and appeal to another (i.e. the silence of history in regard to a "Syrian" recension). The silence of the Fathers, in attesting K readings, was the main external evidence of WH and followers for the non-early existence of such readings. It was claimed that early non-Syrian Fathers never cited the Scripture in the form used later at Antioch; and that Chrysostom was the first Antiochian Father to use it. The silent history, in attesting such a recension as postulated

On some of the editorial procedures followed by the critics of the Alexandrian School see:

Butcher, S. H. *Harvard Lectures on Greek Subjects*. New York: The Macmillan Company (1904), pp. 211-215.

Farmer, William R. *The Last Twelve Verses of Mark*. Cambridge: Cambridge University Press (1974), pp. 13-22.

Grube, G. M. A. *The Greek and Roman Cities*. Toronto: University of Toronto Press (1965), pp. 122-132.

Hadas, Moses. *Ancilla to Classical Reading*. New York: Columbia University Press (1954). He gives an illustration of Alexandrian sensitivity to plagarism or what appears to be "borrowed" material in an author by relating an incident involving Aristophanes, the great Alexandrian scholar, critic and librarian, pp. 54, 55.

Pfeiffer, Rudolph. *History of Classical Scholarship from the Beginnings to the End of the Hellenistic Age*. Oxford: Clarendon Press (1968).

Sandys, Sir John Edwin. *A History of Classical Scholarship*, Vol. I. New York: Hafner Publishing Company (1958). (pp. 104-144 on "The School of Alexandria"; pp. 309-333 on "Greek Scholarship in the Second Century")

Valk, M. van der. *Researches on the Text and Scholia of the Iliad* (2 vols.) *Part I* (1963), *Part II* (1964). Leiden: E. J. Brill. Especially *Part II*, where he sets forth the extensive changes of the Alexandrian critics based on a variety of reasons, and maintains that by and large the "vulgate" text is superior to the Alexandrian! Cf. chapter X, pp. 1-83 on Zenodotus, especially pp. 34-40 and all through *Part II*. Cf. statement (p. 609) that "the koine" has preserved the authentic text. . . ." (Cf. also the "Epilogue," pp. 642, 643.)

by Hort, was the main external evidence (of Burgon and his followers) that such a recension in reality never took place.

Are both arguments equally invalid because they are from silence? Actually, the two seem quite different in their validity. WH's argument from the silence of the Fathers was considered invalid for two reasons: 1) the silence is explainable. It is what one would expect: the Fathers are expected to support their *own* local texts. And 2) the silence is not complete: the early non-Syrian Fathers *do* occasionally support K readings.

However, the silent history, in regard to a recension in the fourth century, is considered a more valid argument from silence because of two opposite reasons: 1) The silence is inexplicable: it is not what one would expect. It seems logical that there should be as great or greater reaction to the replacement of a people's whole Greek New Testament (the original language) than there was to Jerome's revision of the Old Latin (a translation). And 2) the silence is complete: there is not a shred of historical evidence that such a recension was made and then superceded the previous local text(s) of the Antiochian area. And these two things appear incredible if such a recension actually took place!

CHAPTER XVI

Summary Of Section B

In the light of the evidence, the Byzantine text should not be thought of as edited in the WH sense. The "proofs" by which WH defended their theory now appear untenable. As found in Section A, Byzantine readings are demonstrated early in the case of papyri-supported Byzantine readings. The lack of testimony to the Byzantine text-type on the part of early Fathers is neither complete nor decisive as WH had claimed. The invalidity of WH's silence-of-the-Fathers argument is evident from the discovery of non-patristic-supported Byzantine readings in the early papyri. Furthermore, that the longer or conflate readings are unble to prove WH's theory of Syrian editing is apparent for two reasons: first, because this type of reading also has been shown by the papyri to go back into the second century, and second, because such readings are found in other text-types, including the Alexandrian.

Besides the failure of the WH proofs for the secondary nature of the Koine text, there are positive reasons for considering that the Antiochian text has not undergone the radical re-editing called for by their theory. The significant provenance of the "Syrian" text-type (the ancient missionary church at Antioch) raises further doubts about its dependence on Egyptian and Western parts of the Empire for editorial source material. The style of the Byzantine text (WH's third argument) need not always be interpreted as "smoothed-up" but is appropriate to what would normally be expected of authors with a Semitic background writing for broad public consumption in the common language of the day. It is neither artificial nor stilted; it tends to avoid the "Atticisms" of the Alexandrian text on the one hand and the free handling of the text by the Westerns on the other. It appears to reflect a conservative attitude on the part of the School of Antioch in exercising restraint in matters concerning the text of the Scriptures. Finally, the history which records that Origen worked with the Hexapla and Lucian with the LXX and Jerome with the Latin is strangely silent concerning such a formal recension, as conjectured by WH, for the New Testament. In addition, it may be noted that some of those working in the vanguard of textual-criticism are saying that the evidence suggests that deliberate alteration, which has been preserved in the text-types, was restricted to a period prior to the year A.D. 200.

In view of these matters, it does not seem too much to affirm that the Byzantine text did not originate through the mixture of antecedent Alexandrian and Western texts as conjectured by WH, but that it is an independent witness to the second-century tradition of its locale. The Byzantine, no doubt, has undergone editorial treatment, as have the other text-types, but such editing was early (prior to A.D. 200 as in the case of Alexandria) and proceeded along different lines than that characterizing the Alexandrian and Western texts.

Conclusion

Westcott and Hort reasoned that the Byzantine text was made through an editorial process by using previously existing Western and Alexandrian texts. They argued that because the "Syrian" text was late, edited, and therefore *secondary* in origin, it should not be used as evidence in textual criticism of the New Testament.

Burgon and Hills, on the other hand, sought to controvert the WH theory by maintaining that the Byzantine text was the providentially preserved text; for this reason the Byzantine text was not secondary but *primary*. They referred to it as the "Traditional" text, the one which has descended in unbroken procession from the original because it was preserved by God's special care. In their opinion, the peculiar evidence for the primacy of the Byzantine text is its overwhelming superiority in numbers. For Burgon and Hills, the Alexandrian and Western texts are corruptions of the "Traditional" text and are therefore untrustworthy for the recovery of the original.

The thesis that the Byzantine text is primary was examined and felt to be unacceptable because its main argument rests on what appears to be a mis-use of the doctrine of God's providence. It thus excludes from use other types of text which, in the providence of God, have also been preserved.

The thesis that the Byzantine text is late, textually mixed, and therefore wholly secondary in form, though it had been supported by the apparently imposing arguments of conflate readings, patristic silence, and an appeal to intrinsic character, is now inadequate to account for the data which have accumulated since the days of Westcott and Hort.

Contrary to what WH held, *distinctively Byzantine readings of every kind have been shown to be early.* They have been shown to be early by evidence which is more certain than citation by early Fathers. The argument from conflation was found to be inadequate, not only because it is now known that such readings are early, but also because it is now realized that this type of reading is not confined to the Byzantine text. It is found in others also, including the Alexandrian. Finally, now that more is known about the language *milieu* of the New Testament, its Semitisms and Koine style are no longer evidences for editing as they seemed to be in the days of WH.

If the culminative force of the evidence presented sufficiently justifies the two affirmations: 1) the Byzantine readings are early, and 2) the Byzantine text is unedited in the WH sense, then the conclusion which follows logically is that while the Byzantine text is neither primary nor secondary, it is independent. That is to say, since it is not made from the Alexandrian and Western texts, it is not dependent upon them in its attestation of early readings. Therefore, it constitutes an additional, genealogically unrelated witness to second-century readings, along with the Western and Alexandrian text-types. Since it is not the only type of text whose testimony recedes into the obscurity of the second century, it cannot be treated as "primary." However, if it is not "secondary" but "independent" in its attestation to early readings, it appears reasonable to conclude that the Byzantine text should be given equal weight, along with the Alexandrian and "Western" texts, in evaluating external evidence for readings.

Suggested Synopsis Of The History Of The Text

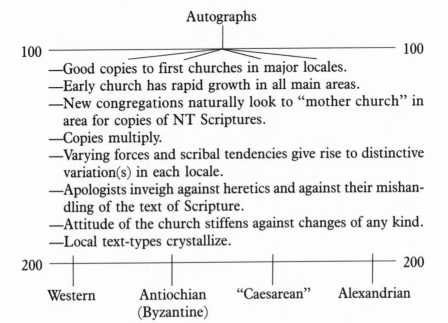

Autographs

100 —————————————————————— 100
—Good copies to first churches in major locales.
—Early church has rapid growth in all main areas.
—New congregations naturally look to "mother church" in area for copies of NT Scriptures.
—Copies multiply.
—Varying forces and scribal tendencies give rise to distinctive variation(s) in each locale.
—Apologists inveigh against heretics and against their mishandling of the text of Scripture.
—Attitude of the church stiffens against changes of any kind.
—Local text-types crystallize.

200 —————————————————————— 200

Western   Antiochian   "Caesarean"   Alexandrian
          (Byzantine)

In places of variation, each text-type, where supported by a concensus of its leading witnesses, is independently preserved from the end of the second century.

Individual readings supported by a concensus of the major text-types should be considered as 1) heavily attested by external evidence and 2) preserved from very early in the second century.

APPENDICES

Contents of the Appendices

135

Charts

Introduction to the Lists

Arrangement of the readings in the lists

In List 1, the first reading after each New Testament reference is the distinctively Byzantine reading supported by the papyrus. Immediately under this the reading of the Alexandrian text-type is found, and it is usually followed by WH. If there are but two readings (the Byzantine and the alternative), the second reading will also be supported by the Western witnesses (e.g., Mark 6:2). If the passage divides three or more ways, other readings are listed under the Alexandrian. If the Western is distinct from the Alexandrian it will be usually found in the third position (e.g., Mark 5:42), and any others will be listed below it (e.g., Matt. 26:22). Occasionally, what might be termed a "Caesarean" as distinct from the Western and Alexandrian readings may be found, and it is usually placed below the Western (e.g., Mark 6:45). This arrangement, however, is not rigidly observed. While the papyrus supported Byzantine is always listed first, occasionally the other readings will be arranged differently because of certain patterns of differences or simiilarities between the variants.

In the other lists a similar procedure is followed, with the main difference being the various combinations into which the leading Byzantine reading enters.

Sigla used in the lists

The following sigla are used consistently throughout the lists. Parentheses around a papyrus or manuscript symbol, e.g., (p^{37}) in Matthew 26:22, has the same force as *vid* or *videtur*, i.e., that there is some uncertainty about the reading of the manuscript but this is what it appears to read. Parentheses ( ) around a Church Father, e.g., (Or) . . . (Or) in Luke 6:28, signifies that the Father uses this reading in some of his quotations, but in other quotation(s) of the same passage he supports another reading. Elsewhere it is used to indicate something parenthetical. Square brackets [ ] indicate a lacuna at the particular place in the manuscript, e.g., Luke 6:39, where [p^{75}] is found for both readings, indicating that the papyrus could have read either way at that point as far as can be told from the photographic facsimile. The reason for including it in this way is to show that the papyrus was consulted for the reading.

Tischendorf's sigla, unc^9, stands for the Byzantine manuscripts EFGHKMSUV (see for example, Mark 5:42; and Matt. 26:22, where it is unc^8, M being found with the third reading listed).[1]

The sigla λ and φ as in the German Nestle apparatus[2] stand for family I and family 13, the lake and Ferrar families, respectively. K = the Koine text-type, von Soden's Kappa groups. H = the Hesychian, Egyptian, or Beta text-type. ς = the reading of Stephanus (The Textus Receptus). WH signifies that Westcott and Hort's Greek Testament follows the particular reading. [WH] indicates Westcott and Hort with some doubt about the reading. WH^{mg} is the reading WH place in the margin.

Besides these, the sigla in the lists are taken over from the various apparatuses with no rigorous effort to shape them into one consistent system. For this reason the abbreviations, particularly for some of the versions and some of the Fathers, will vary. In addition it should be added that in some places Tischendorf's numbering of

---

[1]That unc^9 = EFGHKMSUV seems evident by comparing Tischendorf's Eighth Ed., Vol. III, pages 401, 406, and 408 where Tischendorf lists these and compares and adds a few others to them, but they are the main basis of his "comparing" group. Then, in such a passage as Luke 10:40 (Vol. 1, p. 560), where he cites unc^5 it may be noted that none of the other regular members of this group are cited among those uncials agreeing with unc^5 but four of them (FSUV) are cited with the opposing reading. Compare also Luke 10:41 where, along with uncials listed for each reading, unc^9 is listed with the alternative reading and none of the group (EFGHKMSUV) is listed separately. When a reduced number of the uncials is given, e.g., unc^6 etc., it may usually be inferred that the members of the regular group of unc^9 (EFGHKMSUV) are supporting the reading with which it is cited minus those members which follow the other reading(s) or which are manuscripts which have a lacuna at that point.

[2]Cf. introduction to 25th edition, p. 69.

minuscules has not been changed to Gregory numbers. However, care has been taken to endeavor not to overlap attestation by the use of varying sigla so as to double the attestation of one witness for the same reading.

Attestation of support for readings

a. Order or arrangement. Immediately after each reading, the witnesses for this reading are listed in the following order: papyri that support the reading are placed first. Following this come uncial manuscripts in alphabetical order in accordance with their particular alphabet. ℵ is listed first if it supports the reading. After Aleph, the uncial manuscripts with Latin letter designations, then those of the Greek. Following this, any further uncial manuscripts to be listed are given in numerical order, their designated numbers beginning with zero.

Where any collective symbols are to be used for the uncials, as Tischendorf's "unc^9," they follow the uncial listings. Minuscule attestation follows the uncials: if family 1 (λ) and/or 13 (φ) supports the reading, this is listed first, after which the minuscule manuscripts are listed in numerical order. Following the listing of the Greek manuscripts, the abbreviation indicating the proportionate number of remaining Greek manuscripts is given (*pc al pm pl rell*). An effort has been made to use these with the relative force set forth in the introduction to the English Nestle text (2nd ed), page ix.

Following the Greek manuscripts, the testimony of the versions, earlier and later, is given. After the versional evidence, patristic evidence is set forth, the Fathers being indicated by abbreviations beginning with a capital letter, the earlier ones usually cited first. Following the Fathers, von Soden's symbols are given: K for Koine, and H for the Hesychian. If the reading is in Stephanus, then ς is added at this point. A semicolon (;) separates the manuscript evidence from "WH," "WH" indicating modern editorial judgment.

b. Completeness of attestation. As far as the completeness of recorded witnesses is concerned, all the available evidence that has been found for each reading has been included after that reading. No evidence gathered has been knowingly excluded.

c. Sources. The chief sources that were used for finding the papyri agreements are mentioned below. The rest of the manuscript attestation was gleaned chiefly from the critical apparatuses of Greek Testaments,[3] of which, Tischendorf, von Soden, and the two Nestle texts were the more freqently consulted.

The papyri cited in support of Byzantine readings

All the papyri cited are listed as third century with the exception of p^{46} and p^{66}, which are dated about A.D. 200; p^{75} is also dated early in the third century, not much later than p^{66}; and three others, p^{13}, p^{37}, and p^{72}, which are third and early fourth century in date. Of these last three the one which is of some length is p^{72}, containing Jude and I and II Peter. The papryi range, then, from approximately fifty (minimum in case of p^{72}) to one hundred and fifty (maximum in cases of p^{46}, p^{66}, p^{75}?) years older than the great uncial manuscripts of Aleph and B.[4]

The citation of papyri numbers p^{45}, p^{46}, p^{47}, p^{66}, p^{72}, and p^{75} were all made from facsimiles and/or printed texts of the Chester Beatty and Bodmer series of papyri.[5] The rest of the papyrus citations are for the most part taken from apparatuses chiefly from the

[3]Jose M. Bover, *Novi Testamenti Biblia Graeca Et Latina* (Madrid: Talleres Graficos Montana, 1959); *H KAINH ΔIAΘHKH* (2nd ed.; London: n.n., 1958); S. C. E. Legg, *Novum Testamentum Graece Secundum Textum Wescotto-Hortianum Evangelium Secundum Marcu*, Oxonii: E Typgrapheo Clarendoniano, 1935); and *Evangelium Secundum* (Matthaeum, Oxonii: E Typographeo Clarendoniano, 1940); Augustinus Merk, *Novum Testamentum Graece Et Latine* (Editio Octava, Rome: Sumptibus Pontificii Biblici, 1957); Eberhard Nestle, *Novum Testamentum Graece*, eds. Erwin Nestle and Kurt Aland (25th auflage; Stuttgart: Wurttembergische Bibelanstalt, 1963); Hermann Freiherr von Soden, *Die Schriften des Neuen Testaments* (Text und apparat; Gottingen: Vandenhoeck und Rurecht, 1913); Alexander Souter, *Novum Testamentum Graeca* (London: Oxonii, 1953); Constantine Tischendorf, *Novum Testamentum Graece* (3 vols.; editio octava critica major; Lisae: Giesecke & Derient, 1869); Heinrich Joseph Vogels, *Novum Testamentum Graece Et Latine* (Editio Quarta: Friburgi, Brisgoveae—Barcionone: Herder, 1955).

[4]See Kurt Aland's *Kurzgefasste Liste der griechishen Handschriften des Neuen Testaments*, 1. (Gesamtubersicht, Berlin: Walter De Gruyter & Co., 1963) wherein are listed all the manuscripts (papyri, uncials, minuscules and lectionaries) of the New Testament together with their contents, age, material, other characteristics, and location. The dates for the papyri given above were taken from Aland's *Liste*.

[5]Frederic G. Kenyon, *The Chester Beatty Biblical Papyri Descriptions and Texts of Twelve Manuscripts on Papyrus of the Greek Bible*, Fasciculus I, General Introduction (London: Emery Walker Limited, 1933); Fasciculus II, The Gospels and

two Nestle texts. Of these the German Nestle, though quite incomplete, was the more fruitful source of readings.

Distinctive readings

a. Identification of distinctively Byzantine readings. Briefly stated, distinctively Byzantine readings are those which are supported by the mass of the later manuscripts but are not attested by the best representatives of the Alexandrian and the Western texts. In the section on the "Identification and rejection of Syrian readings" WH work up to this in the following way, Hort says:

> The first point is to decide with respect to each reading is whether it is Pre-Syrian or not. If it is attested by the bulk of the later Greek MSS, but not by any of the uncials אBCDLPQRTZ (Δ in Mark) Ξ (also 33) in the Gospels (the smaller fragments we pass over here), אABCDE² (also 13 61) in Acts, אABC (also 13) in the Catholic Epistles, or אABCD²G³ (also 17 67**) in the Pauline Epistles, and not by any Latin authority (except the latest forms of Old Latin), the Old or the Jerusalem Syriac, or either Egyptian version, and not by any certain quotation of a Father earlier than 250, there is the strongest possible presumption that it is distinctively Syrian, and therefore, on the grounds already explained (#158), to be rejected at once as proved to have a relatively late origin. . . .

Acts, Text, 1933; Fasc. II, The Gospels and Acts, Plates 1934; Fasc. III, Pauline Epistles and Revelation, Text, 1934; Fasc. III Supplement, Pauline Epistles, Text, 1936; Fasc. III Revelation, Plates, 1936; Fasc. III Supplement Pauline Epistles, Plates, 1937.

Victor Martin, *Papyrus Bodmer II: Evangile de Jean. Chap. 1-14* (Geneva: Bibliotheca Bodmeriana, 1956); *Papyrus Bodmer II. Supplement. Evangile de Jean. Chap. 14-21* (Geneva: Bibliotheca Bodmeriana, 1958); *Papyrus Bodmer II. Supplement. Evangile de Jean, Chap. 14-21 (env. 200 ap. J.C.)*, Nouvelle edition augmentee et corigee. Preparee avec l'aede de M. J. Barns, Avec reproduction photographique du manuscrit complet (chap. 1-21) (Geneva: Bibliotheca Bodmeriana, 1961); Michel Testuz, *Papyrus Bodmer VII-IX*, VII: *L'Epitre de Jude*, VIII: *Les deux Epitres de Pierre*, IX: *Les Psaumes 33 et 34* (Geneva: Bibliotheca Bodmeriana, 1959); Victor Martin and Rodolphe Kasser, *Papyrus Bodmer XIV: Evangile du Luc chap. 3-24;* and *Papyrus Bodmer XV. Evangile de Jeane chap. 1-15* (Geneva: Bibliotheca Bodmeriana, 1961).

In the next paragraph, Hort narrows this considerably:

> The Syrian or Post-Syrian origin of a reading is not much less
> certain if one or two of the above Greek MSS, as CLPQR 33 in
> the Gospels, AC (E²) 13 in the Acts and Catholic Epistles, and
> AC 17 Greg. 33 in the Pauline Epistles, are found on the side of
> the later MSS, or even if similar testimony is *prima facie* born by
> such a version as the Memphitic. . . .[6]

In the briefer introduction, appended to their Greek text, WH
make it quite plain that the relatively pure manuscripts of the various text-types by which distinctively Syrian readings may be detected with accuracy are few in number:

> What has to be noted is, first the presence or absence of dis-
> tinctively Syrian or distinctively Pre-Syrian readings; and sec-
> ondly, among Pre-Syrian readings, the presence or absence of
> distinctively Western, or distinctively Alexandrian, or dis-
> tinctively neutral readings.
>
> When the texts of existing documents are tested in this man-
> ner, it becomes evident that they are almost all in some sense
> mixed. One Greek MS in most chapters of the Gospels and Acts
> (D), two in St. Paul's Epistles (D²G³), one in the Epistle to the
> Hebrews (D²) have approximately Western texts. Of the two
> oldest MSS, ℵ is Pre-Syrian and largely neutral, but with con-
> siderable Western and Alexandrian elements, B, is Pre-Syrian
> and almost wholly neutral, but with a limited Western element
> in the Pauline Epistles. All other Greek MSS contain a greater
> or less Syrian element, and their Pre-Syrian elements almost
> always exhibit readings of all three Pre-Syrian types, though in
> different proportions.[7]

For this book, readings regarded as distinctively Syrian are those
readings which are attested by the mass of the later manuscripts and
are without the support of the following leading uncials: ℵBCD(L)
in the Gospels, ℵABCD in Acts, ℵABCDE in General Epistles,
ℵABCD(G) in Pauline Epistles and Hebrews, and ℵAC 0207 in the

---

[6]*Introduction*, pp. 163-64.

[7]B. F. Westcott & F. J. A. Hort, *The New Testament in the Original Greek*
(London: Macmillan and Co., 1895), p. 489.

Revelation. It was also felt that the weight of Latin authorities ought to be of help in discerning the Western reading.

While tabulating the readings, a problem arose in connection with the identity of the Western reading or which reading was to be considered as supported by Western witnesses. It was decided that when the Latin versions divided, it would be best to follow D in the Gospels and Acts as the indication of the Western reading. If D and some other Western witnesses differed from the Koine text, it was then taken that the support of the Western text was thus indicated at that point. This would be the case whether or not it might be joined with the Alexandrian.[8]

Occasionally in the Gospels, as in Mark 6:50, a reading is called Byzantine even though L is included in its witnesses[9] when it seems obvious that the Alexandrian reading is distinct and is read by some of its main witnesses (see also Mark 7:32; Luke 6:28; 11:33 for other examples). No instance of a Byzantine reading attested by C is included in the list. For an instance of a reading supported by C and called Syrian by Hort, see Hebrews 7:1 in his "Notes on Select Readings."[10] This reading (Heb. 7:1) is now papyrus supported.[11]

b. Detection of papyrus-supported Byzantine readings: In the case of the Chester Beatty Papyri p^{45}, p^{46}, p^{47} and the Bodmer Papyri p^{66}, p^{72}, p^{75}, the texts of the papyri were compared with the

[8]For example, see List 1 and Mark 5:42, where "it" is read with the distinctively Byzantine reading, but there is a separate reading attested by D c ff^{22} g^2 i q and a few others. Therefore it was concluded that the Western reading here, and in like instances, was attested by D and its sprinkling of followers and that the rest of the Old Latin manuscripts would be considered as conformed to "the Byzantine norm." See also Mark 6:2, where a similar Western alignment combines with the witnesses of the Alexandrian text. Another example, somewhat different, may be seen in Mark 7:12, where D and Old Latin witnesses are spread across two other readings than the Byzantine reading, though the Byzantine has two Old Latin Manuscripts with it also.

[9]Compare WH's remarks above (p. 113) concerning C and L and others when they forsake the Alexandrian text.

[10]*Introduction*, p. 130.

[11]For an additional sixteen readings which would have been classified as distinctively Byzantine except for the presence of C, consult the following passages in List 4, "Papyrus-Byzantine plus varying support of the Western and/or Alexandrians but opposed by WH:" Mark 5:22; 6:16; Luke 4:35; 10:41, 42a; 10:42; 11:42; John 4:51; Acts 9:37; 10:11; 13:26; 15:40; 11 Cor. 6:16; 7:14; Galatians 4:14; Colossians 4:8 and in List 5 Hebrews 7:1.

text of Scrivener[12] and of WH, together with the apparatuses of Tischendorf and von Soden and the Nestle texts in order to find those places where the papyri agreed with the TR and/or the Byzantine as indicated either by Scrivener's text and/or by von Soden's K groups, while it was, at the same time, opposed by the Alexandrian and Western witnesses. Tischendorf's sigla for Stephanus (ς) was also helpful in identifying the TR reading. A card was made for each of these readings together with other readings where the papyri supported the Byzantine text in places where it was also joined by Western and/or Alexandrian witnesses. Attestation for the individual readings was gleaned from the various apparatuses.

The support of Byzantine readings by papyri other than the Chester Beatty and Bodmer papyri was gleaned largely from the Nestle texts, together with a few other sources wherever such evidence was recorded; i.e., in other apparatuses, in books, and in articles.

c. Limitations. As the following lists are presented, certain limitations may be kept in mind. In the first place it must be acknowledged that they are not exhaustive. No doubt some Byzantine readings in the papyri available have been overlooked; in addition to this, there are, no doubt, other Byzantine-supported readings in papyrus which were not available either in facsimile or by citation in textual apparatuses. A certain amount of subjective judgment may also be reflected in the selection of the readings. An effort has been made, however, to err on the conservative side; therefore many were excluded which might have been included as papyrus supported Byzantine readings.[13]

---

[12]F. H. A. Scrivener, *The New Testament in the Original Greek, According to the Text Followed in the Authorised Version, Together with the Variations Adopted in the Revised Version* (Cambridge: At the University Press, 1902).

[13]See note 11, p. 143 for list of sixteen excluded readings. The occasions where C joins K, and H goes a separate way.

LIST I

Papyrus-Distinctively Byzantine Alignments Opposed by Westerns, Alexandrians, and Westcott and Hort

MATTHEW

26:22 εκαστοσ αυτων $(p^{37})p^{45}AW\Gamma\Delta(\Theta)\Pi\Sigma\Phi$ 074 unc[8] λ φ 28
565 700 1241 1582 *pl* sy[p] Eus *K* ς
 εισ εκαστοσ ℵBCLZ 33 102 892 sa eth (it vg); WH
εισ εκαστοσ αυτων DM(Θ) *al*[10] sy[pmg] bo
εισ αυτων 1200 1424
———— p^{64} (Or)

MARK

5:42 εξεστησαν $p^{45}AW\Theta\Pi\Sigma$ unc[9] λ φ 565 700 *pl* it vg sy sa
geo *K* ς
εξεστησαν ευθυσ ℵBCLΔ 33 579 892 co eth; WH
εξεστησαν παντεσ D c ff[2] g[2] i q gat bo (1 ms)

6:2 εν τη συναγωγη διδασκειν $p^{45}ANWΠΣΦ$ unc[9] *pl* λ φ
28 565 700 1071 g[1,2] i q vg go *K* ς
διδασκειν εν τη συναγωγη ℵBCDLΔΘ 33 569 579 892
f ff[2] sa bo sy arm; WH

6:45 απολυση $p^{45}AE^{2}FHMSUVWΠ$ 33 *pm K* ς
απολυει ℵBL(DΔ) 1 *H;* WH
απολυσει (D?)E*ΚΓ φ 28 700 *al*
απελυσεν Θ 565 *pc*

Note: For the discussion on readings such as these in List I see pp. 61-69. For the arrangement and content of the Lists, see pp. 137-143.

6:48 ειδεν p^{45}EFGHSUΓΠ² λ φ 565 700 *pm* sy arm eth K ϛ
     (ιδεν iticism? AKMVXΠ* *al*)
     ιδων ℵBDΛWΘ *pc* a b f ff² q vg co H; WH

6:50 ειδον (or ιδον iticism) (P⁴⁵)AKLMVXΓΔΠ *pl* K ϛ
     ειδαν ℵB; WH
     _____ (_____ γαρ αυτον also) DΘ 565 700 a b
     c ff² i q

7:12 και ουκετι αφιετε p^{45}AWXΓΠ unc⁹ 579 *pl* f g² vg go sy
     arm *K* ϛ
     ουκετι αφιετε ℵBΔΘ λ φ 565 700 *pc* a b c ff² i q co eth
     H; WH
     ουκ εναφιεται D

7:30 το δαιμ. εξελ. και την θυγ. βεβλ. p^{45}ANWXΠ unc⁹ φ
     pl a n sy^p go arm K ϛ
     το παιδ. (την θυγ. Δ λ 700) βεβλ. . .και το δαιμ. εξελ.
     ℵB(D)LΔ(Θ)(λ) 565 (700) *al*¹⁵ it^*pl* vg co sy eth H; WH

7:30 επι τησ κλινησ p^{45}W λ φ 33 565 *pl K* ϛ
     επι την κλινην ℵBD *pc;* WH
     υπο την κλινην L

7:31 και σιδωνοσ ηλθε p^{45}ANWXΓΠ unc⁹ λ φ *pl* q sy^sp go
     arm (sa) *K* ϛ
     ηλθεν δια σιδωνοσ ℵBDLΔΘ 33 565 700 it(exc q) vg
     co sy^h eth; WH

7:32 μογιλαλον p^{45}ALNXΓΠ unc⁹ λ φ *pl* co sy^sp go
     (arm) *K˙* ϛ
     και μογιλαλον ℵBDWΔΘ 565 700 *pc* it vg (arm)
     eth; WH

7:35 ευθεωσ p^{45}AEFGHKMNSUVWXΓΘΠ 0132 λ φ 565
     700 *pl* c f l vg sy^sp (sa) go eth arm *K* ϛ
     _____ ℵBDLΔ 33 *pc* a b ff² iq co; WH

7:35 διηνοιχθησαν p^{45}ANXΓΠ 0132 unc⁹ φ 579 *pm K* ϛ
     ηνοιγησαν ℵBDΔ λ; WH
     ηνοιχθησαν L
     διηνοιγησαν WΘ 565 700 *pc*

7:36 αυτοσ αυτοισ p^{45}EFGHKMNSUVΓΠ φ *pl* sy go
     arm eth *K* ϛ
     αυτοισ ℵABLWXΔΘ; WH

9:6 ησαν γαρ εκφοβοι p^{45}AKNUWXΓΠΦ unc⁹ λ φ 700 *pl*
     f l g^l vg sy^p co go *K* ϛ

εκφ. γαρ εγενοντο ℵBCDLΔΘ 33 565 *pc* it*pl*; WH

9:20   ευθεωσ το πνευμα   *p*[45]AINWXΓΘΠΦ unc[9] λ φ 700 *pl* ς
      το πνευμα ευθυσ   ℵBCLΔ 33 *pc*; WH
      το πνευμα   D a b ff[2] i q

9:20   εσπαραξεν   *p*[45]AINWXΓΘΠ unc[9] λ φ 565 700 *pl K* ς
      συνεσπαραξεν   ℵBCLΔ 33; WH
      εταραξεν   D

12:6   αγαπητον αυτου   *p*[45]ANWXΓΠΦ unc[9] λ φ 28 *pl K* ς
      αγαπητον   ℵBCDLΔ 565 700 a b ff[2] g[1,2] i l q vg sa co
      sy; WH

12:16   ειπον   *p*[45]NXΓΘΠ unc[9] λ φ *pl K* ς
      ειπαν   ℵBCDLWΔ *pc*; WH
      λεγουσι   A b d i l q vg

LUKE

6:28   καταρωμενουσ υμιν   *p*[75]EHLSUVΔΘΛ *pm* Just
      (Or) *K* ς
      καταρ. υμασ   ℵABDKMPRXΓΞΠ *al* (Or) Eus; WH

6:39   δε   *p*[45][*p*[75]]APΓΔΛΠ unc[7] *pl* co go sy[p] *K* ς
      δε και   [*p*[75]]ℵBCDLRWXΘΞ φ 33 *pc* it*pl* vg arm; WH

9:30   μωσησ   *p*[45]AEGHMPSUVΓΛ λ *pm* (*K*) ς
      μωυσησ   (*p*[75])ℵBCDKLRWXΔΘΠ φ *al*; WH

10:21   τω πνευματι   *p*[45]AEGHMSUVWΓΔΛ φ *pl* f g bo[pt] Cl
      Bas Cyr *K* ς
      τω πν. τω αγιω   *p*[75]ℵBCDKLXΞΠ λ 33 *al*[5] a b c e ff[2] i l
      sy[c, h] arm eth; WH

10:39   του ιησου   *p*[45]*p*[75](—του) AB[3]C[2]PWΓΔΘΛΠ unc[9] λ φ *pl* b
      sy[ptxt] Bas *K* ς
      του κυριου   *p*[3]ℵB*C*DLΞ *pc* it(exc b) vg co sy[c, pmg] arm
      eth; WH

11:12   η και εαν   *p*[45]AWXΓΔΘΛΠ unc[9] *pl K* ς (AΘΛ *pc* αν)
      η και   *p*[75]ℵBL λ φ 33 (item sa bo nil nisi *aut*); WH
      εαν δε και   D (d *et si*)
      η ει   R (it vg *aut si*)

11:12   αιτηση   *p*[45]EFGMSUVWXΠ φ *pm K* ς
      αιτησει   *p*[75]ℵABCDHKLΓΔΘΛ λ *pm* Dial *H*; WH

11:33   το φεγγοσ   *p*[45]ALWΓΔΛΠ unc[8] 28 33 *pm K* ς
      το φωσ   *p*[75]ℵBCDXΘ *al H*; WH

11:50   εκχυνομενον   *p*[75]HKMSVXΓΘΛ λ *pl K* ς

εκχυννομενον ℵACDEGLYWΔΠ *al*

εκκεχυμενον p^{45}B 33 69: [WH]

12:5   εξουσιαν εχοντα p^{45}EGHMSUVΓΔΛ *pm* eth Tert *K* ς

εχοντα εξουσιαν p^{75}ℵABDKLRWXΘΠ λ φ *al* it vg sy^p

arm Or Mcion *H*; WH

12:21   εαυτω p^{75}ℵ^{c}AQXΓΔΘΛΠ λ unc^9 *pl K* ς

αυτω ℵ*BL(εν αυτω) *al*; WH

εν εαυτω FWΓ *pc*

12:22   ψυχη υμων p^{45}XΓΔΛΠ unc^8 φ *pl* a e g^2 vg^{ed} sy^c sa bo

eth Cl Ath *K* ς

ψυχη p^{75}ℵABDLQWΘ λ *pc* b c f ff^2 g^1 i l q am fu for

em tol sy^p arm Amb; WH

12:23   η ψυχη p^{45}AEGHKQUVWΓΔΛΠ *pl* a f ff^2 i q g^1 vg

sy^{ptxt} *K* ς

η γαρ ψυχη p^{75}ℵBDLMSXΦ φ *al* b c e co sy^c arm eth

Cl; WH

οτι η ψυχη 070 sa

ουχι η ψυχη 61 243 254 299 *al*^{15} l sy^{pmg}

12:30   επιζητει p^{45}AQWΓΔΘΛΠ unc^8 λ *pl* Bas Ath *K* ς

επιζητουσιν p^{75}ℵBLX 070 φ 33 *H*; WH

ζητει D Cl (it^{pl} vg Tert Marcion)

12:31   την βασιλειαν του θεου p^{45}AD^{2}QWXΓΔΘΛΠ 070 unc^8

λ φ *pl* d it^{pl} vg sy^c Cl Mcion *K* ς

την β. αυτου ℵBD*L a c co eth Ath; WH

την βασιλειαν p^{75} 892

13:2   οτι τοιαυτα p^{75}AWXΓΔΘΛΠ 070 unc^8 λ (φ) *pm* it vg

Chr *K* ς

οτι ταυτα ℵBDL 12 157 e; WH

τα τοιαυτα λ3 69 124 (τοσαυτα *pc*)

13:19   δενδρον μεγα p^{45}AWXΓΔΘΛΠ unc^9 λ φ *pl* c f q sy^p

eth *K* ς

δενδρον p^{75}ℵBDL 070 251 a b e ff^2 i l co sy^{ch} arm

Amb; WH

13:28   οψησθε p^{75}AB^{2}LRWΓΔΛΠ 070 unc^8 *pl* it vg Ir

K ς; [WH]

οψεσθε B*DX φ *pc* Epiph Lucif; WH^{mg}

ιδητε ℵΘ Mcion

14:3   ει εξεστιν p^{45}AWXΔΛΠ unc^8 λ φ *pl* it^{pl} vg (sa) sy^c *K* ς

εξεστιν p^{75}ℵBDLΘ 59 *al* f am (bo) sy^h eth; WH

14:3   ———— p^{45}AWXΓΔΛΠ unc^8 700 1424 *pl* a c ff^2 i l vg
     sa arm *K* ς
     η ου p^{75}אBDLΘ λ φ b e f q mm (sa) co sy^{chp} eth cat
     Cyr; WH

14:23   ο οικοσ μου p^{45}PWΓΔΛ unc^8 λ φ *pl* lat Bas *K* ς
     μου ο οικοσ p^{75}אABDKLRXΘΠ e co *H;* WH

14:34   εαν δε p^{75}ARWΓΔΛΠ unc^8 *pl* e ff^2 i vg^{ed} co sy^p eth
     arm *K* ς
     εαν δε και אBDLX *pc* a b c g$^{1.2}$q am for fu ing em fac
     gat tol sy^c; WH

15:21   υιοσ σου p^{75}ALPQRWΓΔΘΛΠ unc^7 λ φ *pl* it (vg) go co
     sy^h arm Aug *K* ς
     υιοσ σου ποιησον με ωσ ενα των μισθιων σου
     אBDUX 33 700 1241 *al* gat mm tol bodl cat; [WH]

15:22   την στολην p^{75}D^{2}EGHK^{2}MRSUVXΓΔΛ *pl* Ps Chr
     Dam *K* ς
     στοληv אABD*K*LPQΠ *pc;* WH

23:53   εθηκεν αυτο p^{75}ALPWXΓΔΘΛΠ unc^8 *pl* c *K* ς
     εθηκεν αυτον אBCD f^{scr} a b f ff^2 l q vg (co); WH
     εθηκεν λ φ 33 e arm

24:47   αρξαμενον p^{75}AC^{3}FHKMUVWΓΔ* ΛΠ λ φ *pm* (a c e
     l) (sy^{sp}) arm *K* ς
     αρξαμενοι אBC*LNX 33 co eth sy^{pmg} *H;* WH
     αρξαμενοσ ΘΨ 028 *al*
     αρξαμενων DΔ^2 (d, b f ff^2 q vg)

JOHN

1:39   ηλθαν και p^5PΓΔΠ unc^9 700 *pm* c f q vg arm *K* ς
     ηλθαν ουν και P^{66}אABCLXΛ 083(και ηλ. ουν) 33 124
       262 *al^{10}* a e co sy^{pmgh}; WH
     και απηλθον l sy^{cptxt} Epiph

2:15   ανεστρεψεν p^{75}ALPΓΔΛΠ* unc^9 *pl* (Or) *K* ς
     ανετρεψεν p^{66}BWXΘΠ^2 *al^{10}* (Or) Cyr; [WH]
     κατεστρεψεν p^{59}א φ *pc*

2:24   εαυτον αυτοισ p^{66}א^{3}A^{2}PWΓΔΘΛΠ unc^9 *pm* it^{pc}vg
     Or^{pt} *K* ς
     αυτον αυτοισ א*A*BL 253 440 700 *al;* WH
     αυτοισ p^{75} 579

4:14   διψηση p^{66}C^{3}WΛΠ unc^8 *pm K* ς

διφησει p^{75}ℵABDLMΓ 083 1 28 124 133 157 *al;* WH
διψει Δ

4:31 εν δε τω p^{75}AC³ΓΔΘΛΠ unc⁸ *pl* b f ff² m q co sy^cp (Or)
Chr Cyr *K* ς
εν τω p^{66}ℵBC*DL (a) c e g l vg basm sy^h (Or); WH
και εν τω W *pc* (sy) arm eth Aug

5:37 αυτοσ p^{66}AΓΔΘΛΠ unc⁸ *pl* lat sy Eus *K* ς
εκεινοσ p^{75}ℵBLW 213 *pc* a Ath; WH
εκεινοσ αυτοσ D

6:10 ωσει (p^{28})p^{66}(ωσι)AΓΔΘΛΠ unc⁹ λ φ *pl K* ς
ωσ p^{75}ℵBDL; WH
——————— sy co

6:57 ζησεται p^{66}EGHMSUVWΓΔ(Θ)ΛΩ (unc⁷) λ *pm*
lect.1561 *K* ς
ζησει p^{75}ℵBC²KLT(Θ)Π φ *al H;* WH
ζη (C*) D
vivit b q Amb

7:3 θεωρησωσι p^{66}B³XΓΔΛΠ unc⁸ λ *pm K* ς
θεωρησουσι p^{75}ℵ^cB*DLMWΔ *al;* WH
θεωρουσιν ℵ*

7:39 πνευμα αγιον p^{66} LNWXΓΔΛ unc⁶ λ φ 33 1241 *pl* (sa)
(Or) Ath Did Chr Cyr . . . *K* ς
πνευμα $p^{66c}$$p^{75}$ℵKTΘΠΨ 42 91 280 *al* (co) arm
(Or); WH
πν. δεδομενον a b c ff g l r vg^pl sy^pcs (sa) Eus
πν. αγιον δεδομενον B 053 e q (sy)
πν. αγιον επ αυτοισ D* d f go

7:40 Πολλοι p^{66} ΓΔΛΠ unc⁷ 118 *pl* f q go sy *K* ς
——————— $p^{66c}$$p^{75}$ℵBDLTWX 1 565 vg co arm Or
Cyr; WH

8:21 αυτοισ ο ιησουσ p^{66c}ΓΔΘΛΨ unc⁸ λ φ 33 *pm* lat co
Chr *K* ς
αυτοισ $p^{66}$$p^{75}$ℵBDLTX 0141 b e Or Cyr; WH
ο ιησουσ αυτοισ 1279

8:51 το λογον τον εμον p^{66} ΓΔΘΛΠ unc⁸ λ φ *pm* latt sy *K* ς
τον εμον λογον p^{75}ℵBCDLXWΨ 33 213 258 co Or
(Cyr) (Chr); WH
τον λογον μου 433 *al⁵* (Cyr) (Chr)

8:54 δοξαζω p^{66} $\aleph$ᶜC²LXΓΔΛΠ unc⁸ *pl* ϛ *K*
   δοξασω p^{66}ᶜ$p^{75}$$\aleph$*BC*D 1 69 *pc;* WH
9:16 αλλοι $p^{66}p^{75}$ALXΓΔΘΛΠ unc⁸ 28 *pm* it^{pl} (vg) go arm
   sy^p Chr *K* ϛ
   αλλοι δε $\aleph$BDW 0124 λ φ 565 *al* c ff² vgᶜ co
   (sy); [WH]
9:19 αρτι βλεπει p^{66}AXΓΔΛΠΨ unc⁷ λ φ 565 579 1241 *pm*
   co lat *K* ϛ
   βλεπει αρτι $p^{75}$$\aleph$BDLU 33 892 b c d ff² Chr½
   Cyr; WH
   βλεπει νυν Chr½
9:26 αυτω παλιν $p^{66}$$\aleph$ᶜAXΓΔΘΛ unc⁸ λ φ *pl* f q go (sy) arm
   eth Cyr *K* ϛ
   αυτω $p^{75}$$\aleph$*BDW *pc* vg co sy^{sh} Nonn; WH
9:28 ελοιδορησαν p^{66}AXΓΔΛ unc⁸ φ(—69) 28 *al* b e l q (vg)
   arm Aug *K*
   και ελοιδ. $p^{75}$$\aleph$*BW sa eth sy^h Cyr Am; WH
   οι δε ελοιδ. $\aleph$ᶜDLΘ λ 33 157
   ελοιδ. ουν 69 *al* c ff²vgᶜ go ϛ
9:35 ειπεν αυτω $p^{66}$$\aleph$ᶜAL(X αυτον)ΓΔΘΛ unc⁷ *pl* sy^s lat *K* ϛ
   ειπεν $p^{75}$$\aleph$*BDW bo; WH
10:19 σχισμα ουν παλιν p^{66}AΓΔΘΛΠΨ unc⁷ λ φ *pl* (bo) sy^p
   Chr Cyr *K* ϛ
   σχισμα παλιν $p^{45}p^{75}$$\aleph$BLWX 33 157 213 249 lat sa
   arm; WH
   σχισμα ουν D 1241 r^l sy^s (bo)
10:29 οσ $p^{66}p^{75}$AB²MUXΓΔΘ(Λ ουσ)Π unc⁸ λ φ 33 565 *pl* sa
   sy^{sph} eth *K* ϛ
   ο $\aleph$B*DLW *al* a b c e f ff² g l vg go bo Tert Hil; [WH]
10:29 μειζων παντων εστι p^{66}AΓΔΘΛΠ unc⁸ λ φ 33 565 *pl*
   lat go sa sy^{sph} Bas Dial Chr *K* ϛ
   παντων μειζ. εσ. $p^{75}$$\aleph$BDLWΨ (sy) Cyr *H*; WH
   παντ. εσ. μειζ. X
10:31 εβαστασαν ουν παλιν p^{66}AXΠ unc^{rell}λ 565 *pl* (sy) *K* ϛ
   εβαστ. παλιν (p^{75})$\aleph$BLW 33 go (sa)(sy) Ath Aug; WH
   εβαστ. ουν D φ 28 1780 *pc* (lat) (co)
   εβαστ. δε sy^p
   εβαστ. p^{45}Θ (co) (vg)

10:32   πατροσ μου $p^{66}(p^{75})$א^{c}ALWX unc^{rell} λ φ *pl* lat *K* ς
        πατροσ   [p^{45}]א*BDΘ e sy^h Ath Hil; WH

10:38   πιστευσατε $p^{45}p^{66}$AEGHMSXΓΛ φ 118 209 *pl* Ath Bas
        Chr *K* ς
        πιστευετε p^{75}אBDKLUWΘΠ 1 33 Ps-Ath Dam *H;* WH

10:38   αυτω p^{45}AΓΔΘΛΠ unc^7 λ φ *pl* b f ff^2 1 go sy^p Cyp *K* ς
        τω πατρι $p^{66}p^{75}$אBDLWX 33 157 a c e g vg co (sy) arm
        eth Or Eus Ath Dam Hil; WH

11:19   προσ τασ περι   (p^{45})AC^{3}ΓΔΘΛΠΨΩ unc^7 λ φ 565
        pm K ς
        προσ την p^{66}[p^{75}]אBC*LWX 33 38 157 249 *al H;* WH
        προσ   D lat

11:21   μαρθα p^{45}AΓΔΛ unc^7 *pl K* ς
        η μαρθα $p^{66}p^{75}$אBCDKLWXΘΠΨΩ λ φ 565 *H* ς; WH

11:21   ο αδελφοσ μου ουκ αν $p^{45}p^{66}$C^{3}ΓΔΘΛΠΩ unc^8 φ *pl K* ς
        ουκ αν . . . ο αδελ. μου p^{75}אBC*LW *al;* WH
        ουκ αν . . . μου ο αδελ. λ 565
        ουκ αν ο αδελ. μου   AD

11:29   εγειρεται $p^{45}p^{66}$AC^{2}ΓΔΘΛΠ unc^8 λ φ *pm* 1 vg *K* ς
        ηγερθη p^{75}אBC*DLWX 33 it^{pl} fos mt go sy^p arm
        eth; WH

11:31   λεγοντεσ p^{66}AC^{2}ΓΔΘΛΠΨ unc^8 *pm* it vg sa sy^{ph} *K* ς
        δοξαντεσ   אBC*DLX 1 13 33 sy^{pmg} bo arm eth
        And; WH
        δοξαζοντεσ p^{75}
        νομισαντεσ   1188

11:32   εισ p^{66}AC^{3}ΓΔΘΛΠ unc^8 φ *pl K* ς
        προσ   אBC*DLX 1 33 118 157 249 Cyr *H;* WH
        επι   254 y^{scr} Chr

11:32   απεθανεν μου ο αδελφοσ p^{45}AC^{3}XΓΛΠ unc^8 λ
        (φ) *pl K* ς
        μου απεθ. ο αδελ. $p^{66}p^{75}$אBC*LWΔΘ 33 254 *H;* WH
        απεθ. ο αδελ. μου   69 it vg arm
        μου ο αδελ. απεθ.   D

12:6   ειχεν και p^{66}AIXΓΔΛΠΨ unc^8 *pl* a b c f go arm *K* ς
        εχων p^{75}אBDLQ 33 157 *pc* q vg co (Or) *H;* WH
        εχων και   1 (Or) $_*$

12:9   οχλοσ πολυσ p^{66} p^{75}AB^{3}IQXΘΨ λ φ 33 *pl* f g vg bo go
        sy^{ph} *K* ς

ο οχλοσ πολυσ   אB*L *H*; WH

ο οχλοσ ο πολυσ   *p*66c

οχλοσ ο πολυσ   W 1010

οχλοσ δε πολυσ   D a (b c e ff²) sa

12:36   εωσ   *p*66ΧΓΔΛΠ³ unc⁸ λ φ 1241 *pm K* ς

      ωσ   *p*75אABDLΠ* 33 42 108 *H*; WH

12:36   ο ιησουσ   *p*75אᶜAΧΓΔΛΠ unc⁸ *rell* Libere Chr *K* ς

      ιησουσ   *p*66א**BDLΨ; WH

13:26   και εμβαψασ   *p*66AWΓΘΛΠΨ unc⁸ λ *K* ς

      βαψασ ουν   אBCXΠ²(εμβαψασ) 33 *pc*; WH

      και βαψασ   D φ 258 Oṛ

13:26   ισκαριωτη   *p*66AWΓΔΛΠ* unc⁷ λ φ *pm* vgᶜ go co arm

      Or *K* ς

      ισκαριωτου   אBCIᵇLMXΘΠ² 33 *al* vgˢ *H*; WH

      απο καρυωτου   D

14:5   δυναμεθα την οδον ειδεναι   *p*66AC²LNQWXΓΔΘΛΠ

      unc⁶ λ φ *pl* itᵖᶜ vg *K* ς

      την οδον ειδεναι δυναμεθα   א(K?)

      οιδαμεν την οδον   BC* a; WH

      την οδον οιδαμεν   D b e

19:4   εξηλθεν ουν   *p*66cEGHMSUWYΔΘΛ φ *pm K* ς

      και εξηλθεν   ₊(*p*66)ABKLXΠ 33 *al*; [WH]

      εξηλθεν   (*p*66)אDˢᵘᵖᵖWΓ λ 557 565 *al*; WHᵐᵍ

19:11   απεκριθη   *p*66c AXYΔΛΠ unc⁶ φ *pm* itᵖᶜ vg go co arm

      syᵖ *K* ς

      και απεκριθη   *p*66 ₊θ

      απεκριθη αυτω   *p*60אBDˢᵘᵖᵖΛW λ 33 249 itᵖᶜ

      (sy) *H*; WH

19:35   εστιν αυτου η μαρτ.   *p*66EGKSUΛ 579 *pm* am

      ing Caes *K*

      αυτου εστιν η μαρτ.   אABDˢᵘᵖᵖLMXΓΠ *al* Or; WH ς

      εστιν η μαρτ. αυτου   HY *al* b c f ff² g vg Chr Cyr

20:17   πατερα μου   *p*66ALOXΓΔΘΛΠ unc⁶ λφ *pl* lat syᵖˢ

      sa bo *K* ς

      Πατερα   אBDW *pc* b e Ir; WH

ACTS

   4:33   μεγαλη δυναμει   *p*45EP *pl* Thphyl *K* ς

δυναμει μεγαλη אABD 18 103 242 328 *al*[3scr] cat vg
Chr Ir Aug *H;* WH

7:14 τον πατερα αυτου ιακωβ (*p*[45])HP *pl* sy Chr *K* ς
ιακωβ τ. π. αυτ. *p*[74]אABCDE *al* vg sa bo arm; WH
τον πατ. αυτ. 36 90* 94 307 630 cat eth

9:3 περιηστραψεν αυτον φωσ *p*[45]EHLP *pl* vg sy
arm Chr *K* ς
αυτον περιηστ. φωσ *p*[74](περιηστ.)אBC 69 81 327 630 *l*
cat; WH
αυτ. φωσ περιεστ. A

9:3 απο του ουρανου *p*[45]EHP *pl* Theophl[a] *K* ς
εκ του ουρ. *p*[74]אABCL 81 *al*[15] cat Theophyl[b] *H;* WH

9:38 οκνησαι . . . αυτων *p*[45]C[3]HLP *pl* sy arm eth Bas
Chr *K* ς
οκνησησ . . . ημων *p*[74]אABC*E 81 181 453 vg sa bo
H; WH

10:37 αρξαμενον *p*[45]LP 69 81 *pl* (Dial) Thdrt Chr . . . *K* ς
αρξαμενοσ אBCEH 181 *l*[3] *H;* WH
αρξαμενοσ γαρ *p*[74]AD e vg Ir (Dial)

11:11 ημην *p*[45]EHLP *pl* cat vg sy co eth Chr *K* ς
ημεν *p*[74]אABD[gr](d *erant*) 181; [WH]

13:26 απεσταλη *p*[45]EHLP *pl* Thphyl *K* ς
εξαπεσταλη *p*[74]אABCD 33 453 *al*[30] cat Chr; WH

14:15 τον θεον τον ζωντα *p*[45]HLP *pl* Chr *K* ς
θεον ζωντα *p*[74]א[c]BCD[2]E 33 81 104 181 242 *l* *al*[2scr] cat
Ath *H;* WH
θεον τον ζωντα א*
τον θεον ζωντα D* *pc* Thdrt
τον ζωντα θεον 328

16:16 πυθωνοσ *p*[45]C[3]D[2]EHLP *pl* cat tol sy[pmggr] Chr Eus
Lcif *K* ς
πυθωνα *p*[74]אABC*D* 81 326 vg Or; WH

16:39 εξελθειν *p*[45]EHLP *pl* (e vg *exire*) Chr *K* ς
απελθειν *p*[74]אAB 33 81 *pc* cat arm; WH
. . . εξελθειν . . . D (but in a long addition & a diff.
arrangement than the Byz. reading)

17:13 σαλευοντεσ *p*[45]EHLP *pm* eth Chr *K* ς
σαλ. και ταρασσοντεσ *p*[74]אAB(D) 33 69 *al* cat vg sy co
arm; WH

23:12 τινεσ των ιουδαιων p^{48}HLP 69 102 *pl* sa sy Thphyl *K* ς
οι ιουδαιοι p^{74}אABCE 33 81 *al*[15] cat co arm eth; WH

ROMANS

10:14 επικαλεσονται p^{46}KLP *pl* Cl Chr Thdor Euth Thdrt
       Dam etc *K* ς
       επικαλεσωνται אABDEFG 103 441 a[scr] *H;* WH
       invocabunt d e f g vg Or Ambrst etc

16:23 και τησ εκκλησιασ ολησ p^{46}L *pl* Chr Thdrt Dam *K* ς
       και ολησ τησ εκκλησιασ אABCDEP 1 5 69 241 436
       441 *H;* WH
       και ολαι αι εκκλησιαι FG eth (f g)

I CORINTHIANS

4:11 γυμνητευομεν και p^{46}L *pl* Euth Cl Or Eus . . . *K* ς
      γυμνιτευομεν και אB(*-νει-(also D*))CD EFGP 69
      al[3scr]; WH
      ————γ. και A

5:10 η αρπαξιν p^{46}א[c]D[b,c]EL *pl* e vg sy co arm go Or Chr
      Thdt Dam Lcif . . . *K* ς
      και αρπαξιν א*ABCD*FGP 33 *pc* d f g eth; WH
      η και αρπ. 69

7:5 συνερχεσθε p^{46}876 1022 1799 2401 *al* Or Cyp Chr Meth
     (-χησθε KLPΨ 048 049 *pl* co vg) *K* ς
     ητε אABCDEFG 33 *pc*; WH

7:7 χαρισμα εχει p^{46}KL *pl* vg[c] harl go sy[p] arm Eph Chr
     Thdrt Dam Aug Ambst *K* ς
     εχει χαρισμα אABDEFGP 33 69 lat co Cl Or Cyr Euth
     Cyp; WH
     χαρισμα εκ θεου εχει C

7:7 οσ μεν . . . οσ δε p^{46}א[c]KL *pl* (Or) Ephr Chr Thdr
     Dam *al K* ς
     ο μεν . . . ο δε א*ABCDEFGP 33 *pc* Cl (Or) Cyr
     Euth; WH

9:7 εκ του καρπου p^{46}C[3]D[bc]EKL *pl* c d e t vg[sc] am fu sy co
     arm Or Aug Amb *K* ς
     τον καρπον א*ABC*D*FGP 33 1739 *pc* f g tol harl
     floriac *al* sa go Or; WH

9:21   κερδησω ανομουσ *p*[46]ℵ^cKL *pl* Or Did Chr Euth Thdt
Isid Dam *al K* ς
κερδανω τουσ ανομουσ ℵ*ABCFGP 33 69 *pc;* WH
τουσ ανομουσ κερδησω DE

10:8   επεσον *p*[46]D^cKL *pl* Chr Thphl Oec *K* ς
επεσαν ℵABCD*FGP 33 69 *pc* Chr Thdt Dam *H;* WH
επεσεν 1908

11:26   το ποτηριον τουτο *p*[46]ℵ^cC³D^{bc}EKLP *pl* tol sy co eth go
Bas Chr Nest Thdt (Dam) Phot (Cyp) *K* ς
το ποτηριον ℵ*ABC*D*FG 33 *pc* lat Cyr
(Dam)(Cyp); WH

II CORINTHIANS

9:10   αυξησαι *p*[46]ℵ^cD^cKL *pl* go Chr (Cyr) Thdrt Dam *al K* ς
αυξησει ℵ*BCFD*G *al*[15] d e g r vg co arm eth (Cyr)
Euth Cyp Aug Ambst; WH

GALATIANS

4:31   αρα *p*[46]D^cKL *pm* sy^p Bas Chr Thph Oec *K* ς
διο ℵBD* 33 *pc* arm Tert; WH
αρα ουν FG Thdrt
διάραο E (mingles D* with D^c?)
itaque d e f g vg Ambst Hier *al*
ημεισ δε ACP *pc* co Euth Cyr Mrcn Dam
———— 1912

EPHESIANS

2:12   εν τω καιρω *p*[46]*D^cEKLP *pl* vg co go (Or) Dial (Chr)
Euth Thdt Dam Tert Ambst *K* ς
τω καιρω *p*[46]^cℵABD*FG 33 d e f g tol Mrcn (Or) (Chr)
Cyr Victorin Hier Aug *H;* WH

5:9   πνευματοσ *p*[46]D^cE**KL *pm* sy^{hp} Chr Thdt Dam *K* ς
φωτοσ *p*[49]ℵABD*E*FGP 33 *pc* latt go sy co arm eth
Thaum Euth Lcif Vict Ambst Hier *al;* WH

PHILIPPIANS

1:14   τον λογον λαλειν *p*[46]D^cE**K 1739 *pl* sy^{ph} Chr Thdt
Dam Mrcn *K* ς

τον λογ. του θεου λαλ. ℵABP *al* lat sy sa bo bas arm
eth Cl Chr Euth Ambst; WH

τον λογ. λαλ. του θεου D*E* d e

τον λογ. κυριου λαλειν FᵍʳG g

COLOSSIANS

3:16 τω κυριω p^{46}C²DᶜEKL *pl* demid go co Eph Chr Thdt
Dam Ambst Pelag *K* ς

τω θεω ℵABC*D*FG 33 424 *pc* d e f g m⁸⁸ vg sa sy
arm Cl Chr Euth Ambst *al;* WH

3:22 τον θεον p^{46}ℵᶜDᶜE**K *pl* d e vgᶜ demid tol go co
Thdt *K* ς

τον κυριον ℵ*ABCDᵍʳ FGL 33 *pc* f g am fu harl sy arm
Cl Chr Euth Dam Ambst; WH

4:12 πεπληρωμενοι p^{46}DᶜEKLP *pl* syᵖᵗˣᵗ arm Chr Thdt
Dam *K* ς

πεπληροφορημενοι ℵABCD*FG 33 104 424** *pc* syᵖᵐᵍ
Euth; WH

HEBREWS

3:3 δοξησ ουτοσ p^{13}KLM *pl* f vg Euth Thdt Dam *K* ς

ουτοσ δοξησ p^{46}ℵABCDEP 69 *pc* d e Chr; WH

δοξησ arm Bas

10:17 μνησθω p^{46}ℵᶜDᶜKLP *pl* Chr Thdt Dam *al K* ς

μνησθησομαι p^{13}ℵ*ACD* 33 Euthalᶜᵒᵈ; WH

10:38 εκ πιστεωσ p^{13}DᶜEH**IKLP *pl* sy co eth Eus Chr
Euth Thdt Dam *K* ς

μου εκ πιστεωσ p^{46}ℵAH* f r vg arm Cl Thdt Sed
Prim; [WH]

εκ πιστεωσ μου D⋆ *pc* d e sy Eus

11:4 αυτου του θεου p^{13} p^{46}ℵᶜDᶜEKLP *pl* f vg sy *K* ς; [WH]

αυτου τω θεω ℵ*AD* 33

αυτω του θεου p^{13c}Cl

11:32 γαρ με $p^{13}p^{46}$DᶜEIKLP *pl* Cl Chr Euth Thdt *K* ς

με γαρ ℵAD* 33; WH

12:25 τον επι τησ γησ παραιτησαμενοι p^{46} (—τησ)ℵᶜKLP
pl Chr Thdt Dam *K* ς

επι γησ παραιτη. τον p^{46^c} א*ACDM 33 Euth Cyr; WH
παραιτη. τον επι γησ 69 pc
12:25 πολλω p^{46}D^cKLMP pl Chr Euth Cyr Thdt Dam K ς
πολυ אACD* 33 H; WH

I PETER
2:5 τω θεω p^{72}א^cKLP pl Cl Or K ς
θεω א*ABC pc arm H; WH
3:7 εκκοπτεσθαι p^{72}C²KLΨ 33 69 pm vg Hier Amb
Aug (K) ς
εγκοπτεσθαι ABP al⁵⁰; WH
ενκοπτεσθαι אC^{scr}
5:8 οτι ο αντιδικοσ p^{72}א^cLΨ 33 69 1739 pm vg sy co arm
eth (K) ς
ο αντιδικοσ א*ABKP al; WH

II PETER
2:4 σειραισ p^{72}KL(P) pl K ς
σειροισ ABC 81 917; WH
σιροισ א
2:5 αλλ' ογδοον p^{72}K^{sil} P pl K ς
αλλα ογδοον אABCL 122 al³ˢᶜʳ; WH

JUDE
25 και μεγαλωσυνη p^{72}(-λοσυνη)KLP pl cat vg^c
co sy K ς
μεγαλωσυνη אABC al¹⁰; WH
25 εξουσια p^{72}KP pm K ς
εξ. προ παντοσ του αιωνοσ אABCL al¹⁵ H; WH

REVELATION
9:20 δυναται p^{47}046^c pl (And) Are K ς
δυνανται אA(046*)CP pc (And) H; WH
10:2 βιβλιον p^{47}046 pm K
βιβλαριδιον א*AC**P 1 al²⁰ And Are ς; WH
βιβλιδαριον א^cC* 69 al⁷³⁽in Hosk⁾
10:8 ανεωγμενον p^{47}046 pl (K)
ηνεωγμενον אACP 1 al And ς (H); WH

11:2   εκβ. εξω p^{47} 046 *pm* (And) Are *K* ς
      εκβ. εξωθεν   ℵᶜA *al* (And); WH
      εκβ. εσω   ℵ*
      εκβ. εσωθεν   P

11:6   παση πληγη p^{47} 046 *pm* vg Haym *K* ς
      εν παση πληγη   ℵACP 1 2 *al* co sy arm eth Hipp And
        Are Prim; WH
      ————— 95 *pc*

11:12   ηκουσα p^{47}ℵᶜ 046 *pl* co sy And Tyc Are . . . *K*
      ηκουσαν   ℵ*ACP *pc* vg arm Haym ς; WH
      ακουσονται   38 *pc*

11:19   διαθηκησ του κυριου p^{47} *pm K*
      διαθηκησ αυτου   AP *al* ς; WH
      διαθηκησ κυριου   046 *pc*
      διαθηκησ του θεου   ℵ *pc*

12:7   αυτου[1] p^{47} 046 1 6 *pl* And *K* ς
      αυτου του   ACP *al;* WH

12:9   σατανασ p^{47} 046 *pl* (And) Are *K*
      ο σατανασ   ℵACP 1 *al* (And) *H* ς; WH

12:13   αρρενα p^{47} *pl* Hipp And Are *K* ς
      αρενα   046 28 *pc*
      αρσενα   ℵCEP *al*[20]; WH
      αρσεναν   A

13:13   επι την γην p^{47} 046 *al* (And) Are *K*
      εισ την γην   ℵACP 1 *al* (*pm?*)Hipp (And) *H* ς; WH
      ————— E *pc*

14:8   εκ του p^{47} ℵᶜP 046 *pl* co Prim *K*
      η εκ του   AC *al* (And) Haym *H;* WH
      οτι εκ του   1 36 *pc* (And) Are ς

15:8   εκ του p^{47} 046 *al* sy (And) Are *K*
      ————— ℵACP 1 *pm* vg (And) Prim *H* ς; WH

16:3   εν τη θαλασση p^{47} 046 *pl* (And) Are *K* ς
      τα εν τη θαλ.   ACE *pc* eth (And); WH
      των εν τη θαλ.   95 *pc* sy^sh arm
      επι τησ θαλ.   ℵ

16:10   εμασσωντο p^{47} 046 *al*[100+] (And) Are (*K*) ς
      εμασωντο   ℵACP *pm*[130] (And); WH

LIST II

Papyrus-Byzantine-Western Alignments
Opposed by
Alexandrians and Westcott and Hort

MATTHEW

26:27 το ποτηριον $p^{37}p^{45}$ACDHKMSUVΓΠΦ *pl* 157 565 *K* ς
ποτηριον אBEFGLZΔ 1 28 33 *al* (sa bo) Chr; WH

26:31 διασκορπισθησεται $p^{37}p^{45}$DEFH²KSUVWΓΔΘΠΦ 1
565 *pl* Or Eus *K* ς
διασκορπισθησονται p^{53}אABCGH*ILM 047 067 φ 118
700 *al H*; WH

26:45 το λοιπον p^{37}אADΓΔΘΠ unc⁹ λ φ *pl* Ath *K* ς
λοιπον BCL *al⁶* Chr; WH

MARK

6:22 και αρεσασησ p^{45}AC³DWΓΘΠ unc⁹ λ φ 565 700 *pl* a b
f g² i q vg go (sy eth) *K* ς
ηρεσεν אBC*L 33 c ff² co arm; WH

6:22 ειπεν ο βασιλευσ p^{45c} C³DWΓΘΠ unc⁹ λ φ 565 700 *pl*
a b f ff² go syᵖ arm *K* ς (+ Ηηωρδησ p^{45})
ο δε βασιλευσ ειπεν אBC*LΔ 33; WH
ειπεν δε ο βασιλευσ ΑΣ co

6:41 τοισ μαθηταισ αυτου p^{45}ADᵍʳWΓΘΠ unc⁹ λ φ 565 700
pl it^{pl} vg syˢᵖ eth *K* ς

Note: For the discussion on readings such as these in List 2, see pp. 70-76. For the arrangement and content of the Lists, see pp. 137-144.

τοισ μαθηταισ ℵBLΔ *al*[7] d; WH

6:41 παραθωσιν *p*[45]ℵ^cADM²NΓΘΠ² unc⁸ λ φ 565 700
       pl K ς
       παρατιθωσιν ℵ*BLM*WΔΠ* *pc;* WH

7:5   οι μαθηται σου υο περιπατουσι *p*[45]ADWXΓΘΠ unc⁹ λ
       φ 565 700 *pl* it vg sy arm go *K* ς
       ου περιπατουσι οι μαθηται σου ℵBLΔ 33 *pc*
       co eth; WH

7:6   αποκριθεισ *p*[45]ADWXΓΘΠ unc⁹ λ φ 565 700 *pl* it vg
       go sy^p arm *K* ς
       _____ ℵBL 33 102 co sy eth pers^p; WH

7:6   οτι καλωσ *p*[45]ADWXΓΠ unc⁹ λ φ 565 700 892 *pl* b q
       sy^p arm go (co) *K* ς
       καλωσ ℵBLΔΘ 33 102 a c f ff² i l vg sy eth; WH

7:29 το δαιμονιον εκ τησ θυγατροσ σου *p*[45]ADNWXΓΠ
       unc⁹ φ 565 700 892 *pl* it vg (co) sy arm eth*K* ς
       εκ τησ θυγ. σου το δαιμ. ℵBLΔΘ λ (co); WH

8:13 εισ το πλοιον *p*[45]DHKNUWΓΠ 0131 λ φ 700 *al* it
       sy^{sp} bo^{pt} ς
       εισ πλοιον AEFGMSVXΘ 33 565 579 *al* b c f g² i l q
       vg^{ed} em mg go co sy *K*
       _____ ℵBCLΔ ff² g¹ am tol; WH

8:20 οι δε ειπον *p*[45]ADN(W)XΓ(Θ)Π unc⁹ λ φ 565 700 *pl* i
       q sy^p go arm *K* ς
       και λεγουσιν αυτω BCLΔ 115 g l vg sy^s co eth; WH
       και λεγουσιν ℵ

8:36 κερδηση . . . ζημιωθη *p*[45]ACDWXΓΔΘΠ unc⁹ λ φ 565
       700 *pl* lat sy^{sp} sa bo *K* ς
       κερδησαι . . . ζημιωθηναι ℵBL; WH

8:37 δωσει *p*[45]ACDWXΓΘΠ unc⁹ λ φ 565 700 *rell K* ς
       δοι ℵ*B; WH
       δω ℵ³L

9:3   λευκαναι *p*[45]ADWXΓΠ unc⁹ λ 700 *pl* lat go *K* ς
       ουτωσ λευκαναι ℵBCLNΔΘ φ 28 33 565 *pc* ff² k co ar
       eth Or; WH
       _____ x a n sy^s

9:29 προσευχη και νηστεια *p*[45]ℵ^{cb}ACDLNWXΓΔΠ unc⁹ λ
       φ 565 700 *rell* lat sy go ar eth *K* ς
       προσευχη ℵ*B k geo^{pt} Cl; WH

11:33   αποκριθεισ ο ιησουσ   (𝑝⁴⁵)ADKMΠΦ λ φ *al*
       ο ιησουσ αποκριθεισ   WXΘ unc⁷ *al* lat ς
       ο ιησουσ   ℵBCLNΓΔ *al;* WH

LUKE

5:2   δυο πλοια   𝑝⁷⁵ℵᶜC³DΓΔΘΛΠ unc⁹ *pl K* ς
      πλοια δυο   BW *pc* a e co sy; [WH]
      πλοια   ℵ*
      δυο πλοιαρια   AC*LQR 1* 33 *pc* f

7:6   ο εκατονταρχ. φιλουσ   𝑝⁴⁵ADEGHKMRSUVΓΘΛΠ *pl*
      lat sy arm go *K* ς
      φιλουσ ο εκατονταρχ.   𝑝⁷⁵ℵBCLWXΞ λ 33 *pc* c e
      co eth; WH

9:18   λεγουσιν οι οχλοι   𝑝⁷⁵ℵᶜCDWXΓΔΘΛΠ unc⁸ φ *pl* lat
      syᶜ *K* ς
      οι οχλ. λεγ.   ℵ*BLRΞ λ 131 co; WH
      λεγ. οι ανθρωποι   A *al*⁵ e g¹

9:34   επεσκιασεν   𝑝⁴⁵ACDPRWXΓΔΘΛ unc⁹ λ φ *pl* lat co
      sy *K* ς
      επεσκιαζεν   𝑝⁷⁵ℵBL *pc* a; WH

9:34   εκεινουσ εισελθειν   𝑝⁴⁵ADPRWXΓΔΘΛΠ 9 λ φ *pl* sa
      go *K* ς
      εισελθειν αυτουσ   ℵBCL *pc* bo arm; WH
      αυτουσ εισελθειν   C 157 435
      εισελθειν εκεινουσ   *pc*
      εισελθειν   𝑝⁷⁵S

10:13   καθημεναι   𝑝⁴⁵DEGKMSUVWΔΛΠ λ φ *pl* e mm
      (sy) *K* ς
      καθημενοι   𝑝⁷⁵ℵABCFLRXΓΘΞ 118 *al*¹⁰ *H;* WH
      ————— e q r¹ (sy)

10:19   διδωμι   𝑝⁴⁵(δεδωμι)AC³ΓΔΘΛΠ unc⁷ φ 118 131 *pl* e syᶜ
      Eus ir *K* ς
      δεδωκα   𝑝⁷⁵ℵBC*LW λ *pc* lat go syᵖʰ arm eth Or; WH

10:20   εγραφη   (𝑝⁴⁵)ACDEGHKMSUVWΓΔΛΠ φ 118 113 *pl*
      (Eus) Cyr *K* ς
      εγγεγραπται   (𝑝⁷⁵ℵB ενγεγραπται)LX λ 33 (Eus); WH
      γεγραπται   Θ Or

10:30   υπολαβων δε   𝑝⁴⁵ℵᶜAC²DLWXΓΔΘΛΞΠ unc⁸ λ φ(69 ο
      δε) latt (co) syᵖ go arm *K* ς

υπολαβων p^{75}ℵ*BC* (co) sy^c; WH

10:32 λευιτησ γενομενοσ P⁴⁵ACDEGHKMSUVWΓΔΘΛΠ φ
 pl q sy *K* ς
 λευιτησ p^{75}ℵBLXΞ λ 33 co arm eth *H;* WH

10:39 μαρια p^{45}AB*C³DWΓΔΘΛΠ unc^{rell} φ *pl* latt *K* ς
 μαριαμ p^{75}ℵB³C*LPΞ λ 33; WH

10:39 παρακαθισασα p^{45}C³DPWΓΔΘΛΠ unc⁹ λ *pl* Bas *K* ς
 παρακαθεσθεισα p^{75}ℵABC*LΞ; WH

10:39 παρα p^{45}B³C³DPWΓΔΘΛΙ unc⁹ λ φ *pl* (Bas) *K* ς
 προσ p^{75}ℵB*C*LΞ 33 44 (Bas); WH

11:25 ευρισκει p^{75}ℵ*ADWXΔΘΛΠ unc⁸ *pl* lat sy^c arm *K* ς
 ευρ. σχολαζοντα ℵ BCLRΓ λ 565 *al*¹² f l co sy^p eth
 Or; [WH] (:: Mt 12:44?)

11:30 σημειον τοισ νινευιταισ p^{45}ADWΓΔΘΛΠ unc⁸ λ φ *pl*
 it vg sy co arm eth *K* ς
 τοισ νιν. σημειον p^{75}ℵBCLXΞ 33 *H;* WH

11:44 περιπατουντεσ p^{75}ADWXΓΔΛΠ unc⁷ λ φ *pm* lat sy^c
 arm Lcif *K*
 οι περιπατ. ℵBCLM *al* sy^p ς; WH

11:48 μαρτυρειτε p^{75}ACDWXΓΔΘΛΠ unc⁸ λ φ *pl* lat
 Chr *K* ς
 μαρτυρεσ εστε ℵBL eth(—εστε) Or; WH

12:6 πωλειται p^{45}ADLRWXΓΔΛΠ unc⁸ λ *pl* Or (Epiph)
 Cyr *K* ς
 πωλουνται p^{75}ℵBΘ φ (Epiph); WH

12:22 σωματι $p^{45}p^{75}$ℵADWΘ 1 *pm* lat *K* ς
 σωματι υμων B 070 φ *al* a co (sy) eth Cl; [WH]

12:29 η τι p^{75}ADWXΓΔΘΛΠ unc⁸ *pm* lat sa (bo) sy^p ar eth Cl
 Ath *K* ς
 και τι p^{45}ℵBLQ 070 *al* e (bo) sy^c Bas; WH

12:49 εισ p^{45}DEG^{supp}HRSUVΓΔΛ *pm* (Meth) (Bas) Chr (*in
 terram* it vg Tert) *K* ς
 επι p^{75}ℵABKLMUWXΘΠ λ φ *al* Cl Or Archel (Meth)
 (Bas) Eus Ath Cyr Antioch; WH

12:54 την νεφελην p^{45}DWΓΘΛΠ 070 *pl* Bas *K* ς
 νεφελην p^{75}ℵABLXΔ λ φ 33 arm; WH

12:54 απο δυσμων p^{45}ADWXΓΔΘΛΠ 070 λ φ unc^{rell}
 pl(lat) *K* ς
 επι δυσμων p^{75}ℵBL 64; WH

12:56 ου δοκιμαζετε p^{45}ADWΓΔΛΠ unc[8] λ φ *pl* lat sy[cp]
arm *K* ς
ουκ οιδατε δοκιμαζειν p^{75}אBLΘ 070 33 ff[2] l co sy[sc]
sy[pmg] eth Marc *H;* WH

13:5 ομοιωσ p^{75}ADWXΓΔΘΛΠ 070 unc[7] φ *pl K* ς
ωσαυτωσ אBLM 1 33 71 131 244 248 251 c[scr] g[scr] sy[pmg]
Bas Chr Marc; WH

13:9 ει δε μηγε εισ το μελλον p^{45}ADWXΓΔΘΛΠ unc[8] λ φ
pl it vg sy[c] arm Pet *K* ς
εισ το μελλον ει δε μηγε p^{75}אBL 070 33 69 co
Cyr *H;* WH

13:14 εξ p^{45}ADWXΓΔΛΠ 070 unc[9] λ φ *pl* it vg etc *K* ς
οτι εξ p^{75}אBLΘ gat mm sa bo *H;* WH

13:15 απαγαγων $p^{45}p^{75}$א[c]AB[c]WΓ[2] unc[rell] φ *pl* Hipp Cyr *K* ς
απαγων א*B*Θ λ; [WH]

22:47 ετι δε (p^{69})DEHSVΓΘΛ *pm* b c e ff[2] (sa) arm *K* ς
ετι p^{75}אABGIMRTUXΔΛ *al* l q vg (sa) bo; WH

22:50 τον δουλον του αρχιερεωσ p^{75}ADRWXΓΔΛΠ unc[8] γ
pm it vg *K* ς
του αρχιερεωσ τον δουλον אBLT 69 346; WH

23:5 αρξαμενοσ p^{75}ADRWXΓΔΘΛΠ unc[8] *pl* it vg[c] sa
(bo)*K* ς
και αρξαμενοσ אBLT 0124 (vg) (bo) sy[c]; WH

23:31 εν τω υγρω p^{75}אADPQWXΓΔΘΛΠ unc[9] λ φ *pl* Cyr *K* ς
εν υγρω BC 0124 *pc;* WH

JOHN

4:11 η γυνη p^{66}א ACDL 083 unc[rell] *K* ς
εκεινη א*
——————— p^{75}B sy[s] co; WH

4:29 παντα οσα $p^{66}p^{75}$AC[3]D[gr]LWΓΔΘΛΠ unc[8] *pl* lat *K I* ς
παντα α אBC* sa bo af a d e q; WH
Παντα οσα α 579

4:37 ο αληθινοσ p^{66}AC[3]DΓΘΛΠ[2] unc[7] φ 28 *pm K* ς
αληθινοσ אBC*KLWΔΠ* 083 λ 565 700 *al;* WH

4:39 οσα p^{66}AC[3]DWΓΔΘΛΠ unc[9] *pl* lat sy[p] arm *K* ς
α p^{75}אBC*L b e l q co basm sy[c] eth; WH

4:50 ω p^{66}DWΓΔΛΠ unc[8] γ 13 *pl K* ς
ον p^{75}א ABCLΘ 083 579 *H;* WH
ων F

4:51 σον *p*⁶⁶ᶜDᵍʳLΓΔΘΛΠ unc⁹ λ φ *pl* it syᶜᵖ sa bo *K* ς
αυτου² *p*⁶⁶ P⁷⁵ℵABCW 13 *pc* c d f ff² g l
arm Or; WH

4:53 εν εκεινη *p*⁶⁶ℵᶜADILWΔΘΛΠ unc⁹ *pl* Cyr *K* ς
εκεινη *p*⁷⁵ℵ*BC 1 Chr; WH

5:17 ο δε ιησουσ *p*⁶⁶ACDLΘ *pl* lat *K* ς
ο δε *p*⁷⁵ℵBW *pc*; WH

5:19 εαν μη *p*⁶⁶*p*⁷⁵ADLWΘ uncʳᵉˡˡ *pl K* ς
αν μη ℵB; WH

6:42 πωσ ουν *p*⁶⁶ℵADLΓΔΠ unc⁸ λ φ *pm* lat (syᵖ) Ath Chr
Cyr *K* ς
πωσ νυν *p*⁷⁵BCTWQ bo go arm syʰ (eth) Ath; WH
και πωσ (syᵖ)
πωσ a e sa syᶜ

6:43 ο ιησουσ *p*⁶⁶ACDWΓΔΘΛΠΨ unc⁸ φ 28 *pm K* ς
ιησουσ (*p*⁷⁵)ℵBLT 1 33 sa bo; WH

6:45 με *p*⁶⁶ACDLW uncʳᵉˡˡ λ φ *pl* Orᵖᵗ *K* ς
εμε *p*⁷⁵ℵBΘT *pc* Orᵖᵗ; WH

6:71 ημελλεν *p*⁶⁶DEFGHMVΓΔΛΨ 047 33 579 *pm* it *K* ς
εμελλεν *p*⁷⁵BCKLSUΠ *al*⁵⁰ Cyr; WH
και εμελλον ℵ*(cor-λεν)

7:4 εν κρυπτω τι ποιει *p*⁶⁶DWΓΔΘΛ unc⁸ λ φ *pm* lat *K* ς
τι εν κρυπτω ποιει *p*⁷⁵ℵBLXΠ Chr Cyr; WH
εν κρυπτω ποιει τι Ψ

7:16 ο ιησουσ *p*⁶⁶DLTWXΘ uncʳᵉˡˡ λ φ *pl K* ς
ιησουσ (*p*⁷⁵)ℵB 33 (6*̣*0) Cyr; WH

7:41 αλλοι ελεγον *p*⁶⁶ *ℵDWΓΔΛ²Π uncʳᵉˡˡ *pl* syᶜᵖ *K*
αλλοι δε ελεγον λ φ *pc* bo ς
οι δε ελεγον *p*⁶⁶ᶜ*p*⁷⁵BLXΘ *pc*; WH

7:52 προφητησ εκ τησ Γαλιλαιασ *p*⁶⁶ *ℵDWΓΔΘΛΠ unc⁷ λ
φ *pm K* ς
εκ τησ Γαλιλαιασ προφητησ *p*⁶⁶ *p*⁷⁵BLTX
pc; WH

8:28 ειπεν ουν αυτοισ *p*⁶⁶ᶜ*p*⁷⁵ℵDXΓΔΘΛ unc⁸ φ *pl* lat *K* ς
ειπεν ουν *p*⁶⁶ BLTW 1 565 1241 a; WH

8:38 εωρακατε *p*⁶⁶ (;or-)ℵ*D(EFGHMΔ 070 *al* εορ-)ΓΛΨ
unc⁷ 118 209 579 *pl* lat syˢᵖ sa (bo) (eth) Tert Apol *K* ς
ηκουσατε *p*⁷⁵ℵᶜBCKLX 1 13 33 69 229** 249 *al*¹⁰ f go
(bo) syᵖᵐᵍʰ ar (eth) Or Chr Cyr; WH

9:11 υπαγε *p*⁷⁵ADWXΔΘΛΠΨ unc⁸ λ φ 892 *pl* it vg *K* ς

οτι υπαγε ℵBL *pc* sa bo; WH

9:17　συ τι *p*⁷⁵ADWΓΔΘΛΠ unc⁸ λ φ *pl* it vg etc *K* ς
　　　τι συ *p*⁶⁶ℵBLX bo Cyr; WH

9:35　ο ιησουσ *p*⁶⁶ℵᶜAD *rell K* ς
　　　ιησουσ *p*⁷⁵ℵ*B; WH

10:7　υμιν οτι *p*⁶⁶ℵADEFMSWΓΔΘΛΠ² λ φ *pm* lat *K* ς
　　　υμιν *p*⁷⁵BGKLUXΠ* 33 700 *al* a mm arm eth Cyr Lcif;
　　　WH

10:18　αιρει *p*⁶⁶(ερι)[P⁷⁵]ℵ D *rell K* ς
　　　ηρεν *p*⁴⁵[P⁷⁵]ℵ⃰*B; WH

10:22　εγενετο δε *p*⁶⁶ ℵADXΘ unc*rell* φ *Pl* lat go syᴾ *K* ς
　　　εγενετο τοτε *p*⁶⁶ᶜ*p*⁷⁵BLW 33 *PC* sa bo arm; WH
　　　εγενετο λ　565 *pc* (εγενετο δε τοτε gat (co))

10:22　εν ιεροσολυμοισ *p*⁴⁵[*p*⁷⁵]ℵDXΓΔΛΠ unc⁷ λ φ *pm K* ς
　　　εν τοισ ιεροσολ. *p*⁶⁶[*p*⁷⁵⃰]ABLWΘ ς; WH

10:26　καθωσ ειπον υμιν *p*⁶⁶ ADM²XΓΛΠ²Ψ unc⁶ λ φ *pm* it
　　　go syˢᵖ (bo) *K* ς
　　　————————— *p*⁶⁶ᶜ*p*⁷⁵ℵBKLM*Π*WΘ 33 *pc* c g vg got sa
　　　bo arm; WH

10:28　ζωην αιωνιον διδωμι αυτοισ *p*⁶⁶ ADM²ΓΔΘΠΨ* unc⁷ λ
　　　φ *pl* it vg go syᴾ Or Eus Chr Baş *K* ς
　　　διδωμι αυτοισ ζωην αιωνιον *p*⁶⁶ᶜ⁇ P⁷⁵ℵBLM*X 33 157
　　　249 397 sa bo syʰ arm eth Cyr *H;* WH

10:32　πολλα καλα εργα εδειζα υμιν *p*⁶⁶DLXΓΔ unc⁷
　　　φ *AL K* ς
　　　πολλα εργα καλα εδειζα υμιν *p*⁴⁵ℵAK(Θ)ΛΠ λ
　　　33 *al* lat
　　　Πολλα εργα εδειξα υμιν καλα B 1170; [WH]
　　　Πολλα εδειζα υμιν εργα καλα *p*⁷⁵
　　　(—εργα 244; —καλα W b syˢ Theod)

11:21　τον ιησουν *p*⁴⁵*p*⁶⁶*p*⁷⁵AC²DLWXΘΨΩ unc*rell* λ φ 565
　　　pl K ς
　　　ιησουν ℵBC* 213: WH

11:22　αλλα και *p*⁴⁵*p*⁶⁶ℵᶜAC³DLWΘΨΩ unc*rell* φ 22 33 565 *pl*
　　　lat co *K* ς
　　　και *p*⁷⁵ℵ*BC*X λ 33; WH
　　　αλλα 1780

11:28　ταυτα *p*⁶⁶[*p*⁷⁵]ADΓΔΘΛΠΨΩ unc⁸ λ φ *pl* it vg sa *K* ς
　　　τουτο [*p*⁷⁵]ℵBCLX 59 213 397 *pc* bo eth go; WH

11:29 εκειν. p^{66*}AC²DEGHKSΓΔΛΠΨΩ 0211 λ 28 *pl*
　　　lat *K* ς
　　　εκειν. δε p^{66c}P⁷⁵אBC*LWΘ 33 69 *pc* f go co syᴾ; WH
　　　και εκειν. b ff² l eth

11:29 ερχεται $p^{45}p^{66}$(P⁷⁵)AC²DΓΔΘΛΠ unc⁸ λ φ *pl* lat *K* ς
　　　ηρχετο (p^{75})א̣BC*LWX 33 it^{pc} *H;* WH

11:32 μαρια $p^{45}p^{66}$ אAC³DE²WXΓΔΘΛΠΨ unc⁷ λ φ
　　　1241 *pl K* ς
　　　μαριαμ p^{66c} p^{75}BC*E*L 33 157 sy *H;* WH

11:44 αυτοισ ο ιησουσ $p^{45}p^{66}$אA(C)DXΓΔΘΛΠ unc⁷ λ
　　　φ *pl K* ς
　　　ο ιησουσ αυτοισ LW Or½; WH [o]
　　　ιησουσ αυτοισ p^{75}BC* am for ing² sa bo Or½
　　　αυτοισ 157
　　　ο ιησουσ 700 a r̠ syˢ

11:54 διετριβεν $p^{45}p^{66c}$ADIXΓΔΘΛΠΨ unc^{rell} λ φ 33 *pl*
　　　latt *K* ς
　　　εμεινεν (p^{66*})p^{75}BLW 249 397 398 400 579 892 1241
　　　syᵖᵐᵍ Or; WH

11:57 εντοληv p^{66}[p^{75}]ADLXΓΔΘΛΠ unc⁶ φ 33 *pm* latt
　　　co *K* ς
　　　εντολασ [p^{75}]אBIMW λ (28) 565 *al H;* WH

12:1 ο τεθνηκωσ p^{66}[p^{75}]ADIΓΔΘΛΠ unc⁷ λ *pl* (it) go bo
　　　syˢᴾ arm *K* ς
　　　————— [p^{75}]אBLXW (it) sa (sy) *H;* WH

12:16 οι μαθηται αυτου p^{66}ADLWXΓΔ unc^{rell} λ φ *pl K* ς
　　　αυτου οι μαθηται p^{75}אBΘ 579; WH
　　　οι μαθηται ΚΠ

12:22 λεγουσιν p^{66}DWΘ *pl K I* ς
　　　και λεγουσιν p^{75}אBAL *pc;* WH

12:34 συ λεγεισ p^{66}אADΓΔΘΛΠ unc⁸ λ φ *pm* it vg sa *K* ς
　　　λεγεισ συ p^{75}BLWX bo sy *H;* WH

13:2 γενομενου p^{66}(γεναμενου)א^cADᵍʳΓΔΘΛΠ unc⁸ λ φ 33
　　　pl lat *K* ς
　　　γινομενου א*BLWX *pc* d r¹ *H;* WH

13:3 δεδωκεν p^{66}[p^{75}]ADXΓΔΘΛΠ unc⁷ φ 33 118 209 1241
　　　pl K ς
　　　εδωκεν [p^{75}]אBKLW λ *pc H;* WH

13:18 ουσ p^{66}[p^{75}]ADWΓΔΘΠΨ unc⁷ λ φ *pm K* ς

τιωασ [p^{75}]אBCLM 33 157 Or Cyr; WH

13:18 μετ εμον p^{66}[p^{75}]אADWΓΔΘΛΠΨ unc[8] λ φ *pl* it vg go
sp bo sy[sp] arm *K* ς

μου [p^{75}]BCL *pc* vg[pc] sa; WH

13:20 εαν p^{66c}_{*}DEFGHSUΓΔΘΛ λ φ *pl* Or Chr *K* ς

αν p^{66} (A)BCl KLMXΠ 33 *al* Cyr; WH

13:21 ο ιησουσ p^{66c} ACDWXΓΔΘ unc[rell] λ φ *pl K* ς

ιησουσ p^{66} אBL; WH

13:22 ουν p^{66}א*DLWXΓΔΘΛΠ unc[8] λ φ *pl* lat go (sy) boCyr
K ς

―――――― א[c]BCΨ 16 245 e; WH

σε 61 64 1093 *al*[12] a sy[sp] eth Or

13:23 δε p^{66}אAC[2]DWXΓΔΘΛΠ unc[8] λ φ *pm* a c f ff[2] q go sa
bo sy[p] *K* ς

―――――― BC*LΨ 3 80 87 f[scr] (Or); WH

ουν vg (Or)

13:24 πυθεσθαι τισ αν ειη περι p^{66c}AWΓΔ(Θ)ΛΠ unc[8] λ φ *pl*
(sy) *K* ς

π. τ. αν ειη ουτοσ π. D

και λεγει αυτω ειπε τισ εστιν περι BCILX: WH

πυθεσθαι τισ αν ειη περι ου ελεγεν και λεγει αυτω
ειπε τι̣σ εστιν περι א

(Note: p^{66} obscure here, but not the same as B)

13:25 επιπεσων p^{66c}א*AC[3]DWΓΔΘΛΠ[2] unc[7] λ φ *pm K* ς

αναπεσων (p^{66})א BC*KLXΠ* *H;* WH

13:26 βαψασ το ψωμιον p^{66}(εμβαψασ . . . . ADKWΠ λ 42
565 pc) אXΓΔΘΛ unc[8] φ it vg go sy[p] *K* ς

βαψω το ψωμιον BCL sa bo; WH

13:26 επιδωσω p^{66}א*AD(W)XΓΔΘΛΠ unc[8] λ φ *pm* it vg go
sy[p] *K* ς

και δωσω αυτω BC so bo (arm eth); WH

και δω αυτω L

13:26 το ψωμιον διδωσι p^{66}א*ADWΓΔΘΛΠ unc[7] λ φ *pm* it
vg co *K* ς

το ψωμιον λαμβανει και διδ. א[ca]B(−το)CLMX 33 sy[pmg]
eth Or; WH (B−το) (WH: [το])

13:29 ο ιουδασ p^{66}CDEGHKSΓΔΘΛΠΨ 1241 *al K* ς

ιουδασ אABFLMUX λ φ 33 *al* Or; WH

13:29 ο ιησουσ p^{66}ACDLWΓΔΘ unc[rell]φ *pl K* ς

ιησουσ ℵB *pc* Or; WH. (omit both: λ 565 *pc*)

14:4 και την οδον οιδατε *p*⁶⁶ AC³DNΓΔΘΛΠ unc⁷ υ φ *pl* lat
go sy^sph sa Chr Cyr *K* ς

την οσον *p*⁶⁶ᶜℵBC*LQWXΨ 33 *pc* a r¹ bo; WH

14:7 και απ αρτι *p*⁶⁶ℵAC³DNWΓΔΘΛΠ* unc⁷ φ *pl* lat go
co *K* ς

απ αρτι BC*LQXΠ² λ 33 *H;* WH

14:7 εωρακατε αυτον *p*⁶⁶ℵC³DLNQWXΔΘ λ φ *rell* lat Ath
(Ir) Tert *K* ς

εωρακατε BC* r¹ vg⁽¹⁾ (Ir); WH

14:14 εγω *p*⁶⁶ ℵDEGHKM²QSUXΓΔΠ *pl* a e f ff² sy go *K* ς

τουτο *p*⁷⁵ABLΔ²Ψ 060 33 124 249 262 *pc* lat co; WH

τουτο εγω *p*⁶⁶ᶜ

εγω τουτο M*

14:26 _____ [*p*⁶⁶]*p*⁷⁵ℵADΓΔΘ λ φ *rell K* ς

εγω [*p*⁶⁶]BL 33 127; WH

15:4 μεινη [*p*⁷⁵]*p*⁶⁶ADXΓΔΘΛΠ unc⁷ λ φ *pl* lat *K* ς

μενη ℵBL *pc*; WH

16:23 εν τω ονοματι μου δωσει υμιν (*p*²²)AC³DW ΘΔΛΠΨ λ
φ *pl* it vg bo sy *K* ς (+ all other vss)

δωσει υμιν εν τω ονοματι μου ℵBC*LXYΔ 397 sa Or
Cyr; WH

17:13 εν αυτοισ *p*⁶⁶ℵ*C³DLYΓΔΘΛ unc⁷ λ φ *pm K* ς

εν εαυτοισ ℵᶜABWXΠΨ *al;* WH

εν ταισ καρδιαισ εαυτων C*

18:10 ωτιον (*p*⁶⁶)AC³DYΓΔΘΛΠ unc⁶ λ φ *pl* vss Cyr *K* ς

ωταριον *p*⁶⁰ℵBC*LWX *pc* sy^pmg; WH

18:20 ελαλησα *p*⁶⁶C³D^suppWΓΘΛΠ* unc⁷ φ *pm* Bas Chr *K* ς

λελαληκα ℵABC*LXYΔΛ² 565 *al*¹⁰ Cyr; WH

ACTS

4:34 τισ υπηρχεν *p*⁸DEPΨ 431 623 920 1518 *pm* Chr *K* ς

τισ ην *p*⁷⁴ℵAB(ην τισ)F *al H;* WH

5:3 πετροσ (*p*⁸)DP *pl* Thphl *K* ς

ο πετροσ ℵABE *pc* b^scr cat Chr; WH

5:8 ο πετροσ *p*⁸DEP *pl* Or Chr *K* ς

πετροσ ℵAB *pc*; WH

7:13 το γενοσ του ιωσηφ *p*⁴⁵DHP *pl* Chr *K* ς

το γενοσ ιωσηφ BC 47; WH

το γενοσ αυτου p^{74}ℵAE 40 t vg arm

7:18   ετεροσ (p^{45})DEHP 69 81 *pm* gig sy^p Chr *K* ς
       ετεροσ επαιγυπτον p^{74}ℵABC *al*^{20} cat vg co sy^{pmg}
       arm eth; WH

7:19   εκθετα τα βρεφη p^{45}DEHP *pl* cat Chr *K* ς
       τα βρεφη εκθετα p^{74}ℵABC; WH

8:17   επετιθουν p^{45}D*EHLP *pm* Chr *K* ς
       επετιθεσαν p^{74}ℵAD^2 *al* Eus Did Cyr; WH
       επετιθοσαν B
       επετιθεισαν C

8:18   το αγιον $p^{45}p^{74}$ACΔEHLP *pl* vg sy bo arm eth Bas Chr
       K ς
       ————— ℵB sa Const; WH

10:19 ζητουσιν p^{45}ACDEHLP *pl* Const Did Cyr Chr etc *K* ς
       ζητουντεσ p^{74}ℵB 81; WH

13:9   και ατενισασ p^{45}DEHP *pl* sy arm eth Thphl *K* ς
       ατενισασ p^{74}ℵABCL 33 *pc* cat vg sa Chr Lcif; WH

13:25 τινα με p^{45}CDEHLP *pl* vg bo sy arm Chr *K* ς
       τι εμε p^{74}ℵAB 81 sa eth; WH

14:21 ικονιον p^{45}DHLP *pl* e Bas Chr *K* ς
       εισ ικονιον p^{74}ℵABCE^{gr} *pc* cat sy; WH

16:3   ηδεισαν γαρ απαντεσ τον πατερα αυτου οτι ελλην
       p^{45}DEHLP *pl* sy arm Chr Thphl *K* ς
       ηδ. γαρ απ. οτι ελλην ο πατηρ αυτου p^{74}ℵABC *pc*
       a^{scr} cat; WH

ROMANS

8:34   μαλλον δε και p^{46}DEFGKL *pm* it vg^c sy^p Cyr Chr
       Thdrt Amb Hil *K* ς
       μαλλον δε ℵABC 33 *pc* (3^{scr}: g k l) co arm eth Or;WH

9:11   κακον p^{46}DEFGKL 33 *pl* Chr Euth Thdrt Thphl Oec
       K ς
       φαυλον ℵAB *pc* Or Dam; WH

9:27   καταλειμμα p^{46}ℵ DEFGKLP *pl* Thdrt *K* ς
       υπολειμμα ℵ*AB Eus; WH. (υποκαταλ. 47)

10:5   εκ του νομου p^{46}DEFGKLP *rell* arm Chr Thdrt Dam
       K ς
       εκ νομου ℵB; WH
       εκ πιστεωσ A
       ————— eth

10:5   εν αυτοισ *p*⁴⁶ℵ^cDEFGKLP *pl* sy Chr Thdrt Amb *K* ⲋ

εν αυτη ℵ*AB 33 436 1908 d** e vg go co Or

Dam; WH

11:8   καθωσ *p*⁴⁶ACDEFGLP *rell* Pet Chr etc *K* ⲋ

καθαπερ ℵB 81; WH

11:21   μηπωσ ουδε σου *p*⁴⁶DFGL *pl* vg sy ar go Chr Thdrt

(Antio) Thphl Oec Ir Cyp Ambst *K* ⲋ

ουδε σου ℵABCP *pc* co Or Aug Orcis (Antio) Dam; WH

11:31   αυτοι ελεηθωσιν *p*⁴⁶AD^{bc}EFGL *pl* d e f g vg sy ar eth

go Or Chr Thdrt Amb *al K* ⲋ

αυτοι νυν ελεηθ. ℵBD* 4** bo Dam

αυτοι υστερον ελ. 5 33 88 sa

14:5   οσ μεν *p*⁴⁶ℵ^cBDEFG *pl* sy co ar eth Or Chr Thdrt Aug

K ⲋ

οσ μεν γαρ ℵACP 309 326 d e f g vg go Bas Dam

Ambst; [WH]

15:14   πασησ *p*⁴⁶ACDEFGL *pl* Chr Thdrt *K* ⲋ

πασησ τησ ℵBP 101 462 1739 k^{scr} n^{scr} Cl Dam; WH

15:15   υμιν αδελφοι *p*⁴⁶ℵ^cDEFGLP *rell* lat sy arm Thdrt Dam

Ambst *al K* ⲋ

υμιν ℵ*ABC co eth Or Chr Cyr Aug; WH

I CORINTHIANS

3:3   και διχοστασιαι *p*⁴⁶DEFG *pm* it vg^d sy ir Cyp (Amb)

Thdrt Aug Pel Hier Mar *K* ⲋ

——————— ℵABCP 8min m r vg sa bo eth arm Cl Or

Eus; WH

3:5   τισ . . . τισ *p*⁴⁶CD^{gr}E^{gr}F^{gr}G^{gr}LP *pl* sy co ar Chr Thdt

Thphl Oec *K* ⲋ

τι . . . τι ℵ*AB 33 *pc* d e f g r vg eth Euth Dam Aug

Amb Pel . . .; WH

3:13   πυρ *p*⁴⁶ℵDEL *pl* lat sy^p co arm eth (Cl) (Or) (Chr) Cyr

(Thdt) Dam Ambst *K* ⲋ

πυρ αυτο ABCP 33 *pc* (sy) (Or) Eus Bas (Chr)

Pro (Thdt); WH

4:6   απολλω *p*⁴⁶ℵ^aCDEFGLP *pl* Or Chr Thdt *K* ⲋ

απολλων ℵ*AB*; WH

4:14   νουθετω *p*⁴⁶BDEFGLΨ 105 901 *pl* lat Chr Thdt

Dam Amb *K* ⲋ

νουθετων ℵACP 3 6 *pc* Thphl; WH

4:17 τεκνον μου p^{46}DEFGL *pl* d e f g vg (Or) Thdt . . . *K* ς
   μου τεκνον אABCHP 33 69 1739 *pc;* WH
9:2 τησ εμησ αποστολησ p^{46}DEFGKL *pl K* ς
   μου τησ αποστολησ אBP[AC] 33 1739 *pc;* WH
10:9 χριστον p^{46}DEFGKL *pm* latt sy co Marc Ir Cl Or Aug
   Amb Pel Chr¾ Thphl Oec *K* ς
   κυριον אBCP 2 33 *al* sy^{hmg} arm eth Epiph Chr¼ Theo
   Jo-Dam Sed Cassiod; WH
   θεον A 1288
11:3 χριστου p^{46}CFGKLP *pl* Or Mai Eus Chr Thdt Dam *K* ς
   του χριστου אABDE 33 *pc* Cl Eus Chr Euth; WH
11:15 δεδοται p^{46}DFGKLΨ 6 *al* Tert Pel Aug *K*
   δεδοται αυτη אAB 33 *al H* ς; WH
   αυτη δεδοται CHP 1739 *al*
11:32 κυριου p^{46}ADEFGKLP *pl* Bas Caes Chr (Dam) Cyr
   Euth Thdrt *K* ς
   του κυριου אBC 33 *pc* Cl (Dam); WH
12:3 αναθ. ιησουν p^{46}DEGKLP *pl* d e g harl sa sy^{pmggr} Or
   Chr (Cyr) Thdt Dam Novat Hil Ceter *K* ς
   αναθ. ιησουσ אABC 6 33* *pc* bo ar eth sy Euth
   (Cyr) *H;* WH
   αναθ. ιησου F 33** f m vg (Cyr) Ath Did Hil Amb
12:24 υστερουντι p^{46}א DEFGKL *pl* Marc Or Chr Theo *al K* ς
   υστερουμενω א*ABC 33 1611 1739 *pc* Meletius; WH
13:11 ωσ νηπιοσ (before vb thrice) p^{46}DEFGKLPΨ *pl* vg^{al}
   arm sy Tert Cl½ Amb Pel Heir½ Aug Faust *K* ς
   ωσ νηπιοσ (fol vb thrice) אAB 33 1739 *pc* vg^{pl} sa bo
   Cl½ Hier½; WH
14:21 ετεροισ p^{46}DEFGKLP *pl* latt sy Marc Or Hipp Chr Cyr
   Thdt Dam *al K* ς
   ετερων אAB 33 *pc* Euth; WH
14:39 αδελφοι p^{46}B³D*EFGKL *pm* it vg^{pl} basm arm Amb
   Pel *al K* ς
   αδελφοι μου אABD Ψ 1 1739 *al* vg^{pc} sy sa bo Chr Thdt
   Dam *al;* WH
15:31 καυχησιν p^{46}DEFGL *pm* d e f g (arm) Or Chr Thdt
   Dam *al K* ς
   καυχησιν αδελφοι אABKP 69 r vg sy go sa bo basm
   (arm) eth Dial Euth Aug *al H;* WH

II CORINTHIANS

1:19 ιησουσ χριστοσ p^{46}ℵ^cBDEFGKLP *pl* it vg *K* ς
χριστοσ ιησουσ ℵ*ACΨ 543; WH
ιησουσ 33
_____ Chr

GALATIANS

5:7 τη αληθεια p^{46}ℵ^cCDEFGKL *rell* Euth Thdt Dam *K* ς
αληθεια ℵ*AB 062 33*; WH

5:24 χριστου p^{46}DEFGKLΨ 6 *pl* lat go sy^p arm Cl Marc Chr
Euth Thdt Or Cyp Hier Cyp Amb *K* ς
χριστου ιησου ℵABCN P 33 436 1908 *pc* sa bo Bas Cyr
Dam Aug; WH

6:10 εχομεν p^{46}AB³CDEFGKLP *pl* (*habemus* it vg etc)
Marc Cl *K* ς
εχωμεν ℵB* 6 33 69 *pc*; WH

EPHESIANS

5:2 ημασ p^{46}ℵ^cDEFGKL *pl* lat sy bo ar go Bas Chr Thdt
Dam Hier Amb *K* ς
υμασ ℵ*ABP 69 *pc* sa eth Cl Euth Dam Thphl Vict;
WH

6:5 κυριοισ κατα σαρκα p^{46}DEFGKL *pl* Chr Thdt Oec
K ς (*dominis carnalibus* it vg)
κατα σαρκα κυριοισ ℵABP 33 69 *pc* Cl Bas Chr Euth
Dam Thphl; WH

PHILIPPIANS

2:5 τουτο γαρ φρονει. p^{46}ℵ^cDEFGKLP *pl* d e f g m⁵ go sy^p
Chr Thdt Dam Hil Vict Amb *al K* ς
τουτο φρονει. ℵ*ABC 33 69 *pc* k^{scr} co arm eth Or Euth;
WH

COLOSSIANS

4:12 χριστου p^{46}DEFGK *pl* d e f g go sy eth (ar) Chr Thdt
Dam Amb *K* ς
χριστου ιησου ℵABCL 33 69 *pc* vg co (ar) Euth
Aug Pel; WH
ιησου χριστου P 442 436 arm

HEBREWS

7:22 κρειττονοσ p^{46}ℵ^{c}AC^{c}DEKLP *rell* Ath Chr Thdt Thph
K ς

και κρειττονοσ ℵ*BC*35 1610 1831 2298 Dam; WH
και 920

10:1 δυναται p^{46}D*^{c}EHKL 1739 *pm* lat basm co Or Thdt
Oec Chr K ς

δυνανται ℵACD^b P 33 69 *al* Chr Euth Dam Thph;
[WH]

12:25 εφυγον p^{46}ℵ^{c}D$^{c(\overset{*}{}=εφυγαν)}$KLM *pl* Thdt (Dam) K ς
effugerunt d f vg

εξεφυγον ℵ*ACP 33 *pc* cat^{txt} Chr Cyr (Dam); WH

13:6 και ου p^{46}ℵ^{c}AC^{b}DKLM *pl* arm sy^h Chr Euth Thdt K ς
ου ℵ*C*P 33 209* d f vg sy co eth; WH

LIST III

Papyrus-Byzantine-Alexandrian Alignments
Followed by Westcott and Hort
But Opposed by Westerns

List 3 displays instances where the mainlines of the tradition read together against the Western text. The notation of such alignments is worthwhile for several reasons. First, they show that such readings existed early in Egypt. That is, the Alexandrian text itself goes back that far with the Byzantine witness accompanying it. Second, such alignments help to reveal or set off distinctively Western readings. Third, if the Byzantine text is an independent text-type, then such alignments as these, with or without papyri, would constitute a doubling of the external evidence for readings where the Byzantine and the Alexandrian were together in their support. Finally, a more balanced picture of early Byzantine agreements and kinds of readings can be obtained if all the possible alignments with papyrus and Byzantine readings are tabulated. For the tabulated results as to kinds of readings involved in the alignments of List 3 see the tables, particularly Table 5, and the Charts, which summarize the statistical data of the tables.

MARK

7:6   ωσ γεγραπται p^{45}אABLW φ 700 *pl* ς: WH
     και ειπεν   D (c ff[2] *dicens*, g[2] *dicens* ante hypocrit.)
     ωσ ειπεν   λ 565 arm (a b *qui dixit*)
     οσ ειπεν   Θ

7:29 δια τουτον τον λογον υπαγε p^{45}אABLWΘ φ *rell* ς; WH
υπαγε δια τ. τ. λογον (D) λ 565 700 a b c f g¹i q n sy

8:15 ορατε p^{45}אABCLW φ *rell* ς; WH
——————— DΘ λ 565 it sy^s *pc*

LUKE

7:47 αι αμαρτιαι αυτησ (p^{75})BEGHILMSYVXΓΔΘΛΞ *pm* q
go co Bas *K* ς; WH
αυτησ αι αμαρτιαι אAFKWΠ 69 *al* go co Cl
αυτη πολλα D ff² l

10:36 πγησιον δοκει σοι γεγονεναι p^{75}אABCLWXΓΔΘΛΞ
unc⁹ φ *pm;* WH
δοκει σοι πλησιον γεγ. p^{45} 1 *al* it^{pl} vg Or ς
δοκεισ πλησιον γεγονεναι D e

11:13 υπαρχοντεσ $p^{45}p^{75}$ABCEFGHLRSUVWΓΔΘΛ λ φ *pm*
ς; WH
οντεσ אDKMXΠ *al* Marc

11:43 τοισ φαρισαιοισ $p^{45}p^{75}$ABCLWXΓΔΘΛΠ unc⁸ λ φ *pl* f
l vg ς; WH
φαρισαιοι אD a mm b c e ff² i q sy^c Cl

11:54 ενεδρευοντεσ αυτου $p^{45}p^{75}$ABCLWΔLΠ unc⁸ λ φ *pl* vg
(f) sy eth ς; WH
ενεδρευοντεσ אΘX 130^{gr} am co lat
——————— D a b c e i l q sy^c arm

12:27 πωσ αυξανει . . . νηθει $p^{45}p^{75}$אABLQWXΓΔΛΠ 070
unc⁹ λ φ *pl* f q g¹ vg sy^p bo *K* ς; WH
πωσ ουτε νηθει ουτε υφαιν D a sy^{cs} Cl Tert

14:1 ελθειν $p^{45}p^{75}$אABLW Λ *pm K* ς; WH
εισελθειν DMΘ φ 28 69 157 *al* it vg sa bo arm

14:2 τισ $p^{45}p^{75}$אABLWΘ φ *pl K* ς; WH
——————— D λ b c ff² i l q mt sy^s

16:6 βατουσ p^{75}ABΠΡΓΔΘΛΠ unc⁹ λ φ *pm* co sy^{pmggr} a b
ff² q gat K ς; WH
βαδουσ אLWX 127 237 *pc* Or
καβουσ D² 713
καδουσ D* 1241 *pc* e f i (l) r¹ vg Chr

22:19,20 το σωμα μου + το υπερ . . . εκχυννομενον p^{75}
rell Marc or Tert *K H* ς; [[WH]]
το σωμα μου (om rest of 19 & all of 20) D a ff² i l sy^{sc}

24:6 ουκ εστιν ωδε αλλα ηγερθη *p*⁷⁵ *rell H K* ς; [[WH]]
　　　(C*—αλλα; W ανεστη; αλλ C³ΑΓΔΘ λφ *pm K*)
　　　_____ D a b e ff² l
　　　ηγερθη sa bo Marc; ηγερθη εκ νεκρων c

24:12 ο δε πετροσ . . . γεγονοσ *p*⁷⁵ℵABILWXΓΔΘΛΠ unc⁹
　　　pl c f ff² vg sy^cph sa bo eth Eus *H Ķ* ς; [[WH]]
　　　_____ (om vs 12) D a b e l fu sy^h 6 Marc

24:51 απ αυτων και ανεφερετο εισ τον ουρανον *p*⁷⁵ℵ
　　　ABCLXΓΔ ΘΛΠ unc⁷ *pl* c f q vg sy^h Cyr *H K* ς;
　　　[[WH]]
　　　απ αυτων ℵ*D a b e ff² l sy^s

24:52 Προσκυνησαντεσ αυτον υπεστρεψαν *p*⁷⁵ℵABCΘ unc¹³
　　　rell c f q vg^rell *K H* ς; [[WH]]
　　　υπεστρ. D a b e ff² l Aug (προσκ. υπεστρ. 700 *pc*)

JOHN

4:51 δουλοι αυτου *p*⁶⁶*p*⁷⁵ABCWΓΔΘΛΠ unc⁹ *pl K* ς; WH
　　　δουλοι ℵD L 1 a b c e f ff² l vg

7:8 εγω ουπω *p*⁶⁶*p*⁷⁵BLTWXΓΔΘΛ unc⁷ λ φ 33 *pm* f g² d
　　　sy^ph sa Nonn *K* ς; [WH]
　　　εγω ουκ ℵDKMΠ *al* lat sy^sc bo arm Epip Chr Amb

10:11 τιθησιν *p*⁶⁶*p*⁷⁵ *rell K* ς; WH
　　　διδωσιν *p*⁴⁵ℵ*D e b ff i q vg sy^s bo (Cl)

10:34 νομω υμων *p*⁶⁶*p*⁷⁵ℵ^aABLX unc^rell vg sa bo (sy)*K* ς; WH
　　　νομω *p*⁴⁵ℵ*DΘ 1170 it^pl sy^s geo Tert Eus Hil

11:35 εδακρυσεν *p*⁶⁶(*p*⁷⁵)ABCLX unc^rell *pl* sa sy^p Chr And *K*
　　　ς; WH
　　　και εδακρυσεν ℵ*DΘ 61 346 788 828 1010 lat sy^sp ar
　　　gg bo^pt
　　　εδακρ. δε 1093 1216
　　　εδακρ. ουν 317

ACTS

5:10 εξενεγκαντεσ εθαψαν *p*⁴⁵ℵAB *rell* ς; WH
　　　συστειλαντεσ εξενεγκαν και εθαψαν D^gr sy^ph *

5:16 οιτινεσ εθερα. απαντεσ *p*⁴⁵ℵABEP *pl* vg etc *K* ς; WH
　　　και ειωντο παντεσ D gig p sa Lcf

5:31 δεξια *p*⁴⁵ℵAB *rell* ς; WH
　　　δοξη D* gig p sa Ir^lat

6:2   εστιν ημασ p^8ℵABEHP *pl K H* ς; WH
        εστιν ημιν   CD (υμιν 899 af) g p
        εστιν   Dam

6:9   και ασιασ p^{45}ℵBCD²EHP *pl* vg co sy arm eth ς; WH
        —————— AD* 12ˡᵉᶜᵗ d

6:15   και ατενισαντεσ εισ αυτον παντεσ οι καθεζομενοι
        p^{45}ℵABC *rell* ς; WH
        και ητενιζον δε αυτω παντεσ οι καθημενοι
        Dᵍʳ (gg d)

8:23   εισ γαρ χολην πικριαο και συνδεσμον $p^{45}p^{74}$ℵABC *rell*
        k H ς; WH
        εν γαρ πικριασ χολη και συνδεσμω   D* Irˡᵃᵗ

10:33   παντα τα προστεταγμενα σοι $p^{45}p^{74}$ℵBC *rell* ς: WH
        τα προστ. σοι παντα   A
        τα προστ. σοι   D 96 142 460 sa

10:38   οσ $p^{45}p^{74}$ℵᶜABCEHLP *pl* Chr Thdt *K H* ς; WH
        ωσ   ℵ* 33 *pc* Thphl
        ουτοσ   D tol sy sa Ir

12:20   αυτων την χωραν $p^{45}p^{74}$ℵAB *rell* ς; WH
        τασ χωρασ αυτων   D 242 vg Lcif
        αυτων την πολιν   E 33

13:27   τασ φωνασ p^{45}ℵABC *rell* ς; WH
        τασ γραφασ   DE

13:33   ιησουν p^{45}ℵBC *rell* ς; WH
        τον κυριον ιησουν χριστον   D (614) sa Amb
        τον κυριον ημων ιησουν   137 syᵖᵐᵍ Hil
        ουτον εκ νεκρων   A

13:47   εντεταλται p^{45}ℵABC *rell* ς; WH
        εντελλεται   3 61
        εντεταλκεν   D* 47ᵐᵍ eˢᶜʳ Cyr Thdrt

16:18   εξελθειν p^{45}ℵABC *rell* Eust Chr Ps-Ath Euth ς; WH
        ινα εξελθησ   D g gig Lcif
        εξελθε   33

16:36   εν ειρηνη $p^{45}p^{74}$ABC *rell* ς; WH (εισ ειρηνην ℵ)
        —————— D gig

17:14   πορευεσθαι $p^{45}p^{74}$ℵAB *rell* ς; WH
        απελθειν   D

ROMANS

5:18   δικαιωματοσ p^{46}ℵABC *pl* ς; WH

το δικαιωμα DEG 69 sy^{p}
και δικαιωμα F
5:19$^{(2)}$ ενοσ *p*^{46}ℵABC *pl* ς; WH
ενοσ ανθρωπου D*FG d* f g Ir Cyr Aug
6:2 οιτινεσ *p*^{46}ℵABCD *rell* Cl Tert Aug *al* ς; WH
οιτινεσ γαρ FG d e f g vg sy Or Amb
6:8 συνζησομεν *p*^{46}ℵABDEL *pl* d e m^{94} vg Eus Cl Chr ς; WH
συνζησωμεν CKP 104 205 460 k^{scr} Bas Dam Thphl
συνζησομεθα FG
6:8 αυτω *p*^{46}ℵABCD^{c}EKLP *rell* m^{91} fu dimid tol vg^{s} co ar (sy) eth Tert Or Eus Bas Chr Amb Aug ς; WH
τω χριστω D*EFG d e f g vg^{c} am harl marian (sy)
8:20 ουχ εκουσα *p*^{46}ℵABCD *rell* ς; WH
ου θελουσα FG (Latin^{pl} *non volens*) d e f g vg Ir Or Hil Amb
8:21 οτι *p*^{46}ABCD^{c}EKLP *pl* ς; WH
διοτι ℵD*FG
αλλα 179
8:22 συνωδινει *p*^{46}ℵABCD *pl* ς; WH
οδυνει FG (cf various lat rendreings in Tisch.)
8:32 οσ γε του ιδιου υιου ουκ εφεισατο *p*^{46}ℵABC *pl* ς; WH
οσ ουδε υιου ιδιου εφεισατο (D)FG
8:35 τισ *p*^{46}ℵABCD *pl* Or Eus Cyr Tert Cyp Anti Lcif ς; WH
τισ ουν FG d* f g m^{42} vg^{c} arm Or
8:37 του αγαπησαντοσ *p*^{46}ℵABCKL *pl* sy co arm go Cl Or Eus Bas Chr Thdt Dam Amb Aug *K H* ς; WH
τον αγαπησαντα DEFG d e f g vg Tert Or Cyp Lcif Hil
8:38 αγγελοι *p*^{46}ℵABC *pl* Or Eph Bas Ant Hil Aug Cl ς; WH
αγγελοσ DEFG d e f g co Amb Aug
9:1 χριστω *p*^{46}ℵABCD^{c}KL *pl* vg^{rell} Or Arch Did Aug ς; WH
χριστω ιησου D*EFG d e f g arm Or Ath Amb
9:1 εν πνευματι *p*^{46}ℵABCD *pl* ς; WH
συν πνευματι FG g
9:3 απο *p*^{46}ℵABCFKL *pl* ς; WH
υπο DEG

9:3   συγγενων μου p^{46}אABC *pl* Or Eus Bas Thdr Dam ς; WH

συγγενων   D*FG d* g go Or Chr Cyr Amb Aug

9:3   κατα p^{46}אABC *pl* ς; WH

των κατα   DEFG a^scr   Bas Thdt

9:5   οι   (p^{46})אABCD *pl* ς; WH

——————— FG

9:5   και p^{46}אABCD *pl* Ir Or Chr Caes Ath Hil Aug Amb ς; WH

——————— FG f g Hip Epip Cyp Hil

9:6   ισραηλ$^{(2)}$ p^{46}אABKL *pl* tol co Or Caes Cyr Aug ς; WH

ισραηλιται   DEFG vg arm Or Chr Amb Aug

9:8   του θεου p^{46}אABD *pl* Or ς; WH

θεου   FG Or Chr

9:14   τω θεω p^{46}אABD EKLP *pl* Cl Or Thdr *al* ς; WH

θεω   D*FG

9:17   οπωσ$^{(2)}$ p^{46}אABD *pl* ς; WH

οπωσ αν   FG

10:5   ανθρωποσ p^{46}אABD *pl* ς; WH

——————— FG f g sy ar^e Chr

10:8   λεγει p^{46}אABKLP *pl* tol go sy Chr Cyr Dam Aug ς; WH

λεγει η γραφη   DE 33 *pc* d e vg^c am fu harl arm Or *al*

η γραφη λεγει   FG f g bo eth

10:8   το ρημα εστιν p^{46}אAB *pl* Or Chr Thdt Cyr Dam ς; WH

εστιν το ρημα   DEFG d e f g vg go arm Or Hil Amb

10:20   αποτολμα p^{46}אABCLP *pl* d** vg sy Or ς; WH

——————— D* EFG d* e f g

11:4   τη βααλ p^{46}אABCD *pl* Iust Or Eus ς; WH

τω βααλ   FG

11:7   επιζητει p^{46}אABCD *pl* ς; WH

επεζητει   FG 5 336 441 d e f g vg sy Or Amb

11:14   μου την σαρκα p^{46}אABC *pl* ς; WH

την σαρκα μου   DEFG

11:17   εγενου post ελαιασ p^{46}אABC *pl* vg go sy^p Ir ς; WH

εγενου post συνκοινωνοσ   D*FG k^scr d f g co eth Or Amb

11:31   ουτοι p^{46}אABC *pl* ς; WH

αυτοι D*FG 88 sy^{pmg}

12:3   παρ ο δει φρονειν p⁴⁶אABD *pl* Ir Or ς; WH
_____ FG 425 f g

12:4   καθαπερ p⁴⁶אAB *pl* ς; WH
ωσπερ D*EFG

12:5   εσμεν p⁴⁶אABD *pl* Or Eus ς; WH
_____ FG f g

12:13 χρειαισ p⁴⁶אABD^{bc}ELP *pl* e f vg^c Or Chr Thdr Thdt
Dam Thphl Oec Aug ς; WH
μνειαισ D*FG d* g am ap Or Hil Amb Aug *al*

13:4   εκδικοσ εισ οργην p⁴⁶(εγδικοσ)א^cABLP *pm* guelph vg
sy co ar eth go Ir Or ς; WH
εισ οργην εκδικοσ א*D^{bc}E *al*²⁵ d*** Chr Thdt
εκδικοσ D*FG 1944 d* f g

13:9   το γαρ p⁴⁶אABD *pl* Cl Or ς; WH
γεγραπται γαρ FG f g Amb

13:10 πληρωμα ουν p⁴⁶א(A)BD^{bc}EL *pl* f vg sa bo sy^p Cl Or
Chr Thdt Dam Aug . . . ς; WH
πληρωμα δε D*FG d e g m¹⁶ eth Aug . . .
πληρωμα P 88 12^{lect}

14:16 ουν p⁴⁶אABCD *pl* Cl Or ς; WH
_____ FG 3 f g go arm

15:4   προεγραφη (p⁴⁶)אACD^cELP *pl* ς; WH
προσεγραφη D*FG
εγραφη B d e f g m⁷⁸ vg arm eth Or Cl Amb

15:13 εν τω πιστευειν p⁴⁶אABC *pl* ς; WH
_____ DEFG d* e f g m⁷⁹ arm Vig

15:13 εν⁽²⁾ p⁴⁶אABC *pl* ς; WH
_____ D*EF^{gr} G 104 328 g Chr

15:14 αγαθωσυνησ p⁴⁶ABCD *pl* Cl Or Delar ς; WH
αγαπησ FG d e f g m⁹⁷ vg Amb *al*

15:14 δυναμενοι και αλληλουσ p⁴⁶אABCD^bP *pl* ς; WH
(αλλουσ L *al*⁷⁰ g sy Or *al*)
αλληλουσ δυναμενοι D^{gr c}EFG

15:16 ειναι p⁴⁶אABC *pl* ς; WH
γενεσθαι D*FG

15:18 κατειργασατο p⁴⁶אABCP *pl* ς; WH
κατηργασατο DEFGL

15:20 ουχ οπου p⁴⁶אABCD^cD^b(ουκ) *pl* ς; WH οπου ουκ D*FG f g Chr

15:22 ενεκοπτομην p⁴⁶אABCLP *rell* ς; WH
      ενεκοπην DEFG

15:23 εχων(2) p⁴⁶אABC *pl* ς; WH
      εχω D*FG 69 103 242 oˢᶜʳ d* f g

15:24 πορευωμαι p⁴⁶אABC *pl* Chr Dam *al* ς; WH
      πορευομαι DEFGP *al*¹⁵ Euth
      πορευσομαι L 464**
      πορευσωμαι Thdt

15:24 γαρ p⁴⁶אABCDELP *pl* (co) syᵖ Euth Thdt Dam Thphl
      Oec ς; WH
      ————— FG d e f g vg sy arᵉ (co) arm eth Or

15:30 προσευχαισ p⁴⁶אABC *pl* ς; WH
      προσευχαισ υμων DEFG 356ᵐᵍ nˢᶜʳ** d e f g vgᶜ co
      eth

15:33 ειρηνησ p⁴⁶אABCDᶜ *pl* ς; WH
      ειρηνησ ητω D*EFG

16:1 δε p⁴⁶אABCDᵇᶜELP *pl* d*** e vg sy co Or Chr Thdt
      Dam Amb ς; WH
      ————— D*FG d* f g arm eth

16:5 εισ χριστον p⁴⁶אABCLP *pl* ς; WH
      εν χριστω DEFG *al*¹⁰

16:7 χριστω p⁴⁶אABC *pl* Or ς; WH
      χριστω ιησου DEFG d* f g Amb *al*

16:9 εν χριστω p⁴⁶אABLP *pl* am fu semid harl tol sy co eth
      Or Chr Thdt Dam Amb ς; WH
      εν κυριω CDEFG 69 102 218 1912 d e f g arm Chr

16:17 σκοπειν p⁴⁶אABCLP *pl* vg Or ς; WH
      ασφαλωσ σκοπειτε DEFG d* e f g m⁶¹ Auct

16:18 και ευλογιασ p⁴⁶אABCLP *pl* d*** m⁶¹ vg Or ς; WH
      ————— D*EFG 3 33 76 218 327 336 425 d* e f g Chr

16:20 η χαρισ . . . μεθ υμων p⁴⁶אABCLP *pl* d*** vg Or
      Amb ς; WH
      ————— DEFG d* e f g

16:27 σοφω θεω p⁴⁶אABC *pl* ς; WH
      θεω σοφω DE d e

I CORINTHIANS

1:8 εν τη ημερα p⁴⁶אABCLP *pl* r sy co arm eth Or ς; WH
      εν τη παρουσια DEFG d e f g Amb Cass

1:9   δι p^{46}ℵABC *pl* Or Sev Chr Thdt Eus Phot ς; WH
      υφ   D^{gr} F^{gr}G^{gr}

1:10   του κυριου ημων ιησου χριστου p^{46}ℵABCLP *pl* r vg sy
      co arm eth Or Cyp Amb ς; WH
      χριστου ιησον του κυριου ημων   D^{gr}E e
      ιησου χριστου του κυριου ημων   F(om του)G d f g

1:16   εβαπτισα p^{46}ℵABC *pl* ς; WH
      βεβαπτικα   D*FG

1:26   γαρ p^{46}ℵABC *pl* d e r vg Ir Or Eus ς; WH
      ουν   D^{gr}E^{gr}FG 93 f g eth
      γουν   Pamph

1:29   καυχησηται p^{46}ℵABCDEL *pl* ς; WH
      καυχησεται   FGP b^{scr} o^{scr}

1:30   δικαιοσυνη τε p^{46}ℵABCD*** *pl* Or Dial Eus Cyr
      ς; WH
      και δικαιοσυνη   D**FG Or
      δικαιοσυνη   D*

2:3   εν φοβω και εν τρομω p^{46}ℵABC *pl* ς; WH
      εν φοβω και τρομω   DE 1926 d e
      φοβω και τρομω   FG 76 f g r vg Ambst

2:11   του ανθρωπου$^{(2)}$ p^{46}ℵABCD *pl* Or Eus Bas Ant ς; WH
      _____ FG f g it arm Or Hil Amb

2:11   τα του θεου p^{46}ℵABC *pl* Or ς; WH
      το του θεου   D^{gr}
      τα εν τω θεω   F^{gr}G g Hil

2:12   κοσμου p^{46}ℵABCLP *pl* fu harl* tol sy eth Just Or Eus
      Ath Bas Epip Novat ς; WH
      κοσμου τουτου   DEFG f g it vg^c co arm Bas Cyr

3:3   σαρκικοι p^{46}ℵABCD^{c}ELP *pl* Euth Cl ς; WH
      σαρκινοι   D*FG

3:4   λεγη τισ p^{46}ℵABCLP *pl* (LP = λεγει τισ) ς; WH
      τισ λεγη   DEFG d e f g r Ambst

3:17   τουτον p^{46}ℵBCLP *pl* sa bo sy^p eth Or Eus Chr Cyr Did
      Thdt Dam ς; WH
      αυτον   ADEFG 205 326 sy arm Or

3:19   τω θεω p^{46}ℵABLP *pl* Euth Or Dion Eus Herm Chr
      Thdt Dam ς; WH
      θεω   CDEFG 221 b^{scr} o^{scr} Cl Or

4:5   οσ p^{46}ℵABC *pl* Or Amb Ambst ς; WH
      _____ D*EFG d e f g Aug

4:8   γε p^{46}אABC *pl* ς; WH
     ———— D*FG

4:14 γραφω ταυτα p^{46}אABCLP *pl* ς; WH
     ταυτα γραφω   DEFG d e f g k^{scr} vg

5:1   τινα του πατροσ εχειν p^{46}אABC *pl* ς; WH
     του πατροσ εχειυ τιυα   DEFG

5:3   τουτο p^{46}אABCD *pl* ς; WH
     ———— FG

5:5   τον τοιουτον p^{46}אABD *pl* d e f vg Or Dial Lcf ς; WH
     αυτον   F^{gr}G g sy eth

6:1   πραγμα εχων προσ τον ετερον p^{46}אABC *pl* vg sy Cl
     Dam ς; WH
     προσ τον ετερον πραγμα εχων   DEFG 1926 d e f g co
     go Chr Thdt Thphl Cyp Aug Ambst

6:15 πορνησ μελη p^{46}אABC *pl* Or Dial Meth ς; WH
     μελη πορνησ   DEFG d e f g vg Ant Ir Or Tert
     Cyp Lcif

7:2   τασ πορνειασ p^{46}אABCDLP *pl* Cl Or Meth Tert Chr ς;
     WH
     την πορνιαν   FG f g vg sy Tert Or Cyp Ambst

7:9   ουκ εγκρατευονται p^{46}אAB^{3}CD^{3}KLP (B*D* ενκρ-) *pl*
     Or Meth ς; WH
     ου κρατευονται   FG

7:14 γυναικι p^{46}אABCKLPQ *pl* ς; WH
     γυναικι τη πιστη   DEFG it vg sy ar^e Cl Tert

7:17 διατασσομαι p^{46}אABC *pl* ς; WH
     διδασκω   D*EFG it vg

7:24 εν ω εκληθη αδελφοι p^{46}אAB *pl* ς; WH
     αδελφοι εν ω εκληθη   D(εκληθητε)EFG d e f g Ambst
     εν ω εκληθη   104 206 241 255 326 2831 a^{scr} Thdt

7:26 οτι καλον p^{46}אAB *pl* Or Meth Bas ς; WH
     οτι καλον εστιν   D*FG it vg sy

7:28 γημη p^{46}אAB 459 *pl* Or Meth Bas ς; WH
     γαμη   D*FG

7:28 τη σαρκι p^{46}אAB *pl* Or Meth Bas Dam ς; WH
     εν τη σαρκι   D*FG

7:29 ο καιροσ p^{46}אABKLP *pm* m^{79} vg Meth Eus Bas Thdt
     Tert Ambst ς; WH
     οτι ο καιροσ   DEFGΨ 319 642 *al* it vg^{ms} sy co basm
     arm Dam Tert Or Thphl

7:32   τω κυριω   p⁴⁶ℵABD *pl* Meth Eus Bas Eph Epip ς; WH
        τω θεω   FG f g vg Or Cyp Amb Tert

7:36   γαμειτωσαν   p⁴⁶ℵAB(KLP = γαμητ-) *pl* ς; WH
        γαμειτω   D*FG 1108 1611 g sy arm Epip Aug

7:39   γαμηθηχαι   p⁴⁶ℵABDL*(γαμησαι) *pl* Cl Or Epip Bas
        ς; WH
        γαμηθη   FG d e f g vg Tert

7:40   εχειν   p⁴⁶ℵABD *pl* f vg Or Novat Hier ς; WH
        εχω   FG d* g it Tert Ambst

8:4   ουδεν   p⁴⁶ℵABD *pl* ς; WH
        ουδεν εστιν   FG f g m⁵ vg sy co Ir Or Aug Ambst

8:10   τα ειδωλοθυτα εσθιειν   p⁴⁶ℵAB *pl* ς; WH
        εσθιειν τα ειδωλοθυτα   DEFG d e f g vg Or
        Aug Ambst

8:13   βρωμα   p⁴⁶ℵABD *pl* ς; WH
        το βρωμα   FG

8:13   μου⁽²⁾   p⁴⁶ℵABDᵇᶜ EKLP *pl* sy co basm arm eth Cl Bas
        Aug Amb ς; WH
        _____   D*Fg d e f g vg it Cyp Aug Ambst

9:7   εσθιει   p⁴⁶ℵAB *pl* ς; WH
        εσθιει και πινει   DEFG d e f g

9:9   των βοων   p⁴⁶ℵABC 915 *pl* ς; WH
        περι των βοων   DEFG 104 177 181 326 337 441 618 999
        1311 12ˡᵉᶜᵗ it vg Or

9:16   καυχημα   p⁴⁶ℵᵃABCKLP *pl* vg sy sa bo arm eth Or Chr
        Euth Thdt Dam Aug Ambst ς; WH
        χαρισ   ℵ*DEFG d e f g it Ambst

9:18   τη εξουσια   p⁴⁶ℵABC *pl* ς; WH
        την εξουσιαν   D*FG 38
        τησ εξουσιας   181 1836 1898

9:22   ασθενεσιν   p⁴⁶ℵABC *pl* ς; WH
        ασθενουσιν   DEFG

9:22   παντωσ τινασ   p⁴⁶ℵABC *pl* ς; WH
        παντωσ τινα   1311
        παντασ   DEFG it vg
        τουσ παντασ   33 Cl Or Mac

9:24   ουτωσ   p⁴⁶ℵABCD *pl* ς; WH
        εγω δε λεγω υμιν ουτωσ   DFG f g Ir Cyp Ambst

10:8   πορνευωμεν . . . επορνευσαν   p⁴⁶ℵABDᶜ E *pl* Chr Thdt
        Dam ς; WH

πορνευομεν . . . επορνευσαν KLP

πορνευσωμεν . . . επορνευσαν 33 69 441

πορνευωμεν . . . εξεπορνευσαν 056 1 385 424*

εκπορνευωμεν . . . εξεπορνευσαν D*FG Chr

10:13 ουκ ειληφεν p⁴⁶אABCD *pl* Or ϛ; WH

ου κατειληφεν 206 1758 1835

ου καταλαβη FG e f g vg Or Cyp Aug Hil Ambst

10:13 εασει p⁴⁶אABC *pl* Or Ath Bas Eph Mac ϛ; WH

αφησει DEFG

10:13 ο δυνασθε p⁴⁶אABCD *pl* ϛ; WH

δυνασθε υπενεγκειν FG f g Aug

10:17 αρτου⁽²⁾p⁴⁶אABC *pl* ϛ; WH

αρτου και του ενοσ ποτηριου D(−ενοσ)EFG it vgˢ demid harl tol go Ambst Pelag

10:27 απιστων p⁴⁶אABC *pl* ϛ; WH

απιστων εισ δειπνον D*EFG d e f g fu* vg sa Ambst Pelag

10:33 παντα πασιν p⁴⁶אABC *pl* Or Hil vg ϛ; WH

πασιν παντα DE go it Tert Or

πασιν κατα παντα FG

11:2 παραδοσεισ p⁴⁶אABC(Lp παραδωσεισ) *pl* ϛ; WH

παραδοσεισ μου DFG it vg Ambst

11:5 τη κεφαλη p⁴⁶אABC *pl* ϛ; WH

κεφαλη D*FG

11:13 εν υμιν αυτοισ p⁴⁶אABCFG *pl* fu** tol ϛ; WH

υμεισ αυτοι DE d e vg Ambst Pelag

11:13 τω θεω προσευχεσθαι p⁴⁶אABCHKLP(Ψ 330 −τω) *pm* ϛ; WH

προσευχ. τω θεω DEFG it vg sy

11:18 εν υμιν υπαρχειν p⁴⁶אABCDᵇKLP *pl* ϛ; WH

υπαρχ. εν υμιν D* EFG vg sy arm

υπαρχειν am fu dimid harl tol Or Ambst

11:19 αιρεσεισ εν υμιν ειναι p⁴⁶אABC *pm* ϛ; WH (αιρ. ειν. εν υμιν DᶜE 330 co)(εν υμ. αιρ. ειν. 42 234 522)

om εν υμιν D*FG d e f g vg Tert Or Cyp Aug Ambst

11:20 εστιν p⁴⁶אABC *pl* ϛ; WH

ετι D*FG

——————— d e f vg Ambst

11:21 εν τω p⁴⁶אABC *pl* Cl ϛ; WH

επι τω DEFG Chr
εισ το 3 33 1108 1611

11:22 εσθιειν και πινειν *p*⁴⁶אABCD *pl* ς; WH
      φαγειν και πειν FG

11:23 τη νυκτι η *p*⁴⁶אABC *pl* ς; WH
      η νυκτι D*FG 1912 lat

11:23 αρτον *p*⁴⁶אABC *pl* ς; WH
      τον αρτον D*FG

11:28 ανθρωποσ εαυτον *p*⁴⁶אBKL 88 1912 *pl* sy arm eth (sa
      bo = ανθ. δε δοκιμ. εαυτ.) Cl Or Bas Chr Cyr Thdt
      Dam ς; WH
      εαυτον ανθ. CD(D* = ο ανθ.)EFGP 33 81 181 326 it vg
      go Euth Dam
      om ανθ. 255

12:1 αδελφοι . . . αγνοειν *p*⁴⁶אABC *pl* ς; WH
      αγνοειν αδελφοι D* EFG 336 1739 d e f g vg eth Did
      Ath Ambst

12:3 λαλων *p*⁴⁶אABC *pl* ς; WH
      _____ DEFᵍʳ G d e g Hil Vict

12:9 δε⁽²⁾ *p*⁴⁶אABC *pl* Cl Cyr Chr Thdrt Hil ς; WH
      _____ D*EFG it vg Eus arm Hil (same witt om
      δε⁽¹⁾vs 10)

12:10 ενεργηματα *p*⁴⁶אABC *pl* Cl Or Eus Cyr Bas Caes Aug
      ς; WH
      ενεργεια DEFG (181 = ενεργειαι)(056 = ενεργημα)
      it vg Hil

LIST IV

Papyrus-Byzantine Plus Varying Support
(Western and/or Alexandrian)
But Opposed by Westcott and Hort

Lists 4 and 5 complete the spectrum of alignments and comparisons which have significance for this study. These two lists set forth readings with papyri-Byzantine plus varying support from Alexandrian and/or Western witnesses. The lists are divided on the basis of whether or not the papyrus-Byzantine-plus reading is opposed (4) or supported hesitantly (5) by WH.

In List 4 there are some fifteen or so readings which could have been classified in List 1 as distinctively Byzantine readings supported by the papyri, but they have one or more members of the Alexandrian group, (cf. footnote, no. 11, p. 143.[1] For an outstanding example, see Luke 10:41-42, "but one thing is necessary" ενος δε εστιν χρ). This is the Byzantine reading but it is also read by the first hand of manuscript C which kept it from being classified as a distinctively Byzantine reading. It also has a few Old Latin manuscripts reading with it, as well as the Curetonian Syriac, but this reading in Luke 10:41-42 probably would have been classified as a "Syrian" reading by WH. Their doubt over this passage was not because of the manuscript evidence reading with ενος δε εστιν, but because the other Alexandrians were found dispersed among three

---

[1]They were placed in List 4 to begin with because of the attestation of manuscript C, but compare the statements of WH (quoted pp. 141-142) regarding the identification of distinctive readings.

different readings, and the whole clause is omitted by D, an omission which caused them to put it in half-brackets in their text. The passage is now found to be supported by two papyri, The Chester Beatty p^{45} and p^{75}. These combine to show that the "Syrian" reading was early and was preserved accurately, though almost alone, by the Byzantines.

Here may be seen the striking circumstance of a Byzantine reading existing early in Egypt, as witnessed by the two early papyri, preserved by the first hand of one Alexandrian (C) but the rest of the Alexandrians making changes. B goes one way; Aleph goes still another; and the minor Alexandrians go yet a third way which is really a conflation combining all the elements found in the others, and this is the one followed by WH and placed in half brackets. Then, as mentioned above, the entire passage has dropped out of the geographically Western text-type, though the Sinaitic Syriac also agrees in omitting it. Luke 10:41-42, then, is an example of a reading which previously was thought of as characteristically Byzantine, and therefore late, but it is now seen to reach back deep into the second century. Two papyrus witnesses to the reading are found in Egypt, witnesses which attest that this "Byzantine" reading was known in Egypt at the time the Alexandrian text-type was being formed.

Aside from these passages which might have been classified in List 1, however, the list presents readings where the papyrus-Byzantine reading is supported with some members of the Western and/or Alexandrian text-types but is nevertheless opposed by WH. List 4 is a selection of eighty readings taken from a much larger group, of which about 195 remain. These in the list were selected because they involved variants which would be more likely to show up in translation than the larger number of readings of this type which were left out of the list.

Some of the readings in List 4 (as well as in List 5) illustrate the relatively mixed nature of not only the Western but also the Alexandrian text-type as compared to the Byzantine. Many of the instances in List 4 illustrate cases where, if the Byzantine text's independent weight of external evidence were acknowledged, the doubt surrounding the readings supported by WH would either be increased or the reading adopted by the printed texts would be changed. For some examples of modern editorial change in this direction (i.e., in instances where papyri are involved) compare the following places in List 4 where the American Bible Society's Greek Testament (UBS)[2] departs from the WH reading for the papyrus-Byzantine-plus reading and where, at the same time, ABS treats the variant in its apparatus: Matthew 26:20; Luke 9:59; 10:15; 10:41, 42; 11:24; 16:12; John 9:6; 11:45; 16:28; Acts 16:32; Romans 8:34; 10:5 (change in word order affecting meaning); I Corinthians 6:11; 15:10; II Corinthians 1:14; 2:7; 8:19; Ephesians 3:9; Philippians 2:26; 3:13; Colossians 1:20; I Peter 5:2; II Peter 3:18. In connection with the same List 4, some other instances may be noticed where the text of UBS has quietly[3] changed the WH reading for the one supported by papyrus-Byzantine-plus: Mark 9:30; Luke 11:20; 23:39; 24:49; John 2:12; 2:15; 5:15; 6:71; 8:41; 13:36; 18:29; Acts 7:15; 9:37; 10:19; Romans 8:34; II Corinthians 7:14; I Peter 1:9.

This does not imply that UBS favors the Byzantine text. It is probably doubtful that very many of the above changes would have been made had it not been for the papyri which attested the readings. UBS has a fondness for the shortest readings and also a preference for B which sometimes outstrips WH, as it reveals in passages such as Romans 15:19, where it moves away from WH to the reading found only in B and two Fathers. In other passages, such as I Corinthians 2:16 and II Corinthians 4:6, UBS neither moves from the WH-supported reading nor makes any note that there are significant variants at these points.

Again, in this list as in the others, the corrections of p^{66} call for attention. There are two instances (John 2:15; 12:22) where p^{66*} reads with the Byzantine combination and p^{66c} changes to the Alexandrian combination of p^{75}BL etc. There is one correction (11:45) where the first hand of p^{66} is uncertain, but the correction is to a reading found in two relatively late manuscripts: 0141, a tenth century manuscript (of von Soden's C class), and 473 (a von Soden IKc manuscript) of the thirteenth. There are also two instances in List 4 where the correction is from a definite Alexandrian alignment to the reading supported by the Byzantine text (2:12 and 14:17).

---

[2]Aland, et.al., *The Greek New Testament* (New York: American Bible Society, 1966).

[3]UBS gives no indication in its apparatus that it has forsaken WH in these instances.

MATTHEW

26:20 δωδεκα p^{37} (p^{45})BDΓ unc[8] λ φ 565 700 *pl* sa sy[s] Eus
K ς

δωδεκα μαθητων ℵALMWΔΘΠΦ 074 33 *pc* it vg sa bo
sy[ph] arm eth Chr Or; [WH]

26:39 προσελθων p^{53} ℵACDILWΓΔΘΠ[2] 067 074 unc[8] λ 33 69
pm sy[p] Chr K

προελθων p^{37} BMΠ* φ *al* latt sa bo sy[s] Or Hil *H*
ς; [WH]

MARK

5:22 ιδου p^{46} ACNWΠΣ 0107 unc[9] λ φ 565 700 *pl* c f l sy[p]
arm go K ς

_____ ℵBDLΔΘ 102 892 a b e ff[2] g[1,2] i q vg co sy
eth arr *H*; WH

6:16 οτι p^{45} ACWΔΠΦ unc[9] φ *pl* co go K ς

_____ ℵBDLΘ λ 28 33 69 124 565 700 it vg sy arm
eth Or *H;* WH

9:30 παρεπορευοντο p^{46} ℵAB[3]CLNWXΓΔΘ unc[9] λ φ 565
700 *rell* b d ff[2] g[(1)2] i k l q vg co sy arm K ς

επορευοντο B*D[gr] a c f go eth; [WH]

LUKE

4:35 εξ αυτου p^{75} ACMQXΓΔΛΠ unc[8] *pl* K ς

απ αυτου ℵBDLVΞ 1 13 *al* it vg (latt *exi ab*) Or; WH

9:59 κυριε $p^{45}p^{75}$ ℵAB[3]CLWXΓΔΘΛΞΠ unc[7] λ φ *pl* latt sy[cp]
sa bo *H* K ς

_____ B*DV 57 sy[s] Or; WH

10:15 καταβιβασθηση p^{45} ℵACLRWXΓΔΘΛΞΠ unc[7] λ φ *pl* it
go co arm K ς

καταβηση p^{75} BD 579 sy[sc] eth arm; [WH]

10:41,42 ενοσ δε εστιν χρεια $p^{45}p^{75}$ AC*PWΓΔΘΛΠ unc[9] λ
(exc. 1) φ *pl* f g[1] q vg sy[cp] Chr Antio K ς

ολιγων δε εστιν χρεια 38 sy[pal] arm

ολιγων δε χρεια η ενοσ B

ολιγων δε εστιν χρεια η ενοσ C[2]L 1 33 579 sy[hmg] bo
eth; [WH]

ολιγων δε εστιν η ενοσ p^{3} ℵ

omit whole clause D a b c e ff i l r sy[s]

10:42　απ αυτησ　p^3(p^{45})p^{75}א^cCPWΓΔΘΛΠ unc⁹ λ φ *pl* c d f vg
　　　　Cl Mac Did Bas *K* ς
　　　　αυτησ　א*aBDL a b e ff² i l q; WH

11:20　ει δε. . .(−εγω)　p^{45}א*AWXΓΔΘΛΠ unc⁹ λ *pm* b f ff² i
　　　　vg arm Eus Cyr *K* ς
　　　　ει δε εγω　D *pc* co eth Tert Bas Chr
　　　　ει δε . . . εγω　p^{75}א^aBCLR φ 33 *al* ff² l q r¹ sy^p *H;*
　　　　[WH]

11:24　ευρισκον　p^{45}א*ACDE*GHRSWΓΔΛΠ unc^{rell} φ 118 *pl*
　　　　it^{pl} vg etc *K* ς
　　　　ευρισκον τοτε　p^{75}א^cBLXΘΞ 33 *pc* y^{scr} b l sa bo sy^p;
　　　　[WH]

11:42　αφιεναι　(p^{45}א* 57 y^{scr} αφειναι)B³CWXΓΔΘΛΠ
　　　　unc⁸ γ *pl K* ς
　　　　παρειναι　p^{75}א^cB*L φ 346; WH
　　　　παραφιεναι　A
　　　　omit (with whole phrase from ταυτα on) D Marc

16:12　υμετερον　p^{75}אADPRWXΓΔΘΛΠ unc⁹ λ φ *pl* lat go sy^h
　　　　co ar Bas Cyr Or Cyp *K* ς
　　　　ημετερον　BL 1574 *pc* Or; [WH]
　　　　εμον　157 e i l Marc

23:39　αυτον λεγων　p^{75}אACQRXΓΔΛΠ unc⁸ *rell* a b c f ff² q
　　　　vg sa bo sy^{ch} arm eth Or *K* ς
　　　　αυτον　BDL e l; WH

24:49　αποστελλω　p^{75}א*ACDNWΓΘΛΠ unc⁷ λ φ *pl*
　　　　(*pc* —ελω) *K* ς
　　　　εξαποστελλω　א^cBL(-ελω)XΔ 33 157 *pc;* WH
　　　　mittam　a g² tol ing vg^s co

JOHN

1:19　απεστειλαν　$p^{66}p^{75}$אC³LWΓΔΛΠ unc⁹ *pl K* ς
　　　　απεστειλαν προσ αυτον　ABC*33 249 *pc* sy^c co arm eth
　　　　Chr; WH
　　　　προσ αυτον απεστειλαν　Θ *pc* lat

2:12　αδελφοι αυτου　p^{66c}אAHMVWXΓΔΘΛΠ unc⁹ *pl* b f l vg
　　　　co sy^p OrEpip Cyr *K* ς
　　　　αδελφοι　p^{66} p^{75}_*BL(T)Ψ(0141) 0162 1071 a c e Or; WH

2:15　το κερμα　(p^{66})אAPΓΘΛΠ unc⁹ *pl* it^{pl} vg *K* ς
　　　　τα κερματα　$p^{66c}p^{75}$BLW X 083 33 *pc* b q co Or
　　　　Eus; WH

4:51   αυτω και απηγγειλαν *p*⁶⁶ACWΓΘΛ unc⁸ *pl* Cyr *K* ς
        αυτω και ηγγειλαν אD lat sy^cp sa (אD also om
        λεγ-οντεσ after -γειλαν)
        αυτω και ανηγγειλαν KΠ *pc* λ 33 sa
        αυτω *p*⁷⁵BLN 185 213 *pc* bo eth; WH

5:15   ανηγγειλεν *p*⁶⁶*p*⁷⁵ABΓΘΛΠ unc⁷ λ 28 *al* sa ac² *K* ς
        απηγγειλεν DKUΔ φ 33 *al*
        ειπεν אCL *pc* bo it^pc; [WH]
        ανηγγειλεν και ειπεν αυτοισ W
        nuntiavit it^pl vg etc

6:51   ζησεται *p*⁶⁶BCEGHMSTUVΓΔΛΠΩ unc⁸ λ φ *pm*
        Or *K* ς
        ζησει (*p*⁷⁵)אDLWΘ 33 *al;* WH

6:71   εισ ων *p*⁶⁶אC²WΓΔΘΛΠ ⁹ λ φ *pl* it vg *K* ς
        εισ *p*⁷⁵BC*DL *pc* sy eth; WH

8:41   ειπ. ουν ₊*p*⁶⁶*p*⁷⁵CDXΓΔΘΛΠ unc⁸ φ 33 565 1241 *pl* f vg
        sa sy^pc Or Cyr *K* ς
        ειπ. אBLTW 118 209 *pc* a b e ff² l q fos co sy arm eth;
        WH

9:6   επεχρισεν *p*⁶⁶*p*⁷⁵א(AD -χρεισεν, ΕΔ *pc* -χρησεν) WΘ
        λ φ *pl* Ir^lat laṭt sy *K* ς
        επεθηκεν BC( )1093 sa; [WH]
        εχρισεν 661

10:16   γενησεται *p*⁶⁶*p*⁷⁵א*AΓΔΛΠ unc⁷ φ 28 *pl* it^pl vg sy Rus
        Bas Cyr Thdt *K* ς
        γενησονται *p*⁴⁵א^cBDLXWΘ λ 33 *pc* f vg⁽¹⁾ sa bo arm
        go Cl; WH

11:45   α εποιησεν *p*⁶*p*⁴⁵(P⁶⁶ *)אA*LWXΓΔΘΛΠ unc⁷ φ *pl* lat
        bo arm Or *K* ς₊
        ο εποιησεν (*p*⁶⁶) A^cBC*D λ *pc* e sa ac² go eth; [WH]
        οσα εποιησεν ₊*p*⁶⁶^c 0141 473

12:22   και παλιν *p*⁶⁶ א(+ ερχ.)(D)(W)XΓΔΛΠ unc⁷ λ φ *pl* *K*
        ς
        ————— *p*⁶⁶^c *p*⁷⁵ABLΘ it; WH

13:36   απεκριθη αυτω *p*⁶⁶אAC³WXΓΔΘΛΠ unc⁷ λ φ *pl K* ς
        απεκριθη BC*L 229* lat co go arm sy; WH
        λεγει αυτω D

14:16   ινα μενη *p*⁶⁶A(D)WΓΔΘΛΠ unc⁷ λ φ *pl* vg arm sy^p *K* ς
        ινα η (*p*⁷⁵)אBLQX (060) 33 co go sy^c; [WH]

14:17 γινωσκει αυτο p^{66^c} ΑΧΓΔΘ unc^{rell}pl it^{pl} Did K ς
γινωσκει αυτο*ν* DL
γινωσκπι p^{66} p^{75}ℵBW 579 a Lcif; WH

16:28 παρα του πατροσ p^5p^{22}ℵAC^{2}ΥΓΔΘΛΠ unc^7 λ φ pl
Cyr K ς
εκ του πατροσ BC*LXΨ 33 249 Epip; WH
a patre it vg (but Hil: *ex patre, de patre, a patre*)

18:29 κατα p^{66}ℵ^{a}ACD^{supp}LWXΓΔΘ unc^{rell} λ φ pl b f ff g gat
vg co sy Chr Cyr K
——————— ℵ*B 579 e it^{pc}(a c q); WH

20:19 μαθηται συνηγμενοι (p^{66})EGKMSXΓΘΛ pl it K ς
μαθηται ℵABDIΛ* it^{pc}sy^{ptxt}; WH
μαθηται αυτου συνηγμενοι LUΔ 33 346 pc

ACTS

7:15 εισ αιγυπτον $p^{45}p^{74}$ℵACDEHP *rell* K H ς
——————— B; [WH]

9:37 αυτην εθηκαν $p^{45}p^{58}$ℵ^{c}CEHLP pl Chr K ς
εθηκαν B cat it; WH^{txt}
εθηκαν αυτην p^{74}ℵ*A 81 181; WH^{mg}

10:11 αρχαισ δεδεμενον και p^{45}(C*)LP 81 pl d (sy) Chr K ς
αρχαισ ℵABC^{2}E 181 431 453 12^{lect} vg co eth Or; WH

10:19 αυτω το πνευμα p^{45}DELP pl sy eth Did Chr K ς
το πνευμα αυτω p^{74}ℵAC 69 81 181 431 cat vg sa
το πνευμα B bo; WH

13:26 υμιν ο λογοσ p^{45}CEHLP pl lat sy^{ph} bo arm eth Chr K ς
ημιν ο λογοσ p^{74}ℵABD 33 38 81 326 c^{scr} sa sy^{pmg}; WH

15:40 θεου p^{45}CEHLP pl vg^c bo sy arm Chr (Thphl) K ς
κυριου p^{74}ℵABD 33 81 pc am fu demid tol sa
(Thphl); WH

16:32 κυριου $p^{45}p^{74}$ℵ^{c}ACDEHLP *rell* vg sy co Lcif Chr K ς
θεου ℵ*B; [WH]

ROMANS

8:34 εγερθεισ (p^{27}) p^{46}ℵ^{c}BDEFGKL pl vg sy ar Ir Or Cyr K
ς
εγερθεισ εκ νεκρων ℵ*AC 33 104 326 pc co eth Did
Chr Dam; [WH]

8:34 οσ και εστιν $p^{27}p^{46}$ℵ^{c}BDEFGKL pm d*** e f g am
harl** sy^p Cyr Thphl Oec Max Aug K ς

οσ εστιν ℵ*AC 424 *pc* d* vg go co Ir Or Did Chr Cyr
Thdt Dam Hil etc; WH

10:3 ιδιαν δικαιοσυνην *p*⁴⁶ℵFGKL *pl* d* f g go sy eth Ir
Tert Or Chr Cyr *K* ς

ιδιαν ABDEP *pc* vg co arm Cl Or Bas Chr Cyr Procop
Dam Aug Ambst; WH

10:5 γραφει . . . νομου οτι *p*⁴⁶ℵᶜBDᶜEFGKLP *pl* d e f g sy
go Chr Thdt *K* ς

γραφει οτι . . . νομου ℵ*AD* 33* 424 vg (co) Or Dam
Amb Cass; WH

10:5 ο ποιησασ αυτα *p*⁴⁶ℵᶜBFGKLP *pl* sy ar Chr Thdt
Amb *K* ς

ο ποιησασ ℵ*ADE 6 424** vg Or Dam; WH
(add *eam* d**et*** e co go Cass)

15:19 πνευματοσ θεου *p*⁴⁶ℵDᵇLP *pm* syᵖᵗˣᵗʰ eth Or Euth Cyr
Thdt Dam Thphl Oec *K* ς

πνευματοσ αγιου ACD*ᶜEFG(ᵍʳ αυτου πν. αγ.) 1739 *pc*
lat co syᵖᵐᵍ Ath Bas Did Dial Cyr Thdt Aug
Ambst; [WH]

πνευματοσ B Pelagᶜᵒᵐ(not txt) Vig

I CORINTHIANS

2:16 χριστου *p*⁴⁶ℵACDᶜELP *pl* d e vg sy co ar Ps-Iust Or
Did Epip Chr Cyr Pelag Vig *K* ς

κυριου BDFG f g r Thph Aug Amb Sed Libere
Or; WH

5:4 χριστου *p*⁴⁶ℵDᶜEFGLP *pl* e f g vg sy co arm eth go
Dial Bas Chr Thdt Dam Ambst *K* ς

——————— ABD* d syᵖᵗˣᵗ eth Euth Lcif; WH

6:11 κυριου *p*⁴⁶ℵADEL *pm* d e syᵖᵗˣᵗ Did Cyr Dam Ir Tert
K ς

κυριου ημων B(C)P 33 69 *pc* f m⁹⁴ vg sy co arm eth Ath
Did Epip Chr Thdt Euth Or Cyp [WH]

7:15 ημασ *p*⁴⁶ℵᶜBDEFGL *pl* it vg sy bas arm eth go Nyss
Chr Thdt Phot Oec Ambst *al K* ς

υμασ ℵ*ACK 326 *pc* co Euth Dam Thphl Pelag
al; [WH]

7:34 η αγαμοσ⁽²⁾ *p*⁴⁶ℵADEFGKL 33 *pl* d e f* g m⁷⁹ fu sy
arm eth Or Meth Bas Euth Thdt Dam Thphl Tert Cyp
Amb Ambst Aug *K* ς

——————— p^{15}BP 6 104 *pc* it vg sa bo basm Eus Amb Hier; WH

9:13 εργαζομενοι p^{46}ACD^bcEKLP *pl* d e sy arm Chr Ambst Jer Thdt Dam *K* ς

εργαζαμενοι τα ℵBD*FG 181 1739 f g vg co basm Aug; WH

15:10 του θεου η p^{46}ℵ^cAD^bcEKLP *pl* Bas Ps-Ath Chr Euth Cyr Thdt Antioch Dam *K* ς; WH^mg

του θεου ℵ*BD*FG it vg Or Ambst; [WH]

II CORINTHIANS

1:14 κυριου p^{46}ACDEKL *pm* d e go sy^ptxt Oec *K* ς

κυριου ημων ℵBFGMP 33 69 104 424 *pc* f g vg co sy arm eth Chr Euth Thdt Antioch Dam Thphl Ambst *al;* WH

2:7 μαλλον υμασ p^{46}ℵCKLOP *pl* (f vg) (sy^p) arm Chr Euth Thdt Dam Tert Ambst *K* ς

υμασ μαλλον DEFG 33 go Thdt Tert (f vg)

υμασ AB (sy^p) Aug; WH

2:17 οι λοιποι p^{46}DEFGL 543 *al* g sy arm Chr Marc Thdt *K*

οι πολλοι ℵABCK *pm* d e f vg co eth Ir Did Bas Euth Dam Ambst *al H* ς; WH

4:6 ιησου χριστου p^{46}ℵCHKLP *pl* tol sy co arm^ed go Or Euth Thdt Dam *al K* ς

χριστον ιησου DEFG d e f g r vg Cyr Amb Aug Ambst

χριστου AB 33 arm^cdd Marc Or; WH

6:16 υμεισ . . . εστε p^{46}ℵ^c(εστε θεον)CD^cEFGK *pl* f g vg sy ar go Ath Chr Euth Thdt Dam Or Tert Lcif Ambst *al K* ς

ημεισ . . . εσμεν ℵ*BD*LP 6 33 104 424 *pc* d e co eth Cl Did Philo; WH

7:14 η επι τιτου αληθεια p^{46}ℵ^cCKL *pl* Chr Thdrt Dam *K* ς
η προσ τιτον αληθ. DEFGP 69 *pc* lat sy co arm
επι τιτου αληθ. ℵ*B 103 1926 Euth; WH

8:19 συν τη χαριτι p^{46}ℵDEF^grGKL *pl* d e g go sy Cl Thdt Aug *K* ς

εν τη χαριτι BC(-τη)P *al* f vg co arm eth Euth Dam Ambst *al;* WH

GALATIANS

4:14 πειρασμον μου p^{46}ℵᶜCDᵇᶜEKLP *pm* sy arm eth go Bas
Chr Cyr Thdt Dam Euth Thphl *K* ϛ
πειρ. υμων ℵ*ABD*FG 33 *pc* d e f g vg co *H;* WH
πειρασμον 69 *al*

EPHESIANS

3:9 φωτισαι παντασ p^{46}ℵᶜBCDEFGKLP *pl* it vg sy Dial
Did Chr Euth Marc *al K* ϛ; WHᵐᵍ
φωτισαι ℵ*A 424** 1739 Cyr Aug Hil Hier; WHᵗˣᵗ

PHILIPPIANS

2:26 υμασ p^{46}ℵᶜFGKLP *pm* f g vg go Chr Thdt Vict
Ambst *al K* ϛ
υμασ ιδειν ℵ*ACDE *al* d e sy co arm eth Euth Dam
Thphl Cass *H;* [WH]
υμασ παντασ B

3:13 ου p^{46}BDᶜEFGKL *pm* d e f g vg sy arm Chr Tert Or
Vict Hier *K* ϛ
ουπω (p^{16})ℵADᵍʳP 33 *al* co eth Cl Bas Euth Chr Thdt
Chron Antioch Dam Ambst Hier; [WH]

4:23 αμην p^{46}ℵADEKLP *pl* d e r vg bo sy arm eth Thdt *K* ϛ
_____ BFG 1908 f g sa Chr Euth vict; WH

COLOSSIANS

1:20 δι αυτου⁽²⁾ p^{46}ℵACDᵇᶜEKP *pl* sy bo go Chr Thdt Dam
K ϛ
_____ BD*FGL 104 *al* bˢᶜʳ it vg sa arm eth Or
Euth Cyr Thph Ambst; [WH]

4:8 γνω . . . υμων p^{46}ℵᶜCDᵇᶜEKL *pl* f vg go sy co Chr
Dam (*al* Dam γνω τε) *K* ϛ
γνωτε . . . ημων ℵ*ABD*Fᵍʳ GP 33 69 *pc* d e g arm
eth Euth Thdt Hier; WH

I THESSALONIANS

5:27 τοισ αγιοισ αδεγφοισ (p^{46})ℵᶜAKLP *pl* vg go co sy arm
Chr Euth Thdt . . . *K* ϛ

τοισ αδελφοισ ℵ*BDEFG *pc* d e f g Euth Syn Ambst Cass; WH
τοισ αγιοισ 103 Thphl

HEBREWS

8:8   αυτοισ *p*⁴⁶ℵᶜBDᶜEL *pl* Dam Chr *K* ς
αυτουσ ℵ*AD*KP 33 326 *pc* Euth Thdt Chr; [WH]

I PETER

1:9   πιστεωσ υμων (*p*⁷²)ℵACKLP *pl* lat bo *K* ς
πιστεωσ B 1 *pc* sa Cl Or Aug; WH

1:20   εσχατων *p*⁷²KLP *pl* latt sa arm eth Ir *K* ς
εσχατου ℵABCΨ 33 1739 *pc* dˢᶜʳ sy bo; WH

1:21   πιστευοντασ *p*⁷²ℵCKLPΨ *pl* sy . . . *K* ς
πιστουσ Ab latt; WH
πιστευσαντασ 33 *pc*

1:22   καθαρασ καρδιασ *p*⁷²ℵ*CKLPΨ *pl* it(*vero, puro, certo*) *K* ς
καρδιασ AB *pc* vg; WH

4:8   καλυψει *p*⁷²ℵ(C)LP 69 1739 *al K* ς
καλυπτει ABKΨ 33 *al* lat sy *H;* WH

5:2   θεου επισκοπουντεσ *p*⁷²ℵᶜAKLPΨ 69 1739 *pl* latt sy bo *K* ς
θεου επισκοπευοντεσ 614 *al*
θεου ℵ*B 33 323 *pc* sa Hier; WH

5:8   τινα καταπιη *p*⁷²(-πειη)A *al* latt sy Or Eus Eph Chr *K* ς
τινα καταπιειν ℵᶜ(*-πιν)KLP *al H I*
καταπιειν BΨ 0206 1175 Or; WH
καταπιειν τινα 33* *al*
τινα καταπιει *pc*

5:10   εν χριστω ιησον *p*⁷²AKLPΨ *pm* latt co *K* ς
εν χριστω ℵ 69 0206 614 *al* syᵖ; WH
εν τω χριστω B; WHᵐᵍ

II PETER

3:18   αμην *p*⁷²ℵACKLP *pl* vg sa bo sy arm *K H* ς
———— B 440 522 1175 1739*; WH

REVELATION

14:6   αγγελον p^{47}א* 046 pl^{160} Or And^p ^{bav}Amb K

       αλλον αγγελον   א^{cc} ACP al vg co sy arm eth And^a Cyp

       Vig . . . H ς; WH

       αγγελον αλλον   33 35 And^c

LIST V

Papyrus-Byzantine Plus Varying Support (Alexandrian and/or Western) Followed Hesitantly by Westcott and Hort

One reading in this list (Heb. 7:1) would have been included in List 1 with the distinctively Byzantine readings but for the testimony of C. In their "Notes on Select Readings," WH call this a "Syrian" reading.

> . . . Text (Syrian) C*LP cuᵖ². . . . It seems more likely that oς is a primitive re-duplication (OCC for OC), perhaps suggested by ω in v. 2, and ó a right emendation of the Syrian revisers, than that the writer broke off the sentence two lines below without apparent cause.*

WH's reconstruction of how OC arose (a primitive reduplication) may indeed be correct, but the assumption that the "Syrian revisers" emended does not necessarily follow. The Syrians did not have to emend. The reading was in existence in the second century. It was present also in Egypt but had been rejected by most of the Alexandrians. Such rejection can be seen in C².

If the reading at 1 Corinthians 5:4 were re-arranged in a larger unit of variation as it is in the apparatus of UBS, then B and D* with 1739 d would be removed from the papyrus-Byzantine-supported reading to form a third reading which omits χριστου follow-

---

*Notes Select Readings, p. 130.

ing ιησου. It is this third reading which is followed by UBS and WH. This would mean that the papyrus-Byzantine reading would then classify as a "distinctively" Byzantine reading and in such case could have been included in List 1 also.

The Bodmer papyri are involved in three instances of correction in this list. In John 12:43, p^{66*} is with the Byzantine-plus reading while p^{66c} joins the opposite. In John 5:47, p^{75} may be seen correcting to the Byzantine aligned reading while in 14:11 it is p^{66} again that corrects to the Koine-supported reading. For two instances of p^{46} changing alignments in its corrections in List 5, see 1 Cor. 6:14 and 10:2.

List 5 may have some value in illustrating a kind of reading which would receive more assurance of ancient and wide-spread external evidence of support if the Byzantine testimony were treated as independent. In such instances (other things being equal) the marks of uncertainty around the WH readings could be removed because of such increased weight of evidence.

In many of the readings in List 5, UBS follows the same reading and eliminates the brackets that WH have in their text: Matthew 26:27; John 4:1; Acts 8:27; 16:17; I Corinthians 7:28; 9:7; II Corinthians 8:9; Ephesians 4:7; 5:31; Hebrews 1:8; 11:6; I Peter 4:17; Revelation 11:11. On the other hand, in some cases the brackets are retained, e.g., Luke 13:35; John 13:28; Romans 16:27; I Corinthians 5:4; 10:20. In a few cases UBS moves away from the WH hesitantly followed Byzantine readings to the WH^{mg} or another reading: I Corinthians 9:9; 15:14; 15:49; II Peter 1:3, 2:15.

MATTHEW

26:27 και ευχαριστησασ (p^{37})p^{45}אABDWΓΘΠ unc^9 φ *pl* co
Chr Or *K* ς; [WH]
ευχαριστησασ CLZΔ λ 33 157 252 892 q lat arm Or
Bas

LUKE

7:11 εν τω p^{75}א^{c}ABEFGHLRUVXΓΔΘΛ φ *ala* b ff^2 g^1 l q
vg sy^s sa *K* ς; [WH]
εν τη א*CD-εν)KMSWΠ *pm* c e f go bo sy arm eth

7:16 παντασ p^{75}BDEGHMSUVXΔΛΠ *pm K* ς; [WH]
απαντασ אACFLRWΘΞ *al*

7:20 αλλον p^{75} ABΘ *pm* Cyr *K* ς; [WH]
     ετερον ℵDLWXΞ 1 33 *al H* Cyr

13:26 αρξεσθε p^{75} BEGHUVΛ *pm* K ς; [WH]
     αρξηοθε ℵADKLMSWXΓΔΘΠ *al*

13:35 λεγω δε p^{75} ℵᶜABDRWXΓΔΘΛΠ unc*rell* λ φ *pl* f q vg
     boᵖᵗ syᵖˢ arm *K* ς; [WH]
     λεγω p^{45} ℵ*L 40 253 259 b c ff² i l sa boᵖᵗ syᶜ eth

14:17 ερχεσθε p^{75} BΘ λ *pm* it *K* ς; [WH]
     ερχεσθαι ℵADKLPRWΠ *al* vg syˢᶜ

14:17 εστιν p^{45} ABDPWX unc*rell* φ *pl* ς; [WH]
     εισιν p^{75} ℵLRΘ λ

17:12 απντησαν p^{75} ℵᶜABWXΓΔΛΠ unc⁹ 700 *pl* ς; [WH]
     υπηντησαν ℵ*LΘ λ φ 157 *pc* a Bas Dam
     οπου ησαν D e (*et ecce* a b c ff² i l q s syˢᶜ)

23:51 συγκατατεθειμενοσ p^{75}(συν- with sev. oths)
     ABPWΓΘΛΠ² (Π*-θεμενοσ) unc⁸ *pl K* ς; [WH]
     συγκατατιθεμενοσ ℵCDLXΔΨ 0124 λ φ 28 435
     1424 cˢᶜʳ *al*⁶

JOHN

4:1 η ιωαννησ $p^{66}p^{75}$ *pl K* ς; [WH]
     ιωαννησ B*AGLWΓΨ 262 *al*

5:47 ρημασιν πιστευσετε p^{75c} ℵALΓΛΠ² unc*rell pm* a b c e g
     q vg syʰ Or Cyr Ir Cyp *K H* ς; [WH]
     ρημ. πιστευετε $p^{66}p^{75}$*BVΠ* 235 *pc* f ff² l foss syᶜIr
     ρημ. πιστευσητε DGSWΔΘ λ φ 28 *al* Or Chr

6:36 εωρακατε με $p^{66}(p^{75})$BDL(T μη)WΓΔΘΛΠ unc*rell* λ φ
     pl c f ff² g vg sa bo syᵖʰ go arm eth Chr Cyr *K H*
     ς; [WH]
     εωρακατε ℵA a b e q gat vgᶜᵒᵈ(Lat². . . .) syˢᶜ

8:16 πατηρ $p^{39}p^{66}p^{75}$ℵᶜBLTX unc*rell pl* it vg ς; [WH]
     ———— ℵ*D syˢᶜ co ac²

12:43 ηπερ p^{66}* p^{75}ABDΓΔΠ unc⁸ *pl K* ς; [WH]
     υπερ p^{66c}ℵLW λ 33 69 118 157 565 *pc*

13:26 το ψωμιον⁽²⁾ p^{66} *rell* ς; [WH]
     ψωμιον B

13:28 δε p^{66}ACDLΘ λ φ *pl* latt Or *K H* ς; [WH]
     γαρ 63 253 259
     ———— B(WΨ) 157 248 435 sa

14:11 αυτα p^{66c} *pl* it vg sy^{cp} go Ath Cyr Hil etc ς; [WH]

αυτου $p^{66*}p^{75}$ B 229* sa eth

ταυτα Paris⁹⁷

_____ 24* 157 244 q r sy arm bo diates Tert

19:4 εξω ο πιλατοσ p^{66} ABD^{supp}ΓΔΘΛΠ unc⁷ λ *pl* sy^p go

Cyr *K* ς; [WH]

ο πιλατοσ εξω ℵLWX φ 237 252 a b c f ff² g q vg sy^h

ar eth

ο πιλατοσ 106 131 249 *pc* e sa bo

ACTS

5:32 αγιον ο p^{45} ℵAD²HP *pl K* ς; [WH]

αγιον ον D*E

αγιον B *pc* sa bo

8:27 οσ εληλυθει p^{50} ℵ^cBC²D²EHLP *pl* cat sy^p arm

Chr ; [WH]

εληλυθει p^{74} ℵ*AC*D* sa

12:15 οι δε ελεγον p^{45} ℵAD^{gr}EHLP *rell* cat vg Or Chr

ς; [WH]

οι δε ειπαν B d 12^{lect} gig Chr

13:29 τα περι αυτου γεγρ. $p^{45}p^{74}$ ℵACD *rell* vg sy^p ς; [WH]

τα γεγρ. περι αυτου B sy

16:17 τω παυλω $p^{45}p^{74}$ ℵACDEHLP *rell* ς; [WH]

παυλω B Or

16:19 ιδοντεσ δε $p^{45}p^{74}$ ℵC *pl* sa bo sy^p arm Lcif Chr ς; [WH]

και ιδοντεσ_* B sy eth

ιδοντεσ A^( ) d

ωσ δε ειδαν D (d om ωσ δε)

θεασαμενοι ουν Eust

ROMANS

10:20 εγενομην p^{46} ℵACD^{bc}EFGLP *rell* f g vg Cl Chr Euth

Thdt

Dam Hil ς; WH^{txt}

εγενομην εν B D*; WH^{mg}

inventus sum enter eos d e Ambst

13:13 εριδι και ζηλω p^{46} ℵACDFG *rell* Ir Or etc ς; [WH]

εν ερισι και ζηλοις B sa (Cl) Amb

15:32 θεου p^{46} ℵ^cACD^cLP *rell* vg sy co ar Or Chr Thdt

Dam *al* ς; [WH]

ιησου χριστου ℵ*; χριστου ιησου DEFG d e f g fu
κυριου ιησου B

16:27 ω p⁴⁶ℵACD *pl* ⛿; [WH]

——————— B 33 72 f sy Or

αυτω P 31 54 co Chr

I CORINTHIANS

2:13 πνευματικοισ p⁴⁶ℵACDFG *pl* ⛿; [WH]
πνευματικωσ B 33

5:4 ονοματ. του κυριου ημων p⁴⁶BDEFGLP *pl* d e f g vg sy
Dial Bas Chr Thdt Dam . . . ⛿; [WH]
οναματ. του κυριου ℵA demid syᵖᵗˣᵗ Lcif Pacian

6:14 εξεγερει p⁴⁶ ℵCD³EKL *pl* f vgᶜ sy co arm eth Meth
Ath Chr Thdt Ir Tert Archel K ⛿; [WH]

εξεγειρεν p⁴⁶ B ϲ7** 1739 r t Or; WHᵐᵍ
εξεγειρει p¹¹p⁴⁶⁽ ⁾AD*PQ 69 88 (*suscitat* d e)

7:28 η παρθενοσ p⁴⁶ℵADEKLP *pl* Or Meth Bas ⛿; [WH]
παρθενοσ BFG 429

7:40 δοκω δε p⁴⁶ℵADEFGKLP *pl* vg sy co Or Chr Thdt
Dam Tert Aug ⛿; [WH]
δοκω d* arm
δοκω γαρ B 4 33 69 256 330 424** 441 462 467 999
1319 1739 1845 1912 1004 tol basm syᵖ eth Cyr Or
Amb Ambst

8:6 ου⁽²⁾ p⁴⁶ℵADFG *pl* Ir Or Eus Did Ath Cyr Bas Epip
Hil ⛿; [WH]
ον B eth Epip; WHᵐᵍ

9:7 η τισ p⁴⁶ℵAC*KLP *pl* sy bo basm Bas Cyr Dam
al ⛿; [WH]
τισ BC⁽²⁾DEFG 104 441 1926 it vg sa syᵖ arm go Orth
Chr
Euth Thdt Thphl Aug Amb

9:9 φιμωσεισ p⁴⁶ℵAB³CDᵇᶜEKLP(-σησ) *pl* Or Dial Chr
Euth Cyr Thdt Dam . . . ⛿; [WH]
κημωσεισ B*D*FG 1739 Chr Thdt; WHᵐᵍ

10:2 εβαπτισαντο p⁴⁶ᶜ BKLP 1739 *pm* Or Chr Thdt Dam
Phot Oec K ⛿; [WH]
εβαπτισθησαν ℵACDEFG 33 *al* Ir Bas Chr Euth Cyr
Thdt; WHᵐᵍ
εβαπτιζοντο p⁴⁶*

10:20   τα εθνη δαιμονιοισ p^{46}אACK(L οτι τα εθ . . .) f g sy
       co ar eth go Or Chr Euth Thdt Dam *K* ς; [WH]
       δαιμονιοισ   BDEF^{gr}G^{gr} d e m^{56} Marc Eus Tert Ambst

11:3   ο χριστοσ p^{46}אAB^{3}D^{c}EKLP *pl* Ortho Cl Eph Chr
       al ς; [WH]
       χριστοσ   B*D*FG 103 462 1926 Libere Or; WH^{mg}

15:5   ειτα p^{46}BD^{c}KLP *pl* sy^{pmggr} sa bo Or Eus Cyr
       Thdt Dam *K* ς; [WH]
       επειτα   אA 33 *pc* Eus Cyr Chr Euth Hes; WH^{mg}
       και μετα ταυτα   D*FG

15:14   αρα p^{46}א BL *pm* d e f vg sy co ae eth Ig Epip Cyr Chr
       Thdt Dam Ir Tert Ambst *K* ς; [WH]
       αρα και   א*AD^{gr}E^{gr}F^{gr}GKP *al* g go Dial Euth Oec;
       WH^{mg}

15:49   φορεσωμεν p^{46}אACDEFGKLP *pm* it vg go co Cl Or
       Caes Chr Epip Euth Cyr Ps-Ath Max Dam Ir Cyp Hil
       . . . *K*; [WH]
       φορεσομεν   BI 181 *al* Cyr Thdt Thphl Oec ς; WH^{mg}

II CORINTHIANS

1:8   υπερ τησ θλιψ. p^{46}BKLM *pm* Chr Dam *K* ς; [WH]
       περι τησ θλιψ.   אACDEFGP 33 69^{mg} *al* b^{scr} o^{scr} Or Bas
       Chr Euth Thdt Ant *H*

8:9   ιησου χριστου p^{46}אCDFG *rell* ς; [WH]
       ιησου   B sa: (om both: Chr)

11:3   εισ τον χριστον p^{46}BDEKLP *pl* Cl Or Epip Chr Euth
       Thdt *al K* ς; [WH]
       εισ χριστον   אFGM 1611 1739 *pc* d^{scr}
       in Christo Iesu   r Lcif Ambst *al* (εν χριστω k^{scr})

GALATIANS

1:12   ουτε p^{46}BD^{c}EKL *pl* Oec *K* ς; [WH]
       ουδε   אAD*FGP 69 *pc* cat co Eus Chr Euth Cyr
       Thdt Dam
       _____ 103 1913 Thphl

6:18   του κυριου ημων p^{46}ABCDEFGKL *pl* it vg etc *K* ς;
       [WH]
       του κυριου   אP 69 2^{lect} eth

EPHESIANS

4:7   η χαρισ *p*⁴⁶אACDᶜEKPᶜ *pl* Or Chr Thdt *al K* ς; [WH]
      χαρισ BD*FGLOᵇP* 1 209* 40ˡᵉᶜᵗ kˢᶜʳ arm Euth Dam

5:31 τον πατερα και την μητερα *p*⁴⁶אADᶜEKLP *pl* Marc
      Or Meth Tit Epip Chr Euth Thdt Dam ς; [WH]
      πατερα και μητερα BD*FG

6:1   υμων εν κυριω *p*⁴⁶אADᵇᶜEKLP *pl* vg sy co arm eth Or
      Bas Chr Euth Thdt Dam Ambst Hier ς; [WH]
      υμων BD*FG d e f g Cl Tert Cyp

PHILIPPIANS

1:9   περισσευη *p*⁴⁶אAK**L *pl* Cl Bas Chr Thdt Dam
      ς; [WH]
      περισσευει K*P *pc*
      περισσευοη BDE 69 kˢᶜʳ; WHᵐᵍ
      περισσευσει Euthalᶜᵒᵈ
      περισευοι FG

1:24 επιμενειν *p*⁴⁶אACDFG *pl* Cl Or etc ς; [WH]
      επιμειναι B 1611 *pc* Or Petr Chr Euth Cyr; WHᵐᵍ

2:2   το εν φρονουντεσ *p*⁴⁶אᵃBDFGKLP *pl* d e g sy arm eth
      Cl Bas etc *K* ς; [WH]
      το αυτο φρονουντεσ א*ACI 33 441 f vg go (co?) Euth;
      WHᵐᵍ

COLOSSIANS

2:17 α εστιν *p*⁴⁶אACDEFᵃKLP *pl* f vg Or Eus Chr Euth
      Aug Amb ς; [WH]
      ο εστιν BFᵍʳG d e g m⁶² go Marc Aug

3:16 του χριστου *p*⁴⁶אᶜBC²DEFGL *pm* d e f g m⁸⁸ vg go sa
      syᵖ arm Chr Euth Dam Ambt ς; [WH]
      του θεου AC* 33 *pc* eth ar Thdt Thphl
      του κυριου א*I Cl; WHᵐᵍ

HEBREWS

1:8   του αιωνοσ *p*⁴⁶אAD *rell* ς; [WH]
      ─────── B 33 Tert

2:7   εστιφανωσασ αυτον *p*⁴⁶BDᶜE**KL *al*⁷⁵ (sy) aˢᶜʳ Chr
      Dam Thphl Oec *K*; [WH]

εστιφ. αυτον και κατεστησασ αυτον επι τα εργα των
χειρων σου ℵACD*E*MP *pm* lat (sy) arm eth ς

4:3   γαρ *p*¹³*p*⁴⁶BDEKLP *pl* d e f vg (syᴾ) eth Chr Euth Cyr
Thdt Dam Lcif Prim ς; [WH]
ουν ℵACM *pc* co; WHᵐᵍ
δε (syᴾ): *autem* sy arᵉ arm

7:1   ο συναντησασ *p*⁴⁶C*LP *pl* Euth etc *K* ς; [WH]
οσ συναντησασ ℵABC²DEK 33; WHᵐᵍ

7:27   ανενεγκασ *p*⁴⁶BCDEKLP *pl* Chr Euth Thdt Dam
al ς; [WH]
προσενεγκασ ℵAI 33 *pc* Cyr; WHᵐᵍ

8:10   καρδιασ αυτων *p*⁴⁶ℵᶜADEL *pl* ς; [WH]
καρδιαισ αυτων P 104
καρδια εαυτων B
καρδιαν αυτων ℵ*K 122* 425 gˢᶜʳ f vg eth Cl; WHᵐᵍ

10:1   θυσιαισ *p*⁴⁶ACDEHKL *pl* d e f vg sy Or ς;
θυσιαισ αυτων ℵP; WHᵐᵍ

11:6   τω θεω *p*⁴⁶ℵᶜAD*ᶜEKLP *pl* Chr Thdt Dam *al K* ς;
[WH]
θεω *p*¹³ℵ*Dᵇ 33 1912 kˢᶜʳ

12:25 απ ουρανων *p*⁴⁶ACDKLP *pm* Euth Cyr Thdt Dam
ς; [WH]
απ ουρανου ℵM 234 424 Chr; WHᵐᵍ

I PETER

4:17   ο καιροσ *p*⁷²BKLP *pl K* ς; [WH]
καιροσ ℵA *al*⁴

II PETER

1:3   δια δοξησ και αρετησ *p*⁷²BKL *al* vg⁽¹⁾ *K* ς; [WH]
ιδια δοξη και αρετη ℵACP *pm?*

1:9   αμαρτιων *p*⁷²BCLP *pm* cat Marc *K* ς; [WH]
αμαρτηματων ℵAK 1175 *al*

2:13   απαταισ *p*⁷²ℵA*CKLP *pl* syʰ bo *K* ς; [WH]
αγαπαισ A BΨ 623 1611 *pc* latt syʰᵐᵍ sa
αγνοιαισ 323 424 1739 *pc*

2:15   καταλιποντεσ *p*⁷²B³CKLP *pm K* ς; [WH]
καταλειποντεσ ℵAB* *al*

3:11 υπαρχειν υμασ   p⁷²ᶜℵᶜ ACKLP *pl* vg sa sy *K* ς; [WH]
      υπαρχειν   p⁷²*p⁷⁴B 1175 m
      υπαρχειν ημασ   ℵ* *al*

REVELATION

1:4   πνευματων α   p¹⁸C 046 *pl* Andᵉ Areᵗˣᵗ *K* ς; [WH]
      πνευματων των   ℵA 88 241 2036 Andᵃ; WHᵐᵍ
      πνευματων   2037

11:11 τασ τρεισ   p⁴⁷ AC 046 *pm* Andᵃᵖ Are *K* ς; [WH]
      τρεισ   ℵ 025 1 *al* arm Andᶜ · · · Prim Vig

13:17 και ινα μη   p⁴⁷ℵᶜ A 025 046 *pl* vg(exc tol) arm eth Andᶜᵇ
      Are *K* ς; [WH]
      ινα μη   ℵ*C *pc* tol co sy Hipp Andᵃ Ir Prim

TABLES

In an effort to obtain a complete picture of the kinds of early Byzantine readings, all the papyrus-Byzantine readings in each of the major alignments of the first three lists were tabulated.[1] Five tables were necessary in order to tabulate the readings for the three lists. The charts which follow the tables summarize the data given in the tables.

Tables 1 through 3 constitute a breakdown of the three kinds of alignments in List 1, those with the papyrus-supported distinctively Byzantine readings. Three tables are needed here in order to set off the differences because distinctively Byzantine readings are not supported by either the Alexandrian or the Western text. As these two ancient texts stand against the Koine (K), they are at times separate from each other, but often they are together in their opposition, particularly where the text divides into but two readings, one of which is read by K.

Therefore, in the places in List 1 where the Alexandrian and Western texts are separate, Table 1 delineates K's variation from the Alexandrian text-type. Table 2 gives the papyrus-supported Byzan-

---

[1]Inasmuch as Lists 4 and 5 involve less clear-cut alignments, they therefore have no firm textual basis of comparison (i.e., from which the Pap-Byz-+ varied) which would show up meaningfully in a table. For this reason Lists 4 and 5 were not tabulated.

tine variants as over against the Western. In Table 3 are found the kinds of variations in distinctively Byzantine readings when the two other traditions are combined against it. Table 4 gathers its material from List 2—those papyrus-Byzantine readings which were aligned with the Western text but opposed by the Alexandrians and WH. Table 5 gathers the statistics on kinds of readings involved in List 3, where Papyrus-Byzantine-Alexandrian alignments are followed also by WH but opposed by the Westerns.

The table 1 shows the kinds of variants in Papyrus-supported Byzantine readings (PB) as compared with opposing Alexandrian readings (where the Alexandrian reading is separate from the Western). The other abbreviations and symbols used in this and the other tables are as follows: *art* = article, *pro* = pronoun, *con* = conjunction, *oth* = other (other word or words), *form* = the same basic word but a different form of it), *word* = a substitution of a different word which may or may not be a synonym; *wo* = word order (a different arrangement of the same words); *x* = substitution and/or addition or omission of more than one word and often accompanied by some change in word order.[2]

---

[2]Tables 1-3 are compiled from List 1.

Table 1: Papyrus-Byzantine versus Alexandrian

Reference	PB adds: art	pro	con	oth	PB omits: art	pro	con	oth	PB subst.: form	word	wo	x
Matt. 26:22	x							x				
Mark 5:42								x				
6:45									x			
6:48									x			
6:50									x			
7:30												x
9:20										x		
12:17				x						x		
Luke 11:12				x								
12:30									x			
24:47									x			
John 5:37										x		
6:57									x			
7:39				x								
9:28								x				
10:19			x									
10:31			x									
11:19				x								
11:21												x
11:32											x	
12: 9					x							
13:26									x	x		
14: 5				x								x
19: 4										x	x	
19:35												x
Acts 10:37									x			
16:39										x		
Rom. 16:23											x	
I Cor. 9:21					x				x			

211

Table 1 (cont.)

Reference	PB adds: art pro con oth				PB omits: art pro con oth				PB subst.: form word		wo x
Phil. 1:14								x			
Heb. 10:38						x					

The table below shows the kinds of variants in Papyrus-supported Byzantine readings (PB) as compared with opposing Western readings (where the Western reading is separate from the Alexandrian):

Table 2: Papyrus-Byzantine versus Western

Reference	PB adds: art pro con oth				PB omits: art pro con oth				PB subst.: form word		wo x
Matt. 26:22								x			
Mark 5:42								x			
6:45									x		
6:48									x		
6:50								x			
7:30											x
9:20										x	
12:17										x	
Luke 11:12										x	x
12:30										x	
24:47									x		
John 5:37						x					
6:57									x		
7:39							x				
9:28						x					
10:19			x								
10:31			x								
11:19	x		x								

Table 2 (cont.)

Reference	PB adds: art	pro	con	oth	PB omits: art	pro	con	oth	PB subst.: form	word	wo x
John 11:21											x
11:32											x
12: 9							x				
13:26									x		
14: 5				x							x
19: 4			x								
19:35											x
Acts 10:37							x		x		
16:39											x
Rom. 16:23									x		x
I Cor. 9:21											x
Phil. 1:14								x			
Heb. 10:38											x

The table below shows the kinds of variants in Papyrus-supported Byzantine readings (PB) as compared with opposing Western-Alexandrian alignments:

Table 3: Papyrus-Byzantine versus Western-Alexandrian

Reference	PB adds: art	pro	con	oth	PB omits: art	pro	con	oth	PB subst.: form	word	wo x
Matt. 6: 2											x
7:12		x									
7:30									x		
7:31		x						x			x
7:32							x				
7:35				x							
—										x	
7:36	x										
9: 6									x		x

213

Table 3 (cont.)

Reference	PB adds:				PB omits:				PB subst.:		wo x
	art	pro	con	oth	art	pro	con	oth	form	word	
Matt. 9:20									x		x
12: 6	x										
12:16									x		
Luke 6:28									x		
6:39						x					
9:30									x		
10:21							x				
10:39										x	
11:12									x		
11:33										x	
11:50									x		
12: 5											x
12:21										x	
12:22	x										
12:23						x					
12:31		x									
13: 2										x	
13:19		x									
13:28									x		
14: 3		x									
—							x				
14:23											x
14:24						x					
15:21							x				
15:22	x										
23:53									x		
John 1:39						x					
2:15										x	
2:24										x	
4:14									x		
4:31		x									
6:10										x	
7: 3									x		
7:40		x									

214

Table 3 (cont.)

Reference	PB adds: art	pro	con	oth	PB omits: art	pro	con	oth	PB subst.: form	word	wo x
John 8:21				x							
8:51											x
8:54									x		
9:16							x				
9:19											x
9:26				x							
9:35		x									
10:29									x		
—											x
10:32		x									
10:38									x		
—										x	
11:21					x						
11:29									x		
11:31										x	
11:32										x	
12: 6			x						x		
12:36									x		
—	x										
13:26									x		
19:11						x					
20:17		x									
Acts 4:33											x
7:14											x
9: 3											x
—										x	
9:38										x	
11:11									x		
13:26										x	
14:15	x										
16:16									x		
17:13							x	x			
23:12				x							
Rom. 10:14									x		

Table 3 (cont.)

Reference	PB adds: art	pro	con	oth	PB omits: art	pro	con	oth	PB subst.: form	word	wo x
I Cor. 4:11									x		
5:10										x	
7: 5										x	
7: 7											x
—									x		
9: 7			x						x		
10: 8									x		
11:26			x								
II Cor. 9:10									x		
Gal. 4:31										x	
Eph. 2:12		x									
5: 9										x	
Col. 3:16										x	
3:22									x		
4:12									x		
Heb. 3: 3											x
7: 1										x	
10:17									x		
11: 4									x		
11:32											x
12:25									x		x
—									x		
I Pet. 2: 5	x										
3: 7										x	
5: 8		x									
II Pet. 2: 4									x		
2: 5									x		

Table 3 (cont.)

Reference	PB adds: art pro con oth	PB omits: art pro con oth	PB subst.: form word	wo x
Jude 25	x			
—		x		
Rev. 9:20			x	
10: 2			x	
10: 8			x	
11: 2			x	
11: 6		x		
11:12			x	
11:19			x	
12: 7		x		
12: 9		x		
12:13			x	
13:13			x	
14: 8		x		
15: 8	x			
16: 3		x		
16:10			x	

The table below shows the kinds of variants in Papyrus-Byzantine-Western (PBW) alignments as compared with opposing Alexandrian readings:[3]

Table 4: PBW versus Alexandrian

Reference	PBW adds: art pro con oth	PBW omits: art pro con oth	PBW subst.: form word	wo x
Matt. 26:27	x			
26:31			x	
26:45	x			
Mark 6:22	x		x	
—		x		x

[3]Compiled from List 2.

Table 4 (cont.)

Reference	PBW adds: art pro con oth				PBW omits: art pro con oth				PBW subst.: form word		wo x
Mark 6:41	x										
—									x		
7: 5											x
7: 6			x								
—		x									
7:29											x
8:13			x								
8:20									x		
8:36									x		
8:37									x		
9: 3								x			
9:29		x	x								
11:33			x								
Luke 5: 2											x
7: 6											x
9:18											x
9:34									x		
—										x	x
10:13									x		
10:19									x		
10:20										x	
10:30		x									
10:32			x								
10:39									x		
—									x		
—										x	
11:25								x			
11:30											x
11:44					x						
11:48								x		x	
12: 6									x		
12:22						x					
12:29										x	
12:49										x	
12:54	x										

Table 4 (cont.)

Reference	PBW adds: art	pro	con	oth	PBW omits: art	pro	con	oth	PBW subst.: form	word	wo x
Luke —									x		
12:56							x		x		
13: 5									x		
13: 9											x
13:14							x				
13:15									x		
22:47		x									x
23: 5		x									
23:31	x										
John 4:11				x							
4:29									x		
4:37	x										
4:39									x		
4:50									x		
4:51										x	
4:53				x							
5:17				x							
5:19									x		
6:42										x	
6:43	x										
6:45									x		
6:71									x		
7: 4											x
7:16	x										
7:41					x		x				
7:52											x
8:28		x									
8:38										x	
9:11								x			
9:17											x
9:35	x										
10: 7				x							
10:18									x		
10:22										x	
—					x						

Table 4 (cont.)

Reference	PBW adds: art	pro	con	oth	PBW omits: art	pro	con	oth	PBW subst.: form	word	wo x
John 10:26				x							
10:28											x
10:32											x
11:21	x										
11:22		x									
11:28									x		
11:29							x				
—									x		
11:32									x		
11:44	x										x
11:54										x	
11:57									x		
12: 1				x							
12:16											x
12:22							x				
12:34											x
13: 2									x		
13: 3									x		
13:18										x	
—				x					x		
13:20									x		
13:21	x										
13:22		x									
13:23		x									
13:24											x
13:25										x	
13:26									x		
—					x		x		x		
—							x	x			
13:29	x										
—	x										
14: 4		x	x								
14: 7		x									
—	x										
14:14										x	
14:26							x				

Table 4 (cont.)

Reference		PBW adds: art	pro	con	oth	PBW omits: art	pro	con	oth	PBW subst.: form	word	wo x
John	15: 4									x		
	16:23											x
	17:13										x	
	18:10										x	
	18:20									x		
Acts	4:34									x		
	5: 3					x						
	5: 8	x										
	7:13	x										
	7:18								x			
	—											x
	8:17									x		
	8:18			x								
	10:19									x		
	13: 9		x									
	13:25										x	
	14:21								x			
	16: 3											x
Rom.	8:34		x									
	9:11										x	
	9:27										x	
	10: 5	x										
	—									x		
	11: 8										x	
	11:21				x							
	11:31								x			
	14: 5							x				
	15:14					x						
	15:15				x							
I Cor.	3: 3		x	x								
	3: 5									x		
	3:13						x					
	4: 6									x		

221

Table 4 (cont.)

Reference	PBW adds: art	pro	con	oth	PBW omits: art	pro	con	oth	PBW subst.: form	word	wo x
I Cor. 4:14									x		
4:17											x
9: 2										x	
10: 9										x	
11: 3		x									
11:15			x								
11:32		x									
12: 3									x		
12:24									x		
13:11											x
14:21									x		
14:39			x								
15:31							x				
II Cor. 1:19											x
Gal. 5: 7	x										
5:24							x				
6:10									x		
Eph. 5: 2										x	
6: 5											x
Phil. 2: 5		x									
Col. 4:12							x				
Heb. 7:22						x					
10: 1									x		
12:25										x	
13: 6		x									

The table below shows the kinds of variants in Papyrus-Byzantine-Alexandrian (PBA) alignments as compared with opposing "Western" readings:[4]

Table 5: PBA versus Western

Reference	PBA adds:				PBA omits:				PBA subst.:		wo x	
	art	pro	con	oth	art	pro	con	oth	form	word	wo	x
Mark 7: 6												x
7:29											x	
8:15				x								
Luke 7:47												x
10:36												x
11:13										x		
11:43	x				x							
11:54		x	x									
12:27												x
14: 1										x		
14: 2	x											
16: 6										x		
22:19				x								
24: 6				x								
24:12				x								
24:51				x								
24:52				x								
John 4:51	x											
7: 8										x		
10:11										x		
10:34	x											
11:35							x					
Acts 5:10						x						x
5:16												x
5:31										x		
6: 2						x						
6: 9				x								

[4]Compiled from List 3.

Table 5 (cont.)

Reference	PBA adds: art	pro	con	oth	PBA omits: art	pro	con	oth	PBA subst.: form	word	wo x
Acts 6:15											x
8:23											x
10:33			x								
10:38										x	
12:20									x		x
13:27										x	
13:33					x		x				
13:47									x		
16:18									x		
16:38			x								
17:14										x	
Rom. 5:18					x				x		
5:19								x			
6: 2							x				
6: 8									x		
—										x	
8:20										x	
8:21										x	
8:22										x	
8:32											x
8:35					x						
8:37									x		
8:38									x		
9: 1								x			
—										x	
9: 3										x	
—		x									
—					x						
9: 5	x										
—		x									
9: 6									x		
9: 8	x										
9:14	x										
9:17								x			
10: 5			x								

Table 5 (cont.)

Reference	PBA adds: art	pro	con	oth	PBA omits: art	pro	con	oth	PBA subst.: form	word	wo x
Rom. 10: 8								x			
—											x
10:20		x									
11: 4									x		
11: 7									x		
11:14											x
11:17											x
11:31										x	
12: 3		x									
12: 4										x	
12: 5		x									
12:13										x	
13: 4		x									
13: 9										x	
13:10										x	
14:16										x	
15: 4										x	
15:13		x									
—		x									
15:14										x	
—	x										x
15:16										x	
15:18									x		
15:20											x
15:22									x		
15:23									x		
15:24									x		
—	x										
15:30						x					
15:33							x				
16: 1	x										
16: 5									x	x	
16: 7							x				
16: 9										x	
16:17								x	x		
16:18			x	x							

Table 5 (cont.)

Reference	PBA adds: art	pro	con	oth	PBA omits: art	pro	con	oth	PBA subst.: form	word	wo x
Rom. 16:20				x							
16:27									x		
I Cor. 1: 8										x	
1: 9										x	
1:10											x
1:16									x		
1:26										x	
1:29									x		
1:30										x	
2: 3			x								
2:11			x								
—										x	
2:12						x					
3: 3										x	
3: 4											x
3:17										x	
3:19	x										
4: 5		x									
4: 8			x								
4:14											x
5: 1											x
5: 3		x									
5: 5	x										
6: 1											x
6:15											x
7: 2									x		
7: 9										x	
7:14								x			
7:17									x		
7:24											x
7:26								x			
7:28									x		
—								x			
7:29							x				
7:32										x	

Table 5 (cont.)

Reference	PBA adds: art	pro	con	oth	PBA omits: art	pro	con	oth	PBA subst.: form	word	wo	x
I Cor. 7:36									x			
7:39									x			
7:40									x			
8: 4								x				
8:10												x
8:13					x							
—		x										
9: 7								x				
9: 9								x				
9:16										x		
9:18									x			
9:22									x			
—		x										
9:24								x				
10: 8										x		
10:13										x		
—										x		
—	x							x				
10:17								x				
10:27								x				
10:33												x
11: 2						x						
11: 5	x											
11:13			x						x			
—												x
11:18												x
11:19			x									
11:20			(x)							(x)		
11:21										x		
11:22										x		
11:23	x											x
—					x							
11:28												x
12: 1												x
12: 3				x								
12: 9			x									
12:10										x		

Charts

The following charts are an attempt to draw some statistical conclusions based on the preceding tables of the four basic textual alignments. As in the tables, the charts will use the following symbols: PB = papyrus readings supporting the Byzantine text; A = the Alexandrian text; and W = the Western text. Thus PB/A/W means the Papyrus-Byzantine readings are being compared against the Alexandrian where it differs from the Western readings (see Tables 1 and 2). This aligning of textual readings is also done for PB/AW, PBW/A, and PBA/W (see Tables 3, 4, and 5 respectively).

Chart 1 shows the number of occurrences for each alignment considered in the Tables and the percentage of the total variants each table represents.

Chart 1

Tables	Readings Compared	Number of Occurrences	Percentage of Total
1-2	PB/A/W	31	6.3
3	PB/AW	121	24.7
4	PBW/A	169	34.4
5	PBA/W	170	34.6
	Total:	491	100.0%

Chart 2 shows the number and the relative percentages for each basic textual alignment. The total is greater here than Chart 1 because some verses contain more than one variant. As in the Tables, Chart 2 uses the following symbols: *Add* = a word is added to a reading; *Omit* = a word is omitted; *word* and *form* = either a word form is changed or a word is substituted by a synonym; *x* = substitution and/or addition of more than one word.

Chart 2

Table	Readings Compared	Add	Omit	word form	wo	x	Total
1	PB/A	8	7	15	4	3	37
2	PB/W	6	9	11	6	4	36
3	PB/AW	28	20	64	16	0	128
4	PBW/A	53	34	72	24	2	185
5	PBA/W	50	31	73	21	9	184
	Totals:	145	101	235	71	18	570
1	PB/A	21.6	18.9	40.5	10.8	8.2	100. %
2	PB/W	16.7	25.0	30.6	16.7	11.1	100. %
3	PB/AW	21.9	15.6	50.0	12.5	0.0	100. %
4	PBW/A	28.6	18.4	38.9	12.9	1.1	100. %
5	PBA/W	27.2	16.8	39.7	11.4	4.8	100. %
Average	Percentages:	23.2	18.9	39.9	12.9	5.0	100. %

Charts 3-5 analyze more specifically the nature of the variants among the alignments. For additions and omissions (Charts 3 and 4), the particular variants listed for each alignment are articles (art), pronouns (pro), conjunctions (con), and other miscellaneous changes (oth). Chart 5 shows the numbers of form and word changes for each alignment.

Chart 3: Additions

Table	Readings Compared	art	pro	con	oth	Total
1	PB/A	0	1	2	5	8
2	PB/W	1	0	1	4	6
3	PB/AW	4	6	6	12	28

(Cont'd.)

4	PBW/A	17	3	16	17	53
5	PBA/W	9	9	6	26	50
	Totals:	31	19	31	64	145

1	PB/A	0.0	12.5	25.0	62.5	100. %
2	PB/W	16.7	0.0	16.7	66.7	100. %
3	PB/AW	14.3	21.4	21.4	42.8	100. %
4	PBW/A	32.1	5.7	30.2	32.1	100. %
5	PBA/W	18.0	18.0	12.0	52.0	100. %
Average Percentages:		16.2	11.5	21.1	51.2	100. %

Chart 4: Omissions

Table	Readings Compared	art	pro	con	oth	Total
1	PB/A	2	1	1	3	7
2	PB/W	0	1	3	5	9
3	PB/AW	4	1	7	8	20
4	PBW/A	7	6	8	13	34
5	PBA/W	5	3	5	18	31
	Totals:	18	12	24	47	101

1	PB/A	28.6	14.3	14.3	42.9	100. %
2	PB/W	0.0	11.1	33.3	55.6	100. %
3	PB/AW	20.0	5.0	35.0	40.0	100. %
4	PBW/A	20.6	17.6	23.5	38.3	100. %
5	PBA/W	16.1	9.7	16.1	58.1	100. %
Average Percentages:		17.1	11.5	24.4	46.9	100. %

Chart 5: Changes

Table	Readings Compared	Number: form	word	Total	Percentage: form	word	Total
1	PB/A	9	6	15	60.0	40.0	100 %
2	PB/W	7	4	11	63.6	36.4	100 %
3	PB/AW	38	26	64	59.4	40.6	100 %
4	PBW/A	46	26	72	63.9	36.1	100 %
5	PBA/W	29	44	73	39.7	60.3	100 %
	Totals:	129	106	235	Avg.: 57.3	42.7	100 %

A Bibliography of New Testament Textual Criticism

A Bibliography of New Testament Textual Criticism

This bibliography, while including works and articles consulted in research for the original dissertation, has been expanded considerably to furnish background reading for a course in textual criticism taught by the writer. In addition, it is hoped that the bibliography (while by no means exhaustive, and limited chiefly to works in English) may help to introduce the student to some of the wide-ranging areas of study and information that bear directly or indirectly on the theory and praxis of New Testament textual criticism. For easier access to subject material included in this bibliography, please consult *Subject Index to Bibliography,* page 275, and *Scripture Index to Bibliography,* page 297.

Abbot, Ezra. "On the Reading 'Only-Begotten God,' in John 1:18; with Particular Reference to the Statements of Dr. Tregelles," *Bibliotheca Sacra,* 17 (October, 1861), 840-72.

Aland, Kurt. "The Greek New Testament: Its Present and Future Editions," *Journal of Biblical Literature,* 87 (June, 1968), 179-86.

──────────. "Ein neuer Textus Receptus für das griechische Neue Testament?" *New Testament Studies,* 28 (February, 1982), 145-153.

──────────. *Kurzgefasste Liste der griechischen Handschriften des Neuen Testaments,* 1. Berlin: Walter de Gruyter & Co., 1963.

──────────. "Neue Neutestamentliche Papyri II," *New Testament Studies,* 9:4 (1963), 303-16.

──────────. "Neue Neutestamentliche Papyri III," *New Testament Studies,* 22:4 (July, 1976), 375-96.

──────────. "Der neue 'Standard-Text' in seinem Verhältnis zu den frühen Papyri und Majuskeln," *New Testament Textual Criticism, Its Significance for Exegesis: Essays in Honour of Bruce M. Metzger.* Ed. Eldon Jay Epp and Gordon D. Fee. Oxford: Clarendon Press, 1981

──────────. "The Present Position of New Testament Textual Criticism,"

Studia Evangelica. Ed. K. Aland, et al. Berlin, 1959. (Papers presented to the International Congress on "The Four Gospels in 1957").

—————————. "The Significance of the Papyri for Progress in New Testament Research," *The Bible in Modern Scholarship*. Ed. J. P. Hyatt. Abingdon Press, 1965, 325-46.

—————————. *Studien zur Überlieferung des Neuen Testaments und Seines Textes*. Berlin: Walter de Gruyter & Co., 1967.

—————————. *Synopsis Quattuor Evangeliorum: Locis parallelis evangeliorum apocryphorum et patrum adhibitis*. Stuttgart: Würtenbergshe Bibelanstalt, 1964.

—————————. *Synopsis Quattuor Evangeliorum: Locis parallelis evangeliorum apocryphorum et patrum adhibitis*, 10th ed. Stuttgart: Deutsche Bibelstiftung, 1978.

—————————. "The Twentieth Century Interlude in New Testament Textual Criticism," *Text and Interpretation*. Ed. Ernest Best and Robert McL. Wilson. Cambridge: Cambridge University Press, 1979, 1-14.

—————————, and Barbara Aland. *Der Text des Neuen Testaments*. Stuttgart: Deutsche Bibelgesellschaft, 1982.

Altaner, Berthold. *Patrology*, English Translation by H. C. Graef. Freiburg: Herder, 1960.

The Ante-Nicene Fathers. Ed. A. Roberts and J. Donaldson. 10 Vols. Grand Rapids: Wm. B. Eerdmans Publishing Co., 1951.

Argyle, A. W. "The Elements of New Testament Text Criticism," *The Bible Translator*, 4 (1953), 118-25.

—————————. "Notes on the New Testament Vulgate," *New Testament Studies*, 22:2 (1975-76), 223-28.

Armstrong, C. B. "The Synod of Alexandria and the Schism at Antioch in A. D. 362," *Journal of Theological Studies*, 3 (1902), 206.

Arndt, William F. *Bible Commentary The Gospel According to St. Luke*, Saint Louis, Missouri: Concordia Publishing House, 1956.

Aulie, W. "The Textual Base of Some Spanish Versions of the New Testament," *The Bible Translator*, 23:4 (1962), 212-18.

Aune, David E. "The Text-Tradition of Luke-Acts," *Bulletin of the Evangelical Theological Society*, 7:3 (Summer, 1964), 69-82.

Auvrya, Paul; Pierre Poulain, and Albert Blaise. *Sacred Languages*. Translated by J. Tester. New York: Hawthorn Books, 1960.

Baarda, Tjitze. "Gadarenes, Gerasenes, Gergesenes and the Diatessaron' Traditions," *Neotestamentica et Semitica: Studies in Honour of Matthew Black*. Ed. E. Earle Ellis and Max Wilcox. Edinburgh: T & T Clark, 181-98.

—————————. *The Gospel Quotations of Aphrahat the Persian Sage, I. Aphrahat's Text of the Fourth Gospel*. 2 Volumes. Amsterdam: Druk: Krips Repro B. V. Meppel, 1975.

—————————. "The Gospel Text in the Biography of Rabbula," *Vigilae Christianae*, 14:2 (1960), 102-27.

Baker, Aelred. "One Thing Necessary," *Catholic Biblical Quarterly*, 17:2 (April, 1965), 127-37.

Bakker, Adolphine Henriette Annette. *A Study of Codex Evang. Bobbiensis (k)*, Part 1. Amsterdam: N. V. Noord-Hollandsche Uiteversmaatschappij, 1933.

Bandstra, Andrew J. "The Lord's Prayer and Textual Criticism: A Response," *Calvin Theological Journal*, 17:1 (April 82), 88-97.

——————. "The Original Form of the Lord's Prayer," *Calvin Theological Journal*, 16:1 (April, 1981), 15-37.

Barbour, Ruth. *Greek Literary Hands A.D. 400-1600*. Oxford: Clarendon Press, 1981, Preface, Introduction.

Barclay, William. "The New Testament and the Papyri," *The New Testament in Historical and Contemporary Perspective, Essays in Memory of G. H. C. MacGregor*. Ed. Hugh Anderson and William Barclay. Oxford: B. Blackwell, 1965.

Barnard, P. M. "Text of the Gospels," *A Dictionary of Christ and the Gospels*. Ed. J. Hastings. Vol. 2. Edinburgh: T & T Clark, 1908.

Barns, J. W. B. "Papyrus Bodmer II. Some Corrections and Remarks," *Museon*, 70:3-4 (1962), 327-29.

Barrett, C. K. "Is There a Theological Tendency in Codex Bezae?" *Text and Interpretation*. Ed. Ernest Best and Robert McL. Wilson. Cambridge University Press, 1979, 15-28.

Bartsch, Hans-Werner. "Ein Neuer Textus Receptus für das griechische Neue Testament?" *New Testament Studies*, 27:5 (October, 1981), 585-92.

——————. "Über den Umgang der frühen Christenheit mit dem Text der Evangelien. Das Beispiel des Codex Bezae Cantabrigiensis," *New Testament Studies*, 29:2, (April, 1983), 167-182.

Beare, Frank W. "Some Remarks on the Text of I Peter in the Bodmer Papyrus (P72)," *Studia Evangelica*. Ed. F. L. Cross. 3:22. Berlin: Akademie-Verlag, 1964.

——————. "The Text of I Peter in P72," *Journal of Biblical Literature*, 80 (September, 1961), 253-60.

——————. "The Text of the Epistle to the Hebrews in P46," *Journal of Biblical Literature*, 63 (1944), 379-96.

Becker, Siegbert W. "Verbal Inspiration and the Variant Readings," *Wisconsin Lutheran Quarterly*, 71:3 (1974,), 169-84.

Bell, Albert A. "Jerome's Role in the Translation of the Vulgate New Testament," *New Testament Studies*, 23 (January, 1977), 230-33.

Bell, H. I. "The Gospel Fragments P. Egerton 2," *Harvard Theological Review*, 42 (January, 1949), 53-64.

——————. *Recent Discoveries of Biblical Papyri*. Oxford: The Clarendon Press, 1937. An inaugural lecture delivered before the University of Oxford, November 18, 1936.

Bell, H. I. and T. C. Skeat. *Fragments of an Unknown Gospel and Other Early Christian Papyri*. London: Oxford (1935).

Best, Ernest. "Ephesians 1:1," *Text and Interpretation*. Ed. Ernest Best and Robert McL. Wilson. Cambridge: Cambridge University Press, 1979, 29-42.

Bethune-Baker, James F. *An Introduction to the Early History of Christian Doctrine*. 7th ed. London: Methuen and Company, Ltd., 1942.

Bevenot, Maurice. "An 'Old Latin Quotation' (2 Tim. 3:2), and Its Adventures in the Manuscripts of St. Cyprian's De Unitate Ecclesiae Chapter 16," *Studia Patristica*, I, 249-52.

—————————. *The Tradition of Manuscripts: A Study in the Transmission of St. Cyprian's Treatises*. Oxford: Clarendon Press, 1961.

Bibliography and Textual Criticism, English and American Literature, 1700 to the Present. Ed. O M. Brack, Jr. and Warner Barnes, Chicago: University of Chicago Press, 1969.

Biggs, Charles. *The Christian Platonists of Alexandria, The 1866 Bampton Lectures*. Oxford: Clarendon Press, 1912, 1968.

Birdsall, J. Neville. *The Bodmer Papyrus of the Gospel of John*. London: Tyndale Press, 1960.

—————————. "Current Trends and Present Tasks in New Testament Textual Criticism," *Baptist Quarterly*, 17 (July, 1957), 109-14.

—————————. "Diatessaric Readings in the 'Martyrdom of St. Abo of Tiflis'?" *New Testament Textual Criticism, Its Significance for Exegesis: Essays in Honour of Bruce M. Metzger*. Ed. Eldon Jay Epp and Gordon D. Fee. Oxford: Clarendon Press, 1981, 313-324.

—————————. "Georgian Studies and the New Testament," *New Testament Studies*, 29 (1983), 306-320.

—————————. "The Georgian Version of the Book of Revelation," *Studia Biblica 1978, III: Papers on Paul and Pauline Literature*. Sixth International Congress on Biblical Studies, Oxford, 3-7 April 1978. Ed. by E. A. Livingstone.

—————————. "MS 894: A Collation and an Analysis," *Biblical and Patristic Studies*, Ed. J. N. Birdsall and Robert W. Thomson. Freiberg: Herder, 1963.

—————————. "The New Testament Text," *The Cambridge History of the Bible, From the Beginnings to Jerome*. Ed. P. R. Ackroyd and C. F. Evans. Vol. 1. Cambridge: University Press, 1970, 308-77.

—————————. "Rational Eclecticism and the Oldest Manuscripts: A Comparative Study of the Bodmer and Chester Beatty Papyri of the Gospel of Luke," *Studies in New Testament Language and Text*. Ed. J. K. Elliott. Leiden: E. J. Brill, 1976, 39-51.

—————————. "The Text of the Acts and Epistles in Photius," *Journal of Theological Studies*, 9:2 (October, 1958), 278-91.

—————————. "The Text of the Fourth Gospel: Some Current Questions," *Evangelical Quarterly*, 29:4 (October-December, 1957), 195-205.

—————————. "The Text of the Gospels in Photius: I," *Journal of Theological Studies*, 7 (April, 1965), 42-55.

—————————. "Text and Versions: the New Testament," *The New Bible Dictionary*. Ed. J. D. Douglas. Grand Rapids: Wm. B. Eerdmans Publishing Co., 1962, p. 1269.

Birdsall, J. Neville and R. W. Thomson (eds). *Biblical and Patristic Studies in Memory of Robert Pierce Casey*. New York: Herder, 1963.

Black, David A. "The Peculiarities of Ephesians and the Ephesian Address," *Grace Theological Journal*, 2:1 (Spring, 1981), 59-73.

Black, Matthew. *An Aramaic Approach to the Gospels and Acts*. 3rd ed. Oxford: Clarendon Press, 1967.

_____. "The Holy Spirit in the Western Text of Acts," *New Testament Textual Criticism, Its Significance for Exegesis: Essays in Honour of Bruce M. Metzger*. Ed. Eldon Jay Epp and Gordon D. Fee. Oxford: Clarendon Press, 1981.

_____. "Notes on the Longer and Shorter Text of Acts." *On Language, Culture, and Religion: in Honor of Eugene A. Nida*, eds. M. Black and W. A. Smalley. The Hague: Mouton, 1974.

_____. "The Text of the Peshitta Tetraeuangelium," *Studia Paulina*. Haarlem: De Erven F. Bohn N. V., 1953.

_____. "The United Bible Societies' Greek New Testament Evaluated—A Reply," *The Bible Translator*, 28 (1977), 116-120.

Blackman, E. C. *Marcion and His Influence*. London: n. n., 1948.

Blake, R. P. and Kirsopp Lake. "The Text of the Gospels and the Koridethi Codex," *Harvard Theological Review*, 16 (July, 1923), 267.

Blied, Dan. "The Relationship of P45, P66, and P75 to Distinctively Alexandrian Readings." 1972. Unpublished Paper.

Bodine, Walter Ray. *The Greek Text of Judges—Recessional Development*. Ann Arbor, Michigan: Scholars Press, 1980.

Boismard, M. E. "Present Tendencies in Textual Criticism," *Guide to the Bible*. 2nd ed. Vol. I. New York: Desclie Company, 1960.

_____. "The Text of Acts: A Problem of Literary Criticism," *New Testament Textual Critcism, Its Significance for Exegesis: Essays in Honour of Bruce M. Metzger*. Ed. Eldon Jay Epp and Gordon D. Fee. Oxford: Clarendon Press, 1981.

Bonsetch, N. "Origenistic Controversies," *The New Schaff-Herzog Encyclopedia of Religious Knowledge*. Ed. Sam Macauley Jackson, et al. Vol. 7 New York: Funk and Wagnalls, 1908.

Borland, James A. "Re-examining New Testament Textual Critical Principles and Practices Used to Negate Inerrancy," *Journal of the Evangelical Theological Society*, 25 (1982) 499-506.

Bover, Joseph M. *Novi Testamenti Biblia Graece et Latina*. 4th ed. Madrid: Talleres Graficos Montana-Amor Hermoso, 1959. Freiburg: Herder, 1947.

Bowers, F. T. "Textual Criticism," *Encyclopedia Britannica*, 1962 ed; Vol. 20, 13-19.

Boyer, James Leroy. "The Text of Acts." Unpublished Th.M. thesis, Oberlin College, 1940.

Bradley, John William. *A Dictionary of Miniaturists, Illuminators, Calligraphers, and Copyists, with References to Their Works, and Notices of their Patrons, from the Establishment of Christianity to the 18th Century*. Philadelphia: Franklin, 1973.

Bratcher, Robert G. and Eugene A. Nida. *A Translator's Handbook on the Gospel of Mark*. Leiden: E. J. Brill, 1961.

Bray, William D. *The Weekday Lessons from Luke in the Greek Gospel Lectionary*. Chicago: University of Chicago Press, 1959.

Breidenthal, Henry M. "The Relationship and Significance of the Bodmer Papyrus to the Neutral, Western, and Byzantine Text Types." Unpublished Th.M. Thesis, Dallas Seminary, Dallas, Texas, 1962.

Bristol, Lyle Osborne. "A History of New Testament Textual Criticism: Mill to Westcott and Hort." Unpublished M.A. Thesis, Union Theological Seminary, 1939.

—————————. "New Testament Textual Criticism in the Eighteenth Century," *Journal of Biblical Literature*, 69:2 (June, 1950), 101-12.

—————————. "New Testament Textual Criticism in the Nineteenth Century," *Review and Expositor*, 49 (January, 1952), 36-40.

Brock, Sebastian P. "Origen's Aims as a Textual Critic of the Old Testament," *Studies in the Septuagint: Origins, Recensions, and Interpretations*. Ed. S. Jellicoe. New York: KTAV, 1974, 343-346.

—————————. "The Phenomenon of Biblical Translations in Antiquity," *Studies in the Septuagint: Origins, Recensions, and Interpretations*. Ed. S. Jellicoe. New York: KTAV, 1974, 541-71.

—————————. "The Resolution of the Philoxenian/Harclean Problem," *New Testament Textual Criticism, Its Significance for Exegesis: Essays in Honour of Bruce M. Metzger*. Ed. Eldon Jay Epp and Gordon D. Fee. Oxford: Clarendon Press, 1981, 325-343.

—————————. "The Treatment of Greek Particles in the Old Syriac Gospels, With Special Reference to Luke," *Studies in New Testament Language and Text*. Ed. J. K. Elliott. Leiden: E. J. Brill, 1976, 80-86.

Brown, Kenneth I. *A Critical Evaluation of the Text of the King James Bible*. Allen Park: Detroit Baptist Divinity School, 1975.

Bruce, F. F. *The Books and the Parchments, Some Chapters on the Transmission of the Bible*. London: Pickering & Inglis Ltd., 1953.

—————————. "The End of the Second Gospel," *Evangelical Quarterly*, (July, 1935), 169-81.

—————————. "The Gospel Text of Marius Victorinus," *Text and Interpretation*. Ed. Ernest Best and Robert McL. Wilson. Cambridge: Cambridge University Press, 1979, 69-78.

Bruggen, Jakob van. *The Ancient Text of the New Testament*. Winnipeg: Premier Printing, Ltd., 1976.

—————————. *The Future of the Bible*. Nashville: Thomas Nelson, Inc., Publishers, 1978.

—————————. "The Lord's Prayer and Textual Criticism," *Calvin Theological Journal*, 17:1 (April, 1982), 78-87.

—————————. "The Text-Fixation in the Pericope 'Plucking Grain on the Sabbath,'" *The Identity of the New Testament Text*, Ed. W. N. Pickering. Thomas Nelson, Inc., Publishers, 2nd ed. Appendix E, 201-208.

Buchanan, E. S. *The Four Gospels from the Latin Text of the Irish Codex Harleianus*. London: n. n., 1914.

_____. "More Light from the Western Text," *Bibliotheca Sacra*, 73 (1916), 422-44.

_____. *The Records Unrolled. The Story of the Most Ancient Manuscripts of the New Testament*. London: John Ouseley limited, n. d.

Buck, Harry Merwyn, Jr. *The Johannine Lessons in the Greek Gospel Lectionary.* Vol. 2, No. 4 of *Studies in the Lectionary Text of the Greek New Testament*. Chicago: University of Chicago Press, 1958.

Burgon, John W. *The Last Twelve Verses of the Gospel According to Mark*. Introduction by Edward Hills. Ann Arbor: The Sovereign Grace Book Club, 1959.

_____. *The Revision Revised*, Three Articles Reprinted from the *Quarterly Review*. London: John Murray, 1883.

_____. *The Traditional Text of the Holy Gospels*. London: George Bell & Sons, 1896.

_____. *The Causes of the Corruption of the Traditional Text of the Holy Gospels*. London: George Bell & Sons, 1896.

Burkitt, F. C. "Additional Notes," in Westcott and Hort's *Introduction*, 2nd ed. 325-30.

_____. "The Ancient Versions of the New Testament," *Criticism of the New Testament; St. Margaret's Lectures, 1902*. New York: Charles Scribner's Sons, 1902.

_____. "The Caesarean Text," *Journal of Theological Studies*, 30 (1919), 347-56.

_____. "The Chester Beatty Papyri," *Journal of Theological Studies*, 34 (October, 1933), 363-68.

_____. *Evangelion Da-Mepharreshe*. Vol. 2. Cambridge: University Press, 1904.

_____. *The Gospel History and Its Transmission*. Edinburgh: T & T Clark, 1906.

Burns, Y. "The Greek Manuscripts connected by their Lection Systems with the Palestinians Syriac Gospel Lectionaries," *Studia Biblica 1978, II: Papers on the Gospels*, Sixth International Congress on Biblical Studies, Oxford, 3-7 April 1978. Ed. By E. A. Livingstone.

Burrows, Edward W. "The Use of Textual Theories to Explain Agreements of Matthew and Luke against Mark," *Studies in New Testament Language and Text*. Ed. J. K. Elliott. Leiden: E. J. Brill, 1976, 87-99.

Butcher, Samuel Henry. *Harvard Lectures on Greek Subjects*. London: Macmillan and Co., 1904.

Cadbury, Henry J. "The New Testament and Early Christian Literature," *Interpreters Bible*, 7:32. New York: Abingdon-Cokesbury, 1951-1957.

The Cambridge History of the Bible, From the Beginings to Jerome. Ed. P. R. Ackroyd and F. C. Evans. Vol. I. Cambridge: University Press, 1970, 48-66.

Carder, Muriel M. "A Caesarean Text in the Catholic Epistles?" *New Testament Studies*, 16:3 (April, 1970), 252-70.

Carroll, Kenneth L. "Tatian's Influence on the Developing New Testament," *Studies and Documents, 29 Studies in the History and Text of the New Testament*. Ed.

Boyd L. Daniels and M. Jack Suggs. Salt Lake City: University of Utah Press, 1967.

Carson, D. A. *The King James Version Debate: A Plea for Realism.* Grand Rapids: Baker Book House, 1979.

Casey, R. P. "A Russian Orthodox View of New Testament Textual Criticism," *Theology,* 60:440 (February, 1957), 50-54.

——————. "Tendentiousness in Patristic Collections," *Harvard Theological Review,* 41 (January, 1949), 69.

Chadwick, Henry. "The Shorter Text of Luke 22:15-20," *Harvard Theological Review,* (October, 1957), 249-58.

Champlin, Russell. *Family E and Its Allies in Matthew.* 28 Studies and Documents. Ed. Jacob Geerlings. Salt Lake City: University of Utah Press, 1966. (With collation of Codex 903 by Jacob Geerlings).

——————. *Family II in Matthew.* 24 Studies and Documents. Ed. Jacob Geerlings. Salt Lake City: University of Utah Press, 1964.

Charlot, John. *New Testament Disunity: Its Significance for Christianity Today.* New York: E. P. Dutton & Co., Inc., 1970.

Chase, Frederic Henry. *The Old Syriac Element in the Text of Codex Bezae.* London: Macmillan & Co., 1893.

Clark, A. C. *The Acts of the Apostles.* Oxford: n. n., 1933.

——————. *The Descent of Manuscripts.* Oxford: Clarendon Press, 1918.

——————. *The Primitive Text of the Gospels and Acts.* Oxford: Clarendon Press, 1914.

Clark, Kenneth L. "Transmission of the New Testament," *Interpreter's Bible,* 12. New York: Abingdon-Cokesbury Press, 1951-57.

Clark, Kenneth W. "The Chester Beatty Biblical Papyri," *Journal of Biblical Literature,* 55 (1936), 83.

——————. "The Effect of Recent Textual Criticism Upon the New Testament," *The Background of the New Testament and Its Eschatology.* Cambridge: University Press, 1956.

——————. "Observations on the Erasmian Notes in Codex 2," *Studia Evangelica.* Berlin: Akademie-Verlag, 1959.

——————. "The Text of the Gospel of John in Third Century Egypt," *Novum Testamentum,* 5:1 (January, 1962), 17-24.

——————. "Textual Criticism and Doctrine," *Studia Paulina in Honorem Johannis de Zwaan.* Haarlem: De Erven F. Bohn N. V., 1953.

——————. "The Textual Criticism of the New Testament," *Peake's Commentary on the Bible.* Ed. M. Black and H. H. Rowley. London-New York: Nelson, 1962.

——————. "The Theological Relevance of Textual Variation in Current Criticism of the Greek New Testament," *Journal of Biblical Literature,* 85:1 (March, 1966), 1-16.

——————. "Today's Problems with the Critical Text of the New Testament," *Transitions in Biblical Scholarship.* Ed. J. C. Rylaarsdam. Chicago: The University of Chicago Press, 1968, 157-69.

Collins, J. J. "Papyrus Bodmer II," *Catholic Biblical Quarterly,* 20 (July, 1958), 281-89.

Colwell, Ernest Cadman. "Biblical Criticism: Lower and Higher," *Journal of Biblical Literature,* 67 (March, 1948), 1-12.

_____. "The Caesarean Readings of Armenian Gospel Manuscripts," *Anglican Theological Review,* 16 (1934), 113-32.

_____. "The Complex Character of the Late Byzantine Text of the Gospels," *Journal of Biblical Literature,* 54 (1935).

_____. "A Definite Rule for the Use of the Article in the Greek New Testament," *Journal of Biblical Literature,* 52:1 (1933).

_____. "External Evidence and New Testament Criticism," *Studies and Documents.* Ed. Jacob Geerlings, 29 *Studies in the History and Text of the New Testament in Honor of Kenneth Willis Clark.* By Boyd L. Daniels and M. Jack Suggs. Salt Lake City: University of Utah Press, 1967.

_____. *The Four Gospels of Karahissar.* Vol. I of *History and Text.* Chicago: University of Chicago Press, 1936.

_____. "Genealogical Method: Its Achievements and Its Limitations," *Journal of Biblical Literature,* 66 (1947), 109-33.

_____. "The Greek New Testament with a Limited Critical Apparatus: Its Nature and Uses," *Studies in New Testament and Early Christian Literature.* Ed. David E. Aune. Leiden: E. J. Brill, 1972.

_____. "Is There a Lectionary Text of the Gospels?" *Harvard Theological Review,* 25:1 (1932), 73-84.

_____. "Mark 16:9-20 in the Armenian Version," *Journal of Biblical Literature,* 56 (1937), 369-86.

_____. "The Origin of Texttypes of New Testament Manuscripts," *Early Christian Origins.* Ed. Wikgren. Chicago: Quadrangle Books, 1961.

_____. "Scribal Habits in Early Papyri: A Study in the Corruption of the Text." Paper read before the Society of Biblical Literature and Exegesis at annual meeting in New York, 1964.

_____. "The Significance of Grouping of New Testament Manuscripts," *New Testament Studies,* 4 (January, 1958), 73-92.

_____. *Studies in Methodology in Textual Criticism of New Testament.* Leiden: E. J. Brill, 1969.

_____. "Text and Ancient Versions of the New Testament," *Interpreter's Bible,* I. New York: Abingdon-Cokesbury Press, 1951-57.

_____. *What is the Best New Testament?* Chicago: University of Chicago Press, 1952.

_____. and D. W. Riddle. *Prolegomena to the Study of the Lectionary Text of the Gospels.* Vol. I of *Studies in the Lectionary Text of the Greek New Testament.* Chicago: University of Chicago Press, 1933.

_____. and E. W. Tune. "The Quantitative Relationships Between MS Text-Types," *Biblical and Patristic Studies.* Freiburg: Herder, 1963.

_____. and _____. "Variant Readings: Classification and Use," *Journal of Biblical Literature,* 83 (September, 1964), 253-61.

Conybeare, F. C. *History of New Testament Criticism.* London: Watts & Co., 1910.
──────────. "Three Doctrinal Modifications of the Text of the Gospels," *Hibbert Journal,* I (1902-1903), 96-113.

Cook, Frederick Charles. *The Revised Version of the First Three Gospels.* London: John Murray, 1882.

Cooper, Charles M. "Theodotian's Influence on the Alexandrian Text of Judges," *Journal of Biblical Literature,* 67:1 (March, 1948), 63-68.

Corwin, Virginia. *St. Ignatius and Christianity in Antioch.* New Haven: Yale University Press, 1960.

Craig, C. T. "Continental New Testament Research Today," *Journal of Bible and Religion,* 15 (1947), 232-34
──────────. "Current Trends in New Testament Study," *Journal of Biblical Literature,* 57 (1938), 359-75.

Dahl, Nils Alstrup. "0230 (= PSI 1306) and the Fourth Century Greek-Latin Edition of the Letters of Paul," *Text and Intrepretation.* Ed. Ernest Best and Robert McL. Wilson. Cambridge: Cambridge University Press, 1979, 79-98.

Danielou, Jean. *A History of Early Christian Doctrine Before the Council of Nicea.* Philadelphia: Westminister Press.
──────────. Vol. 2: *Gospel Message and Hellenistic Culture,* 1973.
──────────. Vol. 3: *The Origins of Latin Christianity.* 1964.

Danielou, Jean and Henri Marrou. *"Alexandria," The First Six Hundred Years. The Christian Centuries, Volume One.* London: Paulist Press, 1979.

Daniels, Boyd L. and M. Jack Suggs. *Studies and Documents.* Ed. Jacob Geerlings, 29 *Studies in the History and Text of the New Testament.* Salt Lake City: University of Utah Press, 1967.

Daube, David. "Alexandrian Methods of Interpretation and the Rabbis," *Sonderabzug aus der Festschrift Hans Lewald.* Basel: Verlag Helbing & Lichtenhahan, 1953.

Davies, Margaret. "The Text of the Pauline Epistles in Manuscript 2344 and Its Relationship to the Text of the Other Known Manuscripts, in Particular to 330, 436 and 462," 38: *Studies and Documents.* Ed. Jacob Geerlings, Salt Lake City: University of Utah Press, 1968.

Davison, J. A. "The Transmission of the Text" *A Companion to Homer,* Ed. Alan J. B. Wace and Frank H. Stubbings. London: Macmillan and Co., 1962, 215-33.

Dawe, Roger David. *The Collation and Investigation of Manuscripts of Aeschylus.* Cambridge: University Press, 1964.

Dearing, Vinton A. *A Manual of Textual Analysis.* Berkeley: University of California Press, 1959.
──────────. "Methods of Textual Editing." Paper delivered at a seminar on bibliography held at the William Andrews Clark Memorial Library, University of California, Los Angeles, May 12, 1962.
──────────. *Principles and Practice of Textual Analysis.* Berkeley: University of California Press, 1974.
──────────. "The Synoptic Problem; Prolegomena to a New Solution," *The Critical Study of Sacred Texts.* Ed. W. D. O'Flaherty. Berkeley Religious Studies Series, (1979), 121-37.

Deuel, Leo. *Testaments of Time: The Search for Lost Manuscripts and Records.* Baltimore: Penguin Books, Inc., 1965.

Dicks, Claude Darwin. "The Matthean Text of Chrysostom in His Homilies on Matthew," *Journal of Biblical Literature,* 67:4 (December, 1948), 365-76.

Diringer, D. *The Hand-Produced Book.* New York: n. n., 1953.

Dods, Marcus. *Erasmus and Other Essays.* London: Hodder and Stoughton, 1892.

Downey, Glanville. *A History of Antioch in Syria from Seleucus to the Arab Conquest.* Princeton: Princeton University Press, 1961.

Dumeige, G. *Synopsis Scriptorium Ecclesiae Antiquae.* Uccle, Belgium: Willy Rousseau, 1953. (Chart)

Dunkerley, R. "The Textual Critic in the Pulpit, II," *Expository Times,* 63 (January, 1952), 101-4.

Duplacy, Jean. "Critique Textuelle du Nouveau Testament, I, ""' *Recherches de Science Religieuse,* 50:2 (1962), 242-63.

_____. "Critique Textuelle du Nouveau Testament, II," *Recherches de Science Religieuse,* 50:4 (1962), 564-98.

_____. *Ou-en est la Critique Textuelle du Nouveau Testament?* Paris: Libraire Lecoffre, J. Gabalda et Cie, 1959.

_____. "Res Bibliographicae: Bulletin de critique textuelle du Nouveau Testament, III," *Biblica,* 49 (1968), 515-50. (lre partie).

_____. "Res Bibliographicae: Bulletin de critique textuelle du Nouveau Testament, III," *Biblica,* 51 (1970), 84-129. (2e partie)

_____. "La Prehistoire du texte en Luc 22:43-44," *New Testament Textual Criticism, Its Significance for Exegesis: Essays in Honour of Bruce M. Metzger.* Ed. Eldon Jay Epp and Gordon D. Fee. Oxford: Clarendon Press, 1981

_____. "'Le Texte Occidental' des Epitres Catholiques," *New Testament Studies,* 16 (1970), 397-99.

Ebrhardt, Arnold. "Christianity Before the Apostle's Creed," *Harvard Theological Review,* 55 (April, 1962), 73-119.

Edwards, Elizabeth G. "On Using the Textual Apparatus of the UBS Greek New Testament," *The Bible Translator,* 28 (1977), 121-142.

Ehrman, Bart D. and Plunkett, Mark A, "The Angel and the Agony: The Textual Problem of Luke 22:43-44," *The Catholic Biblical Quarterly,* 45 (1983), 401-416.

Elliott, J. Keith. "Can We Recover the Original New Testament?" *Theology: A Monthly Review,* 77:649 (July, 1974), 338-53.

_____. "The Citation of Manuscripts in Recent Printed Editions of the Greek New Testament," *Novum Testamentum,* 25:2 (April, 1983), 97-132.

_____. "Comparing Greek New Testament Texts," *Biblica,* 62 (1981), 401.

_____. "An Eclectic Textual Commentary on the Greek Text of Mark's Gospel," *New Testament Textual Criticism, Its Significance for Exegesis: Essays in Honour of Bruce M. Metzger.* Ed. Eldon Jay Epp and Gordon D. Fee. Oxford: Clarendon Press, 1981

_____. "An Examination of the 26th Edition of Nestle-Aland Novum Testamentum Graece," *Journal of Theological Studies,* 32 (April, 1981), 19-49.

_____. "The Greek Text of the Epistles to Timothy and Titus," *Studies and Documents*, 36 (1968), iii, 1-14.

_____. "The International Project to Establish a Critical Apparatus to Luke's Gospel," *New Testament Studies*, 29 (1983), 531-538.

_____. "John 1:14 and the New Testament's Use of πλήρης," *The Bible Translator*, 28 (1977), 151-153.

_____. "Moeris and the Textual Tradition of the Greek New Testament," *Studies in New Testament Language and Text*, Ed. J. K. Elliott. Leiden: E. J. Brill, 1976, 144-152.

_____. "Phrynicus' Influence on the Textual Traditions of the New Testament," *Zeitschrift für die neutestamentliche Wissenschaft*, 63 (January-February, 1972), 133-38.

_____. "A Second Look at the United Bible Societies' Greek New Testament," *The Bible Translator*, 26:3 (July, 1975), 325-32.

_____. "The United Bible Societies' Textual Commentary Evaluated," *Novum Testamentum*, 17 (September, 1975), 1312-50.

_____. "When Jesus was Apart from God: An Examination of Heb. 2:9," *Expository Times*, 83 (1972), 339-41.

Elliott, W. J. "The Need for an Accurate and Comprehensive Collation of All Known Greek New Testament Manuscripts with Their Individual Variants noted in Pleno," *Studies in New Testament Language and Text*. Ed. J. K. Elliott. Leiden: E. J. Brill, 1976, 137-143.

Ellis, E. Earle. "The Silenced Wives of Corinth (1 Cor 14:34-5)," *New Testament Textual Criticism, Its Significance for Exegesis: Essays in Honour of Bruce M. Metzger*. Ed. Eldon Jay Epp and Gordon D. Fee. Oxford: Clarendon Press, 1981.

Ellis, E. Earle and Max Wilcox. *Neotestamentica et Semitica, Studies in Honour of Matthew Black*. Edinburgh: T & T Clark, 1969

Ellis, Ian, M. "Codex Bezae and Recent Enquiry" *Irish Biblical Studies*, 4 (April, 1982), 82-100.

Ellingsworth, Paul. "New Testament Text and Old Testament Context in Heb. 12:3," *Studia Biblica 1978, III: Papers on Paul and Pauline Literature*, Sixth International Congress on Biblical Studies, Oxford, 3-7 April, 1978. Ed. by E. A. Livinstone.

Ellison, John William. "The Use of Electronic Computers in the Study of the Greek New Testament Text," 2 vols. Unpublished doctoral dissertation, Harvard Divinity School, Harvard University, Cambridge, Massachusetts, April, 1957.

Emerton, J. A. "το αἱμά μου διαθήκης: The Evidence of the Syriac Versions," *Journal of Theological Studies*, (April, 1962).

Epp, Eldon Jay. "The Ascension in the Textual Tradition of Luke-Acts," *New Testament Textual Criticism, Its Significance for Exegesis: Essays in Honour of Bruce M. Metzger*. Ed. Eldon Jay Epp and Gordon D. Fee. Oxford: Clarendon Press, 1981.

_____. "The Claremont Profile-method for Grouping New Testament Minuscule Manuscripts," *Studies and Documents*, 29 (1967), 27-38.

_____. "A Continuing Interlude in New Testament Textual Criticism?" *Harvard Theological Review*, 73 (January-February, 1980), 131-151.

_____. "Coptic Manuscript G67 and the Role of Codex Bezae as a Western Witness in Acts," *Journal of Biblical Literature*, 85:2 (June, 1966), 197-212.

_____. "The Eclectic Method in New Testament Textual Criticism," *Society of Biblical Literature—1975 Seminar Papers*. Vol. 2. Ed. George MacRae. Chicago: Palmer House.

_____. "The Eclectic Method in New Testament Textual Criticism: Solution or Symptom" *Harvard Theological Review*, 69:3-4. (July-October, 1976), 211-57.

_____. "The 'Ignorance Motif' in Acts and Anti-Judaic Tendencies in Codex Bezae," *Harvard Thelogical Review*, 55:1 (January, 1962), 51-62.

_____. "New Testament Textual Criticism in America: Requiem for a Discipline," *Journal of Biblical Literature*, 98:1 (March, 1979), 94-98.

_____. *The Theological Tendency of Codex Bezae Cantabrigiensis in Acts*. Cambridge: Cambridge University Press, 1966.

_____. "Toward the Clarification of the Term, 'Textual Variant,'" *Studies in New Testament Language and Text* Ed. J. K. Elliott. Leiden: E. J. Brill, 1976, 153-173.

_____. "The Twentieth Century Interlude in New Testament Textual Criticism," *Journal of Biblical Literature*, 93:3 (September, 1974), 386-414.

Epp, Eldon Jay and Gordon D. Fee. *New Testament Textual Criticism, Its Significance for Exegesis: Essays in Honour of Bruce M. Metzger*. Oxford: Clarendon Press, 1981.

Eshbaugh, Howard. "Biblical Criticism and the Computer," *Perspective, A Journal of Pittsburgh Theological Seminary*, 13:1 (Winter, 1972), 34-58.

Estrada, David and William White, Jr. *The First New Testament*. Nashville: Thomas Nelson Inc., 1978.

Erickson, George Thomas. "The Relationship of Papyrus Bodmer XV to the Vatican and Sinaitic Manuscripts." Unpublished Th.M. thesis, Dallas Theological Seminary, 1965.

Everts, William Wallace. "The Westcott and Hort Text Under Fire," *Bibliotheca Sacra*, 78 (January-March, 1921), 23-36.

Farmer, William R. *The Last Twelve Verses of Mark*. Cambridge: Cambridge University Press, 1974.

The Fathers of the Church, New Translation, Vol. 12. Editorial director Roy Joseph Deferrari, *Saint Augustine, Letters*. 5 vols. Translated by Sister Wilfred Parsons, S. N. D. New York: Fathers of the Church, Inc., 1951.

Fee, Gordon D. "Codex Sinaiticus in the Gospel of John: A Contribution to Methodology in Establishing Textual Relationships," *New Testament Studies*, 15 (1968-69), 23-44.

_____. "Corrections of Papyrus Bodmer II and Early Textual Transmission," *Novum Testamentum*, 7:4 (October, 1965), 247-57.

_____. "Corrections of Papyrus Bodmer II and the Nestle Greek Testament," *Journal of Biblical Literature*, 84 (March 1965), 66-72.

_____. "A Critique of W. N. Pickering's, 'The Identity of the New Testament Text,'" *Westminster Theological Journal*, 41:2 (Spring, 1979), 397-423.

_____. "The Majority Text and the Original Text of the New Testament," *The Bible Translator*, 31:1 (January, 1980), 107-118.

_____. "Modern Textual Criticism and the Majority Text: A Rejoinder," *Journal of the Evangelical Theological Society*, 21:2 (June, 1978), 157-160.

_____. "Modern Textual Criticism and the Revival of the Textus Receptus," *Journal of the Evangelical Theological Society*, 21:1 (March, 1978), 19-33.

_____. "On the Inauthenticity of John 5:3b-4," *The Evangelical Quarterly*, 54 (1982), 207-217.

_____. "One Thing is Needful? Luke 10:42," *New Testament Textual Criticism, Its Significance for Exegesis: Essays in Honour of Bruce M. Metzger.* Oxford: Clarendon Press, 1981.

_____. "Origen's Text of the New Testament and the Text of Egypt," *New Testament Studies.* 28 (1982), 348-364.

_____. *Papyrus Bodmer II* (P66): *Its Textual Relationships and Scribal Characteristics. Studies and Documents*, 34 ed. by Jacob Geerlings. Salt Lake City: University of Utah Press, 1968.

_____. "P75, P66, and Origen: the Myth of Early Textual Recension in Alexandria," *New Dimensions in New Testament Study*, Ed. Richard N. Longenecker, and Merrill C. Tenney. Grand Rapids: Zondervan Publishing House, 1974, 19-45.

_____. "Rigorous or Reasoned Eclecticism—Which?" *Society of Biblical Literature—1975 Seminar Papers.* Vol. 2. Ed. George MacRae. Chicago: Palmer House.

_____. "The Text of John and Mark in the Writings of Chrysostom," *New Testament Studies*, 26:4 (1980), 525-47.

_____. "The Text of John in the Jerusalem Bible," *Journal of Biblical Literature*, 90:2 (June, 1971), 163-73.

_____. "The Text of John in Origen and Cyril of Alexandria," *Biblica*, 52:3 (1971), 357-95.

_____. "The Text of the New Testament and Modern Translations," *Christianity Today* (June 22, 1973), 6-11.

_____. "A Text-Critical Look at the Synoptic Problem," *Novum Testamentum*, 22:1 (January, 1980), 12-28.

_____. "The Use of the Definite Article with Personal Names in the Gospel of John," *New Testament Studies*, 17:2 (1971), 168-83.

Filson, F. V. "More Bodmer Papyri," *Biblical Archaeologist*, 25:2 (1962), 50-57.

_____. "New Greek and Coptic Manuscripts," *Biblical Archaeologist*, 24 (February, 1961), 2-18.

_____. "A New Papyrus Manuscript of the Gospel of John," *Biblical Archaeologist*, 20 (September, 1957), 54-63.

Finegan, Jack. *Encountering New Testament Manuscripts: A Working Introduction to Textual Criticism.* Grand Rapids: William B. Eerdmans Publishing Co., 1974.

Fischer, Bonifatius. "The Use of Computers in New Testament Studies, with Special Reference to Textual Criticism," *The Journal of Theological Studies*, New Series, 21 (October, 1970), 297-308.

Fitzmyer, J. A. "Papyrus Bodmer XIV: Some Features of Our Oldest Text of Luke," *Catholic Biblical Quarterly*, 24:2 (1962), 170-79.

Flack, Elmer E., et al. *The Text, Canon and Principal Versions of the Bible*. Grand Rapids: Baker Book House, 1956.

Flatt, Dowell, "Thoroughgoing Eclecticism as a Method of Textual Criticism," *Restoration Quarterly*, 18:2 (1975), 102-14.

Fotheringham, D. R. "The Chester Beatty Papyri," *Expository Times* (March, 1935), 285.

Fox, Adam. *John Mill and Richard Bentley, a Study of the Textual Criticism of the New Testament 1675-1729*. Oxford: Basil Blackwood, 1954.

Frank, K. W. "Papyrus Bodmer II (P66) and John 8:25," *Harvard Theological Review*, 51 (April, 1958).

Frede, Hermann J. "Neutestamentliche Zitate in Zeno von Verona," *New Testament Textual Criticism, Its Significance for Exegesis: Essays in Honour of Bruce M. Metzger*. Ed. Eldon Jay Epp and Gordon D. Fee. Oxford: Clarendon Press, 1981, 297-304.

Freed, Edwin D. "John 4:51 παις or υιος?" *Journal of Theological Studies*, 16:2 (October, 1965), 448-49.

Friedrichsen, G. W. S. "The Gothic Text of Luke in Its Relation to the Codex Brixianus (f) and the Codex Palatinus (e)," *New Testament Studies*, 11 (October, 1964-September, 1965), 281-90.

——————————. "The Gothic Version and the Fourth-Century Byzantine Text," *Journal of Theological Studies*, 34 (1938), 42-44.

Fritsch, Charles T. "Bengel, V., the Student of Scripture," *Interpretation, A Journal of Bible and Theology*, (April, 1951), 203-15.

Fromow, G. H. "Samuel Prideaux Tregelles: His Life and Letters," *Evangelical Quarterly*, 22 (October, 1950).

Froude, J. A. *Life and Letters of Erasmus, Lectures Delivered at Oxford 1893-94*. London: Longmans, Green, and Co., 1894.

Fuller, David Otis (ed.) *Counterfeit or Genuine? Mark 16? John 8? Grand Rapids: Grand Rapids International Publications, 1975.*

——————————. *True or False, The Westcott-Hort Textual Theory Examined*. Grand Rapids: Grand Rapids International Publications, 1973.

——————————. *Which Bible?* 3rd ed. Grand Rapids: Grand Rapids International Publications, 1972.

Funk, R. W. "Papyrus Bodmer II (P66) and John 8:25," *Harvard Theological Review*, 51 (April, 1958), 95-100.

Gallagher, J. Tim. "A Study of von Soden's H-Text in the Catholic Epistles," *Andrew's University Seminary Studies*, 8:2 (1970), 97-119.

Gamble, Harry. *The Textual History of the Letter to the Romans. Studies and Documents*, 42. Ed. I. A. Sparks. Grand Rapids: Wm. B. Eerdmans, 1977.

Gaumer, T. "An Examination of Some Western Textual Variations Adopted in the Greek Text of the New English Bible," *Bible Translator*, 16:4 (1965), 184-89.

Geerlings, Jacob. *Family E and Its Allies in Luke.* (Appendix A: Collation of Sinai 148. (Greg 1185) by Kenneth W. Ogden). *Studies and Documents,* 35. Salt Lake City: University of Utah Press, 1968.

——————. *Family E and Its Allies in Mark. Studies and Documents,* 31. Salt Lake City: University of Utah Press, 1968.

——————. *Family II in John. Studies and Documents,* 23. Salt Lake City: University of Utah Press, 1963.

——————. *Family II in Luke. Studies and Documents,* 22. Salt Lake City: University of Utah Press, 1962.

——————. *Family 13 The Ferrar Group, The Text According to Luke. Studies and Documents,* 20. Salt Lake City: University of Utah Press, 1962.

——————. *Family 13 the Ferrar Group, The Text According to Matthew. Studies and Documents,* 19. Salt Lake City: University of Utah Press, 1961.

Geerlings, J. and Silva New. "Chrysostom's Text of the Gospel of Mark," *Harvard Theological Review,* 24 (1931), 121-42.

Giese, Rachel. "Erasmus' Greek Studies," *The Classical Journal,* 29 (April, 1934), 517-26.

Gignac, Francis Thomas. *A Grammar of the Greek Papyri of the Roman and Byzantine Periods. II: Morphology.* Cisalpino-Goliardica, 1981.

——————. "The Language of the Non-Literary Greek Papyri," *12th International Congress on Papyrology.* Vol. 7. *Studies in Papyrology.* Ed. Deborah H. Samuel. Toronto: A. M. Hakkert Ltd., 1970.

Gingrich, F. W "The Greek New Testament as a Landmark in the Course of Semantic Change," *Journal of Biblical Literature,* 73 (December, 1954), 189-96.

Globe, Alexander. "The Caesarean Omission of the Phrase 'Son of God' in Mark 1:1," *Harvard Theological Review,* 75:2 (1982) 209-18.

——————. "The *Dialogue of Timothy and Aquila* as Witness to a Pre-Caesarean Text of the Gospels," *New Testament Studies,* 29:2 (April 1983), 233-246.

Glover, R. "'Luke the Antiochene' and Acts," *New Testament Studies* 10 (1964-65), 97-106.

Gochee, Wm. J. "The Latin Liturgical Text: A Product of Old Latin and Vulgate Textual Interaction," *Catholic Biblical Quarterly,* 34 (1973), 206-11.

Granstrom, E. E. "Some Methods of Preparing Byzantine Manuscripts," *International Congress of Orientalists,* 25. Moscow: Oriental Literature Publishing House, 1960.

Grant, Frederick. "Where Form Criticism and Textual Criticism Overlap," *Journal of Biblical Literature,* I (1940), 11-22.

Grant, Robert M. "The Appeal to the Early Fathers," *Journal of Theological Studies,* 9:1 (April, 1960), 13-24.

——————. "The Bible of Theophilus of Antioch," *Journal of Biblical Literature,* 66 (June, 1947), 172-96.

——————. *The Earliest Lives of Jesus.* New York: Harper and Brothers, 1961.

——————. "The Fragments of the Greek Apologists and Irenaeus," *Biblical and Patristic Studies in Memory of Robert Pierce Casey,* Ed. J. Neville Birdsall and Robert W. Thomson. Freiburg: Herder, 1963.

_____. "The Heresy of Tatian," *Journal of Theological Studies*, 5:1 (April, 1954), 62-67.

_____. *A Historical Introduction to the New Testament*. New York and Evanston: Harper and Row, Publishers, 1963.

_____. "The Oldest Gospel Prologues," *Anglican Theological Review*, 23:41 (1941), 231-45.

_____. "The Problem of Theophilus," *Harvard Theological Review*, 52 (July, 1959), 179.

_____. "Scripture, and Tradition in St. Ignatius of Antioch," *Catholic Biblical Quarterly*, 25:3 (1963), 322-35.

_____. "Scripture Rhetoric and Theology in Theophilus," *Vigiliae Christianae*, 13 (1959), 33-45.

_____. *A Short History of the Interpretation of the Bible*. New York: The Macmillan Company, 1966.

_____. "The Textual Tradition of Theophilus of Antioch," *Verbum Caro*, 6 (1952), 146-49.

The Greek New Testament. Ed. Aland, Black, Metzger, Wikgren. New York: American Bible Society, 1966.

The Greek New Testament. 2nd ed. Ed. Aland, Black, Martini, Metzger, and Wikgren. New York: United Bible Societies, 1968.

The Greek New Testament. 3rd ed. Ed. Aland, Black, Martini, Metzger, and Wikgren. New York: United Bible Societies, 1975.

The Greek New Testament According to the Majority Text. Ed. Zane C. Hodges and Arthur L. Farstand. Nashville: Thomas Nelson Publishers, 1982.

Green, Thomas Sheldon. *A Course of Developed Criticism on Passages of the New Testament Materially Affected by Various Readings*. London: Samuel Bagster and Sons, n. d.

Greenlee, J. H. "The Catena of Codex Zacynthius," *Biblica*, 40:4 (1959), 992-1001.

_____. "A Corrected Collation of Codex Zacynthius (Cod. Ξ)," *Journal of Biblical Literature*, 76:3 (1957), 237-41.

_____. *The Gospel Text of Cyril of Jerusalem. Studies and Documents*, 17. Ed. Silva Lake and Carsten Hoeg. Copenhagen: Ejnar Munksgaard, 1955.

_____. *Introduction to New Testament Textual Criticism*. Grand Rapids: Wm. B. Eerdmans Publishing Co., 1964.

_____. "Some Examples of Scholarly Agreement in Error," *Journal of Biblical Literature*, 70 (December, 1958), 363-64.

Greg, Walter Wilson. *The Calculus of Variants, An Essay on Textual Criticism*. Oxford: Clarendon Press, 1927.

Gregory, Caspar Rene. *Cannon and Text of the New Testament*. Edinburgh: T & T Clark, 1907.

Grenfell, B. P. "The Value of Papyri for the Textual Criticism of Extant Greek Authors," *The Journal of Hellenistic Studies*, 39 (1919).

Groningen, Bernhard Abraham van. *Short Manual of Greek Palaeography*, 4th printing. Leyden: A. W. Sijthoff, 1967.

Growwouw, Willem. *The Coptic Versions of the Minor Prophets*. Rome: Pontifical Biblical Institute, 1938.

Grube, G. M. A. *The Greek and Roman Critics*. Toronto: University of Toronto Press, 1965.

Hadas, Moses. *Ancilla to Classical Reading*. New York: Columbia University Press, 1954.

Hall, Basil. "The Trilingual College of San Ildefonso and the Making of the Complutensian Polyglot Bible," *Studies in Church History*. Vol. 5. *The Church and Academic Learning*. Ed. G. J. Cuming. Leiden: E. J. Brill, 1969, 114-46.

Hall, F. W. *Companion to Classical Texts*. Chicago: Argonaut Inc., Publishers, 1970. (First published in 1923: Oxford, n. n.).

Hall, Isaac H. "On Mill's Statement of the Origin of Elzevir's Greek Text of 1624," *Journal of Biblical Literature*, 6 (June, 1887), 41-46.

Hanson, R. P. C. "The Provenance of the Interpolator in the 'Western' Text of Acts and of Acts Itself," *New Testament Studies*, 12 (October, 1965-July, 1966), 211-30.

Harkins, P. W. "The Text Tradition of Chrysostom's Commentary on John," *Theological Studies*, 19:3 (1958), 404-12.

Harley, John E. "Textual Affinities of Papyrus Bodmer XIV (P75)," *Evangelical Quarterly*, 50:2 (April-June, 1968), 99-102.

Harnack, Adolph. *Bible Reading in the Early Church*. Trans. J. R. Wilkinson. New York: G. P. Putnam's Sons, 1912.

——————————. *History of Dogma*. 7 Vols. Translated from the third German edition by Neil Buchanan. New York: Dover Publications, Inc., 1900-61.

Harris, B. F. "Richard Bentley and the Text of the Greek Testament," *Evangelical Quarterly*, 34:4 (1962), 214-20.

Harris, James Rendel. *The Annotators of the Codex Bezae*. London: C. J. Clay and Sons, 1901.

——————————. "Conflate Readings of the New Testament," *The American Journal of Philosophy*, 6:21 (1885).

——————————. *The Diatessaron of Tatian, A Preliminary Study*. London: C. J. Clay & Sons, Cambridge University Press, 1890.

——————————. *Further Researches Into the History of the Ferrar Group*. London: C. J. Clay and Sons, 1900.

——————————. *On the Origin of the Ferrar Group*. London: C. J. Clay and Sons, 1893.

——————————. "Tatianic Reactions in the Pauline Epistles," *Bulletin of the Bezan Club*, 2 (1926), 12-14.

Harvie, George Frederick. "Investigation of the Text of Papyrus Bodmer XV, Chapters Six through Nine." Unpublished Th.M. Thesis, Dallas Theological Seminary, 1965.

Hastings, James. *Dictionary of the Bible*. Revised and edited F. C. Grant and H. H. Rowley. New York: Charles Scribner's Sons, 1963.

Hatch, William Henry Paine. *Facsimiles and Descriptions of Miniscule Manuscripts of the New Testament*. Massachusetts: Harvard University Press, 1951.

——————————. *The Greek Manuscripts of the New Testament in Jerusalem, Facsimiles and Descriptions*. Paris: Librairier Orientaliste Paul Geuthner, 1934.

_____. *The Principal Uncial Manuscripts of the New Testament*. Chicago: University Press, 1939.

_____. "A Recently Discovered Fragment of the Epistle to the Romans," *Harvard Theological Review*, 45 (April, 1952), 81-86.

_____. "The 'Western' Text of the Gospels." The 23rd annual Hale memorial sermon, delivered March 4, 1937, at Seabury Western Theological Seminary, Evanston, Illinois.

_____. "A Hitherto Unpublished Fragment of the Epistle to the Ephesians," *Harvard Theological Review*, 51:1 (January, 1958), 33-38.

Heard, R. G. "The Old Gospel Prologues," *Journal of Theological Studies*, 6:1 (April, 1955), 1-16.

Hedley, P. L. "The Egyptian Text of the Gospels and Acts," *Church Quarterly Review*, 118 (1934), 23-39, 188-230.

Higgins, A. J. B. "The Persian and Arabic Gospel Harmonies," *Studia Evangelica*. Berlin: Akademie-Verlag, 1959, 793-810.

_____. "Tatian's Diatessaron and the Arabic and Persian Harmonies," *Studies in New Testament Language and Text*. Ed. J. K. Elliott. Leiden: E. J. Brill, 1967, 246-261.

Hills, Edward. F. *Believing Bible Study*. Des Moines: The Christian Research Press, 1967.

_____. "The Caesarean Family of New Testament Manuscripts." Unpublished Ph.D. Dissertation, Harvard University, 1946.

_____. "Harmonization in the Caesarean Text of Mark," *Journal of Biblical Literature*, 2 (1957), 135-52.

_____. "The Inter-relationship of the Caesarean Manuscripts," *Journal of Biblical Literature*, 68 (June 1949), 141-59.

_____. "Introduction" to a reprint of *The Last Twelve Verses of the Gospel According to St. Mark*. John W. Burgon. n. p.: The Sovereign Grace Book Club, 1959, 17-72.

_____. *The King James Version Defended! A Christian View of the New Testament Manuscripts*. Copyright by E. F. Hills, The Christian Research Press, 1956.

_____. *The King James Version Defended: A Space-Age Defense of the Historic Christian Faith*. Des Moines: The Christian Research Press, 1973.

_____. "A New Approach to the Old Egyptian Text," *Journal of Biblical Literature*, 69 (1950), 354-62.

Hirunuma, Toshio. "Matthew 16: 2b-3," *New Testament Textual Criticism, Its Significance for Exegesis: Essays in Honour of Bruce M. Metzger*. Ed. Eldon Jay Epp and Gordon D. Fee. Oxford: Clarendon Press, 1981

Hodges, Zane C. "The Angel at Bethesda—John 5:4," *Biblioitheca Sacra*, 136:541 (January-March, 1979), 25-39.

_____. "The Critical Text and the Alexandrian Family of Revelation," *Bibliotheca Sacra*, 119:474 (April-June, 1962), 129-38.

_____. "A Defense of the Majority Text." A revised edition of a paper originally called "Introduction to the Textus Receptus," with mathematical formulations by David M. Hodges, an unpublished paper.

——————————. "The Ecclesiastical Text of Revelation—Does It Exist?" *Bibliotheca Sacra*, 118:470 (April-June, 1961), 113-22.

——————————. "The Greek Text of the King James Version," *Bibliotheca Sacra*, 125:500 (October-December, 1968), 339-45.

——————————. "Introduction to the Textus Receptus with Critical Apparatus of the General Epistles," an unpublished paper.

——————————. "Light on James Two from Textual Criticism," *Bibliotheca Sacra*, 120 (October-December, 1963), 341-51.

——————————. "Modern Textual Criticism and the Majority Text: A Response," *Journal of the Evangelical Theological Society*, 21:2 (June, 1978), 143-155.

——————————. "Modern Textual Criticism and the Majority Text: A Surrejoinder," *Journal of the Evangelical Theological Society*, 21:2 (June, 1978), 161-164.

——————————. "Rationalism and Contemporary New Testament Textual Criticism," *Bibliotheca Sacra*, 128:509 (January-March, 1971), 27-35.

——————————. "The Text of Aleph in the Apocalypse." Unpublished thesis, Dallas Theological Seminary, 1958.

——————————. "The Women and the Empty Tomb," *Bibliotheca Sacra*, 123:492 (October, 1966), 306-07.

——————————. "The Woman Taken in Adultery (John 7:53-8:11): the Text," *Bibliotheca Sacra*, 136:544 (October-December, 1979), 318-332.

——————————. "The Woman Taken in Adultery (John 7:53-8:11): Exposition," *Bibliotheca Sacra*, 173-545 (January-March, 1980), 41-53.

Holmes, Michael W. "The 'Majority Text Debate': New Form of an Old Issue," *Themelios* 8:2 (1983), 13-19.

Horst, P. W. van der. "Can a Book End with γάρ? A Note on Mark 16:8," *Journal of Theological Studies*, 23:1 (1972), 121-24.

Hort, Fenton John Anthony. *Six Lectures on the Ante-Nicene Fathers*. London: Macmillan and Co., 1895.

Hoskier, J. C. "The Authorized Version of 1611," *Bibliotheca Sacra*, 68 (1911), 693-704.

——————————. *Codex B. and Its Allies, A Study and an Indictment*. London: Bernard Quaritch, 1914.

——————————. *A Commentary on the Various Readings in the Text of the Epistle to Hebrews in the Chester-Beatty Papyrus P⁴⁶*. London: n. n., 1938.

——————————. *Concerning the Date of the Bohairic Version*. London: n. n., 1911.

——————————. *Concerning the Text of the Apocalypse*. 2 Vols. London: Bernard Quaritch, 1929.

——————————. "A Note on 'Eastern' and 'Caesarean' Texts," *Bulletin of the Bezans Club*, 5 (1928), 13-21.

——————————. "A Study of the Chester-Beatty Codex of the Pauline Epistles," *Journal of Theological Studies*, 38 (April, 1937), 148-63.

House, Wayne H. *Chronological and Background Charts of the New Testament*. Grand Rapids: Zondervan, 1981.

Housman, A. E. "The Application of Thought to Textual Criticism," *Classical Association Proceedings*, 18:68 (Morning Session, August 4, 1921). London: n. n., 1922.

Howard, George. "Harmonistic Readings in the Old Syriac Gospels," *Harvard Theological Review*, 73:3-4 (July-October, 1980), 473-491.

Howard, Wilbert F. "The Influence of Doctrine Upon the Text of the New Testament," *London Quarterly and Holborn Review*, 166 (1941), 1-16.

Huffman, Norman. "Suggestions from the Gospel of Mark for a New Textual Theory," *Journal of Biblical Literature*, 56:4 (1937), 347-59.

Hull, Stephen. "A Catalogue of Greek New Testament Manuscript Collations in the Biola College Library." La Mirada: Biola College, 1974, an unpublished research paper.

Hurtado, Larry. W. "The Doxology at the End of Romans," *New Testament Textual Criticism, Its Significance for Exegesis: Essays in Honour of Bruce M. Metzger.* Ed. Eldon Jay Epp and Gordon D. Fee. Oxford: Clarendon Press, 1981.

_____. "Text Critical Methodology and the Pre-Caesarean Text: Codex W. in Mark," *Studies and Documents*, 43. Ed. by I. A. Sparks, Grand Rapids: Wm. B. Eerdmans, 1981.

Husselmann, E. M. "A Bohairic Text on Papyrus," *Journal of Near Eastern Studies*, 6 (1949), 129.

_____. *The Gospel of John in Fayumic Coptic.* Ann Arbor: Kelsey Museum of Archaeology, 1962.

Huston, Hollis W. "Mark 6 and 11 in P45 and in the Caesarean Text," *Journal of Biblical Literature*, 74 (December, 1955), 262-71.

Hutton, E. A. *An Atlas of Textual Criticism.* Cambridge: The University Press, 1911.

Janeway, John R. "An Investigation of the Textual Criticism of the New Testament Done by Spanish Scholars, with Special Relation to the Theories and Text of Westcott and Hort." Unpublished dissertation, University of Southern California, 1958.

Jellicoe, S. "The Hesychian Recension Reconsidered," *Journal of Biblical Literature*, 82:4 (1963), 409-18.

_____. "Some Reflections on the ΚΑΙΓΕ Recension," *Vestus Testamentum*, 23:1 (1973), 15-24.

_____. *The Septuagint and Modern Study.* Oxford: At the Clarendon Press, 1968.

Jenkins, C. "A Newly Discovered Reference to the 'Heavenly Witnesses' (I John 5:7-8)," *Journal of Theological Studies*, 43 (1942), 42-45.

Jeremias, Joachim. *The Rediscovery of Bethesda.* New Testament Archaeology Monograph No. 1, Louisville: Southern Baptist Theological Seminary, 1966.

Johnson, Alan Frank. "A Re-examination of the *Pericope Adulterae*, John 7:53-8:11." Unpublished Th.D. dissertation, Dallas Theological Seminary, 1964.

_____. "A Stylistic Trait of the Fourth Gospel in the Pericope Adulterae?" *Bulletin of Evangelical Theological Studies*, 9 (Spring, 1966), 91-96.

Johnson, George. "The Language of the New Testament," *A Companion to the Bible.* 2nd ed. by H. H. Rowley. Edinburgh: T & T Clark, n. d.

Jones, A. "The Problem of the Vulgate Readings In I Corinthians 15:51," *Scripture,* 2 (1947), 45-48.

——————. "St. John Chrysostom's Parentage and Education," *Harvard Theological Review,* 46:3 (July, 1953), 171-73.

Junack, Klaus. "Abschreibpraktiken und Schreibergewohnheiten in ihrer Auswirkung auf die Textüberlieferung," *New Testament Textual Criticism, Its Significance for Exegesis: Essays in Honour of Bruce M. Metzger.* Ed. Eldon Jay Epp and Gordon D. Fee. Oxford: Clarendon Press, 1981, 277-295.

Kahle, P. E. "End of St. Mark's Gospel. The Witness of the Coptic Versions," *Journal of Theological Studies,* 2 (April, 1951), 49-57.

——————. "The Greek Bible Manuscripts Used by Origen," *Journal of Biblical Literature,* 79 (June, 1969), 111-18.

Η ΚΑΙΝΗ ΔΙΑΘΗΚΗ, second edition with revised critical apparatus, Ed. G. D. Kilpatrick, London: The British and Foreign Bible Society, 1958.

Kennedy, Roland G. "Latin Versions, the Old," *Dictionary of the Bible,* Ed. James Hastings. 3:54 New York: Charles Scribner's Sons, 1900.

Kent, Roland G. "The Textual Criticism of Inscriptions," *Language Monographs.* New York, 1966.

Kenyon, F. G. *Books and Readers in Ancient Greece and Rome.* Oxford: n. n., 1951.

——————. *The Chester Beatty Biblical Papyri Descriptions and Texts of Twelve Manuscripts on Papyrus of the Greek Bible.* Fasciculus I, General Introduction; (London: Emery Walker Limited, 1933); Fasciculus II, The Gospels and Acts, Text, 1933; Fasc. II, The Gospels and Acts, Plates, 1934; Fasc. III, supplement, Pauline Epistles, Text, 1936; Fasc. III, Revelation, Plates, 1936; Fasc. III Supplement Pauline Epistles, Plates, 1937.

——————. "The Evidence of Greek Papyri with Regard to Textual Criticism," *Proceedings of the British Academy.* London: Published for the British Academy by Henry Frowle, Oxford University Press, 1904. Vol. I, 1-28.

——————. *Handbook to the Textual Criticism of the New Testament.* 2nd ed. Grand Rapids: Wm. B. Eerdmans Publishing Co., 1912.

——————. "Hesychius and the Text of the New Testament," *Memorial Lagrange.* Paris: Librairie Lecoffre, J. Gabalda et Cie, Editeurs, 1940.

——————. *Our Bible and the Ancient Manuscripts.* Revised by A. W. Adams. London: Eyre & Spottiswoode, 1958.

——————. *Recent Developments in the Textual Criticism of the Greek Bible.* London: Oxford University Press, 1933.

——————. *The Text of the Greek Bible.* London: Gerald Duckworth and Co., Ltd. 1949.

Kepple, Robert J. "An Analysis of Antiochene Exegesis of Galatians 4:24-26," *Westminster Theological Journal,* 39:2 (Spring, 1977), 239-49.

Kilpatrick, G. D. "Acts of the Apostles: Codex Bezae and Mill," *Journal of Theological Studies,* 6 (1955), 233-38.

——————. "ΑΝΑΚΑΙΣΘΑΙ and ΚΑΤΑΚΑΙΣΘΑΙ in the New Testament," *Journal of Theological Studies,* 17:1 (April, 1966), 67-69.

_____. "Atticism and the Future of ZHN," *Novum Testamentum* 25:2, (April 1983), 146-151.

_____. "Atticism and the Text of the Greek New Testament," *Neutestamentliche Aufsätze*, Festschrift für Prof. Josef Schmid. ed. by J. Blinzler, O. Kuss, F. Mussner. Regensburg: Pustet, 1963, 125-37.

_____. "The Bodmer and Mississippi Collection of Biblical and Christian Texts," *Greek, Roman, and Byzantine Studies*, 5:1 (Winter, 1963), 33-47.

_____. "Conjectural Emendation in the New Testament," *New Testament Textual Criticism, Its Significance for Exegesis: Essays in Honour of Bruce M. Metzger*. Ed. Eldon Jay Epp and Gordon D. Fee. Oxford: Clarendon Press, 1981, 349-360.

_____. "An Eclectic Study of the Text of Acts," *Biblical and Patristic Studies In Memory of Robert Pierce Casey*. Ed. J. Neville Birdsall and Robert W. Thompson. New York: Herder, 1963.

_____. ἐπιθύειν and ἐπικρίνειν in the Greek Bible," *Zeitschrift für die Neutestamentliche Wissenschaft*, 74 (1983), 151-153.

_____. "The Greek New Testament Text of Today and the Textus Receptus," *The New Testament in Historical and Contemporary Perspective*, Ed. Anderson Barclay. Oxford: Basil Blackwell, 1965. Chapter 8, 189-208.

_____. "Griesbach and the Development of Textual Criticism," *Synoptic and Text Critical Studies, 1776-1976*. Ed. Bernard Orchard and Thomas Longstaff. Cambridge: Cambridge University Press, 1978, 136-53.

_____. "The Historic Present in the Gospel and Acts and in Hebrews," *Zeitschrift für die neutestamentliche Wissenschaft*, 68 (1977), 258-65.

_____. "ἰδού and ἴδε in the Gospels," *Journal of Theological Studies*, 18 (October, 1967), 425-46.

_____. "John 1:3,4 and Jerome," *Journal of Theological Studies*, 66 (1945), 191.

_____. "The Order of Some Noun and Adjective Phrases in the New Testament," *The Bible Translator*, 16 (July, 1965), 117-19.

_____. "The Possessive Pronouns in the New Testament," *Journal of Theological Studies*, 42 (1941), 184-86.

_____. "Some Problems in New Testament Text and Language," *Neotestamentica et Semitica: Studies in Honour of Matthew Black*, Ed. E. Earle Ellis and Max Wilcox, Edinburgh: T & T Clark, 1969, 198-208.

_____. "Some Thoughts on Modern Textual Criticism and the Synoptic Gospels," *Novum Testamentum*, 19:4 (1977), 275-92.

_____. "Style and Text in the Greek New Testament," *Studies and Documents, 29 Studies in the History and Text of the New Testament*. Salt Lake City: University of Utah Press, 1967, 153-160.

_____. "A Textus Receptus Redivivus?" *The Center for Hermaneutical Studies in Hellenistic and Modern Culture*, 32 (1978), 1-17. Ed. Edward C. Hobbs, The Graduate Theological Union and the University of California, Berkeley.

_____. "Western Text and Original Text in the Epistles," *Journal of Theological Studies*, 65 (1943), 60.

_____. "Western Text and Original Text in the Gospels and Acts," *Journal of Theological Studies*, 64 (1943), 24-36.

Kim, Kwang Won. "Codices 1582, 1739, and Origen," *Journal of Biblical Literature*, 69:2 (June, 1950), 167-75.

_____. "The Matthean Text of Origen in His Commentary on Matthew." Unpublished doctoral dissertation, University of Chicago, 1946.

_____. "The Matthean Text of Origen in His Commentary on Matthew," *Journal of Biblical Literature*, 68 (1949), 125-39.

King, Marchant A. "Notes on the Bodmer Manuscript of Luke," *Bibliotheca Sacra*, 122 (July-September, 1965), 234-41.

_____. "Should Conservatives Abandon Textual Criticism?" *Bibliotheca Sacra*, 130 (January, 1973), 35-40.

_____. and Richard Patterson. "Textual Studies in the Bodmer Manuscript of John," *Bibliotheca Sacra*, 117 (April-June, 1960), 164-71; (July-September, 1960), 258-266.

Klein, Ralph W. *Textual Criticism of the Old Testament: From the Septuagint to Qumran*. Philadelphia: Fortress Press, 1974.

Klijn, A. Frederick Johannes. "Papyrus Bodmer II (John 1-14) and the Text of Egypt," *New Testament Studies*, 3:4 (July, 1957), 327-34.

_____. "Patristic Evidence for Jewish Christian and Aramaic Gospel Tradition," *Text and Interpretation*. Ed. Ernest Best and Robert McL. Wilson. Cambridge: Cambridge University Press, 1979, 169-78.

_____. "In Search of the Original Text of Acts," *Studies in Luke-Acts: Essays in Honor of Paul Schubert*. Nashville: Abingdon Press, 1966, 103-10.

_____. "Matthew 11:25/Luke 10:21," *New Testament Textual Criticism, Its Significance for Exegesis: Essays in Honour of Bruce M. Metzger*. Ed. Eldon Jay Epp and Gordon D. Fee. Oxford: Clarendon Press, 1981.

_____. *A Survey of the Researches into the Western Text of the Gospels and Acts*. Drubkerij: Utrecht, 1949.

_____. *A Survey of the Researches into the Western Text of the Gospels and Acts*. Part Two. Leiden: E. J. Brill, 1969.

_____. "The Text of the New Testament," *An Introduction to the New Testament*. Leiden: E. J. Brill, 1967, 185-201.

_____. "The Value of the Versions for the Textual Criticism of the New Testament," *The Bible Translator*, 8 (1957), 127-30.

Knox, John. "A Note on the Text of Romans," *New Testament Studies*, 2 (1956), 191-93.

Kraft, Benedikt. *Die Zeichen für die wichtigeren Handschriften des griechischen Neuen Testaments*. Freiburg im Breisgau: Druckerei von Herder and Co., GmbH., 1955.

Kubo, Sakae. "Identification of Scrivener's Collated Manuscripts," *Andrews University Seminary Studies*, 16 (1978), 397-400.

_____. "Jude 22-3: Two-division Form or Three?" *New Testament Textual Criticism, Its Significance for Exegesis: Essays in Honour of Bruce M. Metzger*. Ed. Eldon Jay Epp and Gordon D. Fee. Oxford: Clarendon Press, 1981.

_____. "The Nature and Quality of the Text of the New English Bible," *Andrews University Seminary Studies*, 5 (July, 1967), 131-157.

_____. *P72 and the Codex Vaticanus.* Salt Lake City: n. n., 1965.

_____. "Textual Relationships in Jude," *Studies in New Testament Language and Text.* Ed. J. K. Elliott. Leiden: E. J. Brill, 1976, 276-82.

Kümmel, Werner Georg. *Introduction to the New Testament.* Founded by Paul Feine and Johannes Behm, completely re-edited by Kümmel. 14th revised edition, translated by A. J. Mattill, Jr. New York: Abingdon Press, 1966.

Labriolle, Pierre De. *History and Literature of Christianity from Tertullian to Boethius.* Trans. Herbert Wilson. New York: Barnes & Noble, Inc., 1968.

Lake, Kirsopp. "Codex 1 of the Gospels and Its Allies," *Texts and Studies*, 7:3 (1902). Cambridge: The University Press.

_____. *Codex Sinaiticus: Petropolitanus, the New Testament, the Epistle of Barnabas and the Shepherd of Hermas.* Oxford: Clarendon Press, 1911.

_____. "Excursus on 'The Ecclesiastical Text,'" *Harvard Theological Review*, 21 (1928), 345.

_____. *The Influence of Textual Criticism on the Exegesis of the New Testament.* Oxford: n.n., 1904.

_____. "The Sinaitic and Vatican Manuscripts and the Copies Sent by Eusebius to Constantine," *Harvard Theological Review*, 11 (January, 1918), 32-35.

_____. "The Text of the Gospels," *Porter-Bacon: Studies in Early Christianity.* Ed. Shirley Jackson Case. New York: The Century Co., 1928.

_____. *The Text of the New Testament.* 6th ed. revised by Silva New. London: Rivingtons, 34 King St., Covent Garden, 13th imprint, 1959.

_____. R. P. Blake. "The Text of the Gospels and the Koridethi Codex," *Harvard Theological Review*, 16 (1932), 267-86.

_____. and R. P. Blake and S. New. "The Caesarean Text of the Gospel of Mark," *Harvard Theological Review*, 21 (October, 1928), 207-404.

_____. and Silva Lake. "The Byzantine Text of the Gospels," *Memorial Lagrange.* Paris: Librairie Lecoffre, J. Gabalda et Cie, Editeurs, 1940.

_____. and _____. *Family 13 (The Ferrar Group).* The Text According to Mark with a Collation of Codex 28 of the Gospels. Studies and Documents, 11. Salt Lake City: University of Utah Press, 1965.

_____. and _____. "The Text of Mark in Some Dated Lectionaries," *Amicitiae Corolla (A Volume of Essays Presented to Jas. Rendel Harris)*, Ed. H. G. Wood. London: University of London Press, 1933.

_____. and Silva New. *Six Collations of New Testament Manuscripts.* Cambridge: Harvard University Press, 1932.

Lake, Silva. *Family II and the Codex Alexandrinus. Studies and Documents*, 5. London: Christophers, 1936.

Lattey, Cuthbert. "The Antiochene Text," *Scripture*, 4 (1951), 273-77.

_____. "The Codex Ephraemi Rescriptus in Romans 9:5," *Expository Times*, 35 (1923-24), 42-43.

_____. "The Codex Vaticanus on Romans 9:5," *Expository Times*, 34 (1922-23), 331.

Lawlor, Hugh Jackson and J. E. L. Oulton (trans.). *Eusebius, Bishop of Caesarea, The Ecclesiasticsl History and the Martyrs of Palestine.* Translated with introduction and notes. 2 vols. London: Society for Promoting Christian Knowledge.

Legg, S. C. E. (ed.). *Novum Testamentum Graece Secundum Textum Westcotto-Hortianum.* Evangelium Secundum Marcum. Oxonii: E. Typographeo Clarendoniano, 1935.

——————————. *Novum Testamentum Graece Secundum Textum Westcotto-Hortianum.* Evangelium Secundum Mattaeum. Oxonii: E. Typographeo Clarendoniano, 1940.

Lehmann, Robert Louis. "An Application of Electronic Data Processing to Textual Criticism." Unpublished Th.M. thesis, Dallas Theological Seminary, 1962.

Lewis, Agnes Smith. *Light on the Four Gospels from the Sinai Palimpsest.* London: William Norgate, 1913.

Lieberman, Saul. "How Much Greek in Jewish Palestine?" *Biblical and Other Studies.* Ed. Alexander Altmann; Cambridge: Harvard University Press, 1963.

Lightfoot, Neil, R. "The Textual Base of the RSV New Testament," *Restoration Quarterly,* 5:2 (1961), 62-66.

Linton, Olof. "Evidence of a Second-Century Revised Edition of St. Mark's Gospel," *New Testament Studies,* 14:3 (April, 1968), 321-55.

Logachev, K. I. "Greek Lectionaries and Problems in the Oldest Slavonic Gospel Translations," *New Testament Textual Criticism, Its Significance for Exegesis: Essays in Honour of Bruce M. Metzger.* Ed. Eldon Jay Epp and Gordon D. Fee. Oxford: Clarendon Press, 1981, 345-348.

Loisy, Alfred Farmin. *The Origins of the New Testament.* Translated from French by L. P. Jacks. New York: Collier Books, 1962.

Lowe, Malcolm. "The Demise of Arguments from Order for Markan Priority," *Novum Testamentum,* 24:1, (January, 1982), 27-36.

Maas, Paul. *Textual Criticism.* Oxford: Clarendon Press, 1958.

Macgilvray, Walter. *John of the Gold Mouth: Preacher of Antioch and Primate of Constantinople.* London: James Nisbet & Co., 1871.

MacGregor, Geddes. *The Bible in the Making.* n. p.: J. B. Lippincott, 1959.

MacLean, Sutherland. "Is There a Byzantine Family of New Testament Manuscripts?" Unpublished Th.M. thesis, Dallas Theological Seminary, 1962.

Maldfeld, G. and B. Metzger. "Detailed List of Greek Papyri of New Testament," *Journal of Biblical Literature,* 68 (December, 1949), 359-70.

Mandilaras, Basil G. *Studies in the Greek Language, Some Aspects of the Development of the Greek Language up to the Present Day.* Athens, 1972.

Manson, T. W. *A Companion to the Bible.* 2nd ed. Ed. H. H. Rowley. Edinburgh: T & T Clark, 1963.

Marcovich, M. "Textual Criticism on the Gospel of Thomas," *Journal of Theological Studies,* 20 (April, 1969), 53-74.

Martin, Alfred. "A Critical Examination of the Westcott and Hort Textual Theory." Unpublished doctoral dissertation, Dallas Theological Seminary, 1951.

——————————. "A Critical Examination of the Westcott-Hort Textual Theory," *Which Bible?* Ed. David Otis Fuller; 3rd ed., revised and enlarged: Grand Rapids: Grand Rapids International Publications, 1973, 144-73.

Martin, Ralph P. *New Testament Foundations: A Guide for Christian Students.* 2 Vols. Grand Rapids: William B. Eerdmans, 1975, Vol. 1, 161-173.

Martin, Victor. *Papyrus Bodmer II: Evangile de Jean Chap. 1:14,* Geneva: Bibliotheca Bodmeriana, 1956; *Papyrus Bodmer II. Supplement. Evangile de Jean Chap. 14-21,* Geneva: Bibliotheca Bodmeriana, 1958; *Papyrus Bodmer II. Supplement. Evangile de Jean Chap. 14-21 (env. 200 ap. J. C.),* Nouvelle edition et corigee. Preparee avec l'aede de M. J. Barns, Avec reproduction photographique du manuscrit complet (chap. 1-21), Geneva: Bibliotheca Bodmeriana, 1961.

——————. and Rodolphe Kasser. *Papyrus Bodmer XIV: Evangile du Luc chap. 3-24; and Papyrus Bodmer XV. Evangile du Jean chap. 1-15,* Geneva: Bibliotheca Bodmeriana, 1961.

Martini, Carlo M. "Eclecticism and Atticism in the Textual Crticism of the Greek New Testament," *On Language, Culture and Religion: In Honor of Eugene A. Nida,* Eds. M. Black and W. A. Smalley. The Hague: Mouton, 1974, 149-156.

——————. "Is There a Late Alexandrian Text of the Gospels?" *New Testament Studies,* 24-3 (April, 1978), 285-96.

Mattill, A. J. and Mary Beford Mattill. "A Classified Bibliography of Literature on the Acts of the Apostles," *Textual Studies.* Leiden: E. J. Brill, 1966, 95-121.

McNight, Edgar V. "The New Testament and 'Biblical Greek,'" *Journal of Bible and Religion,* 34:1 (January, 1966), 36-42.

McNeile, A. H. *An Introduction to the Study of the New Testament.* 2nd edition revised by C. S. C. Williams. Oxford: Clarendon Press, 1953.

McReynolds, Paul R. "The Claremont Profile Method and the Grouping of Byzantine New Testament Manuscripts." Unpublished Ph.D. dissertation for Claremont Graduate School, 1968.

——————. "John 1:18 in Textual Variation and Translation." *New Testament Textual Criticism, Its Significance for Exegesis: Essays in Honour of Bruce M. Metzger.* Ed. Eldon Jay Epp and Gordon D. Fee. Oxford: Clarendon Press, 1981

——————. and Frederik Wisse. "Family E and the Profile Method," *Biblica,* 51:1 (1970), 67-75.

Meeks, Wayne A. "Jews and Christians in Antioch in the First Four Centuries," *Society of Biblical Literature, 1976 Seminar Papers,* Ed. George MacRae. Missoula: Scholars Press, 1976, 33-65.

Mees. Michael. "Realer oder irrealer Kondizionalsatz in John 8:39?" *New Testament Textual Criticism, Its Significance for Exegesis: Essays in Honour of Bruce M. Metzger.* Ed. Eldon Jay Epp and Gordon D. Fee. Oxford: Clarendon Press, 1981.

Merk, Augustinus, S. J. *Novum Testamentum Graece Et Latine.* Editio Octava. Rome: Sumptibus Pontificii Biblici, 1957.

Metzger, Bruce M. *An Annotated Bibliography of the Textual Criticism of the New Testament, 1914-1939. Studies and Documents,* 16. Copenhagen: Ejnar Munksgaard, 1955.

——————. "Bible Versions: Ancient, Modern," *The Text, Canon and Principal Versions of the Bible.* Grand Rapids: Baker Book House, 1956.

——————. "Bibliographic Aids for the Study of the Manuscripts of the New Testament," *Anglican Theological Review,"* 48 (October, 1966), 339-55.

_____. "The Bodmer Papyri of Luke and John," *Expository Times*, 73:7 (1962), 201-03.

_____. "The Caesarean Text of the Gospels," *Journal of Biblical Literature*, 64 (1945), 457-89.

_____. *Chapters in the History of New Testament Textual Criticism.* Vol. IV of *New Testament Tools and Studies.* Grand Rapids: Wm. B. Eerdmans, 1963.

_____. "An Early Coptic Manuscript of the Gospel According to Matthew," *Studies in New Testament Language and Text*, Ed. J. K. Elliott. Leiden: E. J. Brill, 1976, 301-312.

_____. "Early Arabic Versions of the New Testament," *On Language, Culture and Religion: In Honor of Eugene A. Nida*, Eds. M. Black and W. A. Smalley. The Hague: Mouton, 1974.

_____. *The Early Versions of the New Testament: Their Origin, Transmission, and Limitations.* Oxford: Clarendon Press, 1977.

_____. "The Evidence of the Versions for the Text of the New Testament," *New Testament Manuscripts Studies.* Ed. M. M. Parvis and A. P. Wikgren. Chicago: University of Chicago, 1950.

_____. "Explicit References in the Works of Origen to Variant Readings in New Testament Manuscripts," *Biblical and Patristic Studies.* Ed. J. Neville Birdsall and Robert W. Thomson. Freiburg: Herder, 1963.

_____. *Historical and Literary Studies: Pagan, Jewish and Christian.* Vol. VIII of *New Testament Tools and Studies.* Grand Rapids: Wm. B. Eerdmans, 1968.

_____. *Index of Articles on the New Testament and the Early Church Published in Festschriften.* Philadelphia: Society of Biblical Literature, 1951.

_____. *Index to Periodical Literature on Christ and the Gospels.* Vol. VI of *New Testament Tools and Studies.* Leiden: E. J. Brill, 1966.

_____. *Index to Periodical Literature on the Apostle Paul.* Vol. 1 of *New Testament Tools and Studies.* Grand Rapids: Wm. B. Eerdmans Publishing Co., 1960.

_____. "Jerome's Explicit References to Variant Readings in Manuscripts of the New Testament," *Text and Interpretation.* Ed. Ernest Best and Robert McL. Wilson. Cambridge: Cambridge University Press, 1979, 179-90.

_____. "The Language of the New Testament," *Interpreter's Bible*, 7. New York: Abingdon-Cokesbury, 1953.

_____. "Literary Forgeries and Canonical Pseudepigrapha," *Journal of Biblical Literature*, 91:1 (1972), 3-24.

_____. "Lucian and the Lucianic Recension of the Greek Bible," *New Testament Studies*, 8 (April, 1962), 189-203.

_____. *Manuscripts of the Greek Bible. An Introduction to Greek Palaeography.* Oxford: Oxford University Press, 1981.

_____. "Names for the Nameless in the New Testament; a Study in the Growth of Christian Tradition," *New Testament Studies: Philological, Versional, and Patristic*, Vol. X, *New Testament Tools and Studies.* Leiden: E. J. Brill, 1980, 23-45.

_____. "On the Citation of Various Readings of Matthew 1:16," *Journal of Biblical Literature*, 77 (December, 1958), 361-63.

_____. "Patristic Evidence and the Textual Criticism of the New Testament," *New Testament Studies*, 18 (1971-72), 379-400.

_____. "The Practice of Textual Criticism Among the Church Fathers," Chapter 12 in *New Testament Studies Philological: Versional, and Patristic*. Leiden: E. J. Brill, 1950.

_____. "The Punctuation of Romans 9:5," Chapter 4 in *New Testament Studies: Philological, Versional, and Patristic*, Vol. X, *New Testament Tools and Studies*. Leiden: E. J. Brill, 1980, 57-74.

_____. "Recent Contributions to the Study of the Ancient Versions of the New Testament," *The Bible in Modern Scholarship*. Ed. J. P. Hyatt. Nashville: Abingdon Press, 1965, 347-69.

_____. "Recent Discoveries and Investigations of New Testament Manuscripts," *Journal of Biblical Literature*, 78 (March, 1959), 13-20.

_____. "Recent Spanish Contributions to the Textual Criticism of the New Testament," *Journal of Biblical Literature*, 66 (1947), 401-23.

_____. "Second Thoughts, The Textual Criticism of the New Testament, Part I," *Expository Times*, 78:11 (August, 1967), 324-27; Part 2, 78:12 (September, 1967), 372-75.

_____. "A Survey of Recent Research on the Ancient Versions of the New Testament," *New Testament Studies*, 2 (September, 1955), 1-16.

_____. "Taitian's Harmony of the Gospels," *Text, Canon, and Principal Versions of the Bible*. Grand Rapids: Baker Book House, 1956.

_____. "The Text of Matthew 1:16," *Studies in New Testament and Early Christian Literature*. Ed. David E. Aune. Leiden: E. J. Brill, 1972, 16-24.

_____. *The Text of the New Testament, Its Transmission, Corruption, and Restoration*. 2nd ed. New York: Oxford University Press, 1964, 1968.

_____. *A Textual Commentary on the Greek New Testament*. New York: United Bible Societies, 1971.

Meye, Robert P. "Mark 16:8—The Ending of Mark's Gospel," *Biblical Research*, 14 (1969), 33-43.

Michaels, J. Ramsey. "Origen and the Text of John 1:15," *New Testament Textual Criticism, Its Significance for Exegesis: Essays in Honour of Bruce M. Metzger*. Ed. Eldon Jay Epp and Gordon D. Fee. Oxford: Clarendon Press, 1981.

Migne, Jacques Paul. *Patrologiae Cursus Completus*. Turnholti: Brepols, 1800-75.

Millard, Alan R. "In Praise of Ancient Scribes," *Biblical Achaeologist* (Summer, 1982), 143-153.

Miller, Edward. *A Guide to the Textual Criticism of the New Testament*. Collingswood: The Dean Burgon Society, Inc., 1979.

Milligan, W. and A. Roberts. *The Words of the New Testament as Altered by Transmission and Ascertained by Modern Criticism*. London: n. n., 1873.

Milne, H. J. M. and T. C. Skeat. *Scribes and Correctors of the Codex Sinaiticus*. Oxford: University Press, 1938.

Moir, Ian A. "Can We Risk Another 'Textus Receptus'?" *Journal of Biblical Literature*, 100 (April, 1981), 614-618.

──────────. "Orthography and Theology: The Omicron-Omega Interchange in Romans 5:1 and Elsewhere," *New Testament Textual Criticism, Its Significance for Exegesis: Essays in Honour of Bruce M. Metzger.* Ed. Eldon Jay Epp and Gordon D. Fee. Oxford: Clarendon Press, 1981.

──────────. "The Text of Ephesians Exhibited by Minuscule Manuscripts Housed in Great Britain—Some Preliminary Comments," *Studies in New Testament Language and Text.* Ed. J. K. Elliott. Leiden: E. J. Brill, 1976, 313-18.

──────────. "Tischendorf and the Codex Sinaiticus," *New Testament Studies,* 23 (1976), 108-15.

Morris, Leon. *The New Testament and the Jewish Lectionaries.* London: Tyndale Press, 1964.

Moulton, Harold K. *Papyrus, Parchment and Print.* "World Christian Books," No. 57. London: United Society for Christian Literature (Lutterworth Press), 1967.

──────────. "The Present State of New Testament Textual Criticism," *The Bible Translator,* 16:4 (1965), 193-98.

Mowry, L. "The Early Circulation of Paul's Letters," *Journal of Biblical Literature,* 63 (1944), 73-86.

Muncey, Raymond Waterville. *The New Testament Text of Saint Ambrose.* Cambridge: At the University Press, 1959.

Murphy, Harold S. "Eusebius' New Testament Text in the Demonstratio Evangelica," *Journal of Biblical Literature,* 73 (September, 1954), 162-68.

──────────. "On the Text of Codices J and 93," *Journal of Biblical Literature,* 67 (September, 1959), 228-37.

──────────. "The Text of Romans and I Corinthians in Minuscule 93 and the Text of Pamphilus," *Harvard Theological Review,* 52:2 (April, 1959), 119-31.

Murray, Gilbert. *Greek Studies.* Oxford: the Clarendon Press, 1946.

Murray, J. O. F. "Textual Criticism of the New Testament," *Dictionary of the Bible,* Extra Volume, Ed. James Hastings. Edinburgh: T & T Clark, 1901.

Mussies, Gerard. "Greek as the Vehicle of Early Christianity," *New Testament Studies,* 29 (1983), 356-369.

Musurillo, Herbert S. J. "The Problem of the Itala," *Theological Studies,* 17:1 (March, 1956), 93-97.

──────────. "Some Textual Problems in the Editing of the Greek Fathers," *Texte und Untersuchungen,* 77 (1961), 85-96.

Nash, Henry S. "The Exegesis of the School of Antioch," *Journal of Biblical Literature,* 11:2 (1892), 23-37.

Nestle, Eberhard. *Introduction to the Textual Criticism of the Greek New Testament.* London: Williams and Norgate, 1901.

Nevius, R. C. "The Use of the Definite Article with 'Jesus' in the Fourth Gospel," *New Testament Studies,* 12 (October-July, 1964-66), 81-85.

New, Silva. "The New Chester Beatty Papyrus," *Journal of Biblical Literature,* 51 (1932), 73.

Newman, B. M. "Some Hints in Solving Textual Problems," *Bible Translator,* 33 (1982), 430-35.

Newton, Benjamin Wills. *Remarks on the Revised English Version of the Greek New Testament.* London: Houlston and Sons, 1881.

Nida, Eugene A. "The New Testament Greek Text in the Third World," *New*

Testament Textual Criticism, Its Significance for Exegesis: Essays in Honour of Bruce M. Metzger. Ed. Eldon Jay Epp and Gordon D. Fee. Oxford: Clarendon Press, 1981, 375-380.

―――――――――. "Spiritual Values in Better Manuscript Readings of the New Testament," *Bible Translator,* 3:2 (April, 1952), 81-86.

Novum Testamentum E Codice Vaticano Graeco 1209 (Codex B). In Civitate Vaticana: ex Bibliotheca Apostolica Vaticana, 1968.

Novum Testamentum Graece. Ed. Erwin Nestle and Kurt Aland. 25th Auflage. Stuttgart: Würtembergische Bibelanstalt, 1963.

Novum Testamentum Graece. Ed. Erwin Nestle and Kurt Aland and Barbara Aland. 26th auflage. Stuttgart: Würtembergische Bibelanstalt, 1979.

O'Callaghan, Jose. "New Testament Papyri in Qumran Cave 7?" trans. William L. Holladay; Supplement to *Journal of Biblical Literature,* 91:2 (1972), 1-14. Accompanied by Carlo M. Martini, "Notes on the Papyri of Qumran Cave 7," trans. Holladay.

―――――――――. "Papiros Neotestamentarios en la Cueva 7 de Qumran," *Biblica,* 53:1 (1972), 91-100.

O'Flaherty, Wendy Doniger. *The Critical Study of Sacred Texts.* Berkeley Religious Studies Series, Berkeley: Lancaster-Miller Publications, Graduate Theological Union, 1979.

Oikonomides, A. N. *Abbreviations in Greek Inscriptions: Papyri, Manuscripts and Early Printed Books.* Chicago: Ares Publishers, 1974.

Oliver, Harold H. Review of *Family II in Luke,* by Jacob Geerlings, *Journal of Biblical Literature,* 82 (1963), 220-22.

―――――――――. "Implications of Redaktionsgeschichte for the Textual Criticism of the New Testament," *Journal of the American Academy of Religion,* 36:1 (March, 1968), 41-45.

―――――――――. "Present Trends in the Textual Criticism of the New Testament," *Journal of Bible and Religion,* 30:4 (October, 1962), 308-20.

―――――――――. "The Text of the Four Gospels as Quoted in the Moralia of Basil the Great." Unpublished Ph.D. dissertation, Emory University, 1961.

Omanson, Roger Lee. "The Claremont Profile Method and the Grouping of Byzantine New Testament Manuscripts in the Gospel of Mark," Ph.D. dissertation, The Southern Baptist Theological Seminary, 1975. His first chapter (pp. 1-23) recounts "The Formation of the International Greek New Testament Project".

―――――――――. "A Perspective on the Study of the New Testament Text," *The Bible Translator,* 34:1 (January 1983), 107-122.

O'Neil, J. C. "The Prologue to St. John's Gospel," *Journal of Theological Studies,* 20: Part 1, (April, 1969), 41-51.

Orchard, J. B. (Ed.). *A Synopsis of the Four Gospels in a New Translation Arranged According to the Two-Gospel Hypothesis.* Macon: Mercer University Press, 1982, viii.

Orlinsky, Harry M. "Current Progress and Problems in Septuagint Research," *Studies in the Septuagint: Origins, Recensions, and Interpretations.* Ed. S. Jellicoe. New York: KTAV, 1974, 3-20.

―――――――――. "The Textual Criticism of the Old Testament," *Studies in the*

Septuagint: Origins, Recensions, and Interpretations. Ed. S. Jellicoe. New York: KTAV, 1974, 239-258.

Osburn, Carroll D. "The Text of I Corinthians 10:9," *New Testament Textual Criticism, Its Significance for Exegesis: Essays in Honour of Bruce M. Metzger.* Ed. Eldon Jay Epp and Gordon D. Fee. Oxford: Clarendon Press, 1981.

──────────. "The Text of Jude 5," *Biblica*, 62:1 (1981), 107-15.

──────────. "The Text of the Pauline Epistles in Hyppolytus of Rome," *Second Century*, 2 (1982), 97-124.

Pack, Frank. "The Contributions of Textual Criticism to the Interpretation of the New Testament," *Restoration Quarterly*, 5:4 (1961), 179-92.

──────────. "The Methodology of Origen as a Textual Critic in Arriving at the Text of the New Testament," Unpublished Ph.D. dissertation, University of Southern California, 1948.

──────────. "Origen's Evaluation of Textual Variants in the Greek Bible," *Restoration Quarterly*, 4:3 (1960), 139-46.

──────────. "The 'Western' Text of Acts," *Restoration Quarterly*, 4:4 (1960), 220-33.

Palmer, Humphrey. *The Logic of Gospel Criticism.* London: Macmillan and Co., Ltd., 1968.

Parker, David C. "The Development of Textual Criticism Since B. H. Streeter," *New Testament Studies*, 24 (1977), 149-162.

Parvis, Merrill M. "The Nature and Tasks of New Testament Textual Criticism; An Appraisal," *Journal of Religion*, 32:3 (1952), 165-74.

──────────. "Text, New Testament," *The Interpreter's Dictionary of the Bible.* 4 Vols. New York: Abingdon Press, 1962.

──────────. and A. P. Wikgren, (eds.). *New Testament Manuscript Studies, the Materials and the Making of a Critical Apparatus.* n. p.: University of Chicago Press, 1950.

Patrick, G. A. "1881-1981: The Centenary of the Westcott and Hort Text," *Expository Times*, 92 (December, 1981), 359-364.

Payne, D. F. "Semitisms in the Book of Acts," *Apostolic History and the Gospel*, Chapter 8. Ed. W. Ward Gasque and Ralph P. Martin. Grand Rapids: Wm. B. Eerdmans Publishing Co., 1970, 134-50.

Payne, J. Barton. "The Relationship of the Chester Beatty Papyri of Ezekiel to Codex Vaticanus," *Journal of Biblical Literature*, 68 (September, 1949), 251-67.

Peacock, Herbert F. "The Text of the Sermon on the Mount," *Review and Expositor*, (January, 1956), 9-23.

Perumalil, A. C. "Are Not Papias and Irenaeus Competent to Report on the Gospels?" *The Expository Times*, 91:11 (August, 1980), 332-37.

Peterson, T. "The Biblical Scholar's Concern with Coptic Studies," *Catholic Biblical Quarterly*, 23:2 (1961), 241-49.

──────────. "An Early Coptic Manuscript of Acts: An Unrevised Version of the Ancient So-called Western Text," *Catholic Biblical Quarterly*, 26:2 (April, 1964), 225-41.

Pfeiffer, Rudolph. *History of Classical Scholarship From the Beginnings to the End of the Hellenistic Age.* Oxford: Clarendon Press, 1968. (Reprinted 1978).

Pickering, Wilbur Norman. "Contribution of John William Burgon to New Testament Textual Criticism," *True or False*. Ed. David Otis Fuller. Grand Rapids: Grand Rapids International Publications, 1973. (Edited form of Th.M. thesis for Dallas Theological Seminary.)

——————. "An Evaluation of the Contribution of John William Burgon to New Testament Textual Criticism." Th.M. Thesis, Dallas Theological Seminary, 1968.

——————. *The Identity of the New Testament Text*. Nashville: Thomas Nelson Inc., Publishers, 1977. Second revised and enlarged ed. 1980.

——————. "Queen Anne . . .' And All That: A Response," *Journal of the Evangelical Theological Society*, 21:2 (June, 1978), 165-67.

Pietersma, Albert. *Two Manuscripts of the Greek Psalter In the Chester Beatty Library Dublin Analecta Biblica*. Rome: Biblical Institute Press, (1978).

Porter, Calvin L. "An Analysis of the Textual Variation between Pap⁷⁵ and Codex Vaticanus in the Text of John," *Studies and Documents*, 29. Salt Lake City: University of Utah Press, 1967, 71-80.

——————. "Papyrus Bodmer XV (P⁷⁵) and the Text of Codex Vaticanus," *Journal of Biblical Literature*, 81 (1962), 363-76.

Postgate, J. P. "Textual Criticism," *Encyclopedia Britannica*. 14th ed., 1919, Vol. 22 pp. 6-11.

Price, Ira M. "Textual Criticism and the Printed Text," *The Ancestry of Our English Bible*. Harper and Bros. 3rd. ed., 1947, 202-11.

Quasten, Johannes. *Patrology*. Westminster, Maryland: The Newman Press, 1960. Vol. 1 *The Beginnings of Patristic Literature*. Vol. 2 *The Ante-Nicene Literature After Irenaeus*. Vol. 3. *The Golden Age of Greek Patristic Literature from the Council of Nicaea to the Council of Chalcedon*.

Quinn, Jerome D. "Notes on the Text of the P⁷², I Pt. 2,3; 5,14; and 5,9;" *Catholic Biblical Quarterly*, 27:3 (July, 1965), 241-49.

——————. "The Diatessaron of Romans," *New Testament Textual Criticism, Its Significance for Exegesis: Essays in Honour of Bruce M. Metzger*. Ed. Eldon Jay Epp and Gordon D. Fee. Oxford: Clarendon Press, 1981, 305-313.

Quispel, G. "The Latin Tatian or the Gospel of Thomas in Limburg," *Journal of Biblical Literature*, 88:3 (September, 1969), 321-30.

Rabil, Albert, Jr. *Erasmus and the New Testament: The Mind of a Christian Humanist*. San Antonio: Trinity University Press, 1972.

Read, William Merritt. *Michigan Manuscript 18 of the Gospels*. Seattle: University of Washington Press, 1942.

Reicke, Bo. "Erasmus und die neutestamentliche Textgeschichte," *Theologische Zeitschrift*, 22 (1966), 254-65.

——————. "The Synoptic Reports on the Healing of the Paralytic, Matthew 9:1-8 with Parallels," *Studies In New Testament Lanugage and Text*. Ed. J. K. Elliott. Leiden: E. J. Brill, 1976, 319-29.

Reneham, Robert. *Greek Textual Criticism, A Reader*. Cambridge: Harvard University Press, 1969.

Reynolds, L. D. and N. G. Wilson. *Scribes and Scholars, A Guide to the Transmission of Greek and Latin Literature*. Oxford: University Press, 1968.

264   THE BYZANTINE TEXT-TYPE

Reuss, Edward Wilhelm Eugen. *History of the Sacred Scriptures of the New Testament.* Translated from 5th ed. by Edward L. Houghton. Boston: Houghton, Mifflin & Co., 1884.

Rhodes, Erroll F. "Conjectural Emendations in Modern Translations," *New Testament Textual Criticism, Its Significance for Exegesis: Essays in Honour of Bruce M. Metzger.* Ed. Eldon Jay Epp and Gordon D. Fee. Oxford: Clarendon Press, 1981, 361-374.

Richards, W. Larry. *The Classification of the Greek Manuscripts of the Johannine Epistles.* Missoula: Scholars Press, 1977.

──────────. "Gregory 1175: Alexandrian or Byzantine in the Catholic Epistles?" *Andrews University Seminary Studies,* 21 (1983), 155-168.

──────────. "Manuscript Gouping in Luke 10 by Quantitative Analysis," *Journal of Biblical Literature,* 98:3 (1979), 379-91.

──────────. "Textual Criticism on the Greek Text of the Catholic Epistles: A Bibliography," *Andrews University Seminary Studies,* 12 (February, 1974), 103-11.

Riddle, D. W. "Textual Criticism as a Historical Discipline," *Anglican Theological Review,* 18 (1936), 220-34.

Riesenfeld, Harald. "The Text of Acts 10:36," *Text and Interpretation,* Ed. Ernest Best and Robert McL. Wilson. Cambridge: Cambridge University Press, 1979, 191-94.

Roberts, Colin H. "Books in the Graeco-Roman World and in the New Testament," *The Cambridge History of the Bible, From the Beginnings to Jerome.* Ed. by P. R. Ackroyd and C. C. Evans. Vol. 1. Cambridge: University Press, 1970, 48-66.

──────────. "An Early Papyrus of the First Gospel," *Harvard Theological Review,* 46:4 (October, 1953), 203-15.

──────────. *Greek Literary Hands 350 B.C.—A.D. 400.* Oxford: The Clarendon Press, 1956.

──────────. *Manuscript, Society and Belief in Early Christian Egypt.* London: The Oxford University Press, 1979.

──────────. *An Unpublished Fragment of the Fourth Gospel.* Manchester: The Manchester University Press, 1935.

Roberts, W. Rhys. *Demetrius on Style.* English translation by W. Rhys Roberts. The Loeb Classical Library. Cambridge: Harvard University Press, 1953.

──────────. *Greek Rhetoric and Literary Criticism.* New York: Longmans, Green & Co., 1928.

Robertson, A. T. *An Introduction to the Textual Criticism of the New Testament.* Nashville: Broadman Press, 1925.

──────────. "Some Interesting Readings in the Washington Codex of the Gospels," *Studies in the Text of the New Testament.* New York: George H. Doran Co., 1969, 94-101.

──────────. *Studies in the Text of the New Testament.* New York: George H. Doran Co., 1969.

──────────. "Why Textual Criticism for the Preacher," *Studies in the Text of the New Testament.* New York: George H. Doran Co., 1969, 54-64.

Ropes, James Hardy. *The Text of Acts.* Vol. 3 of *The Beginnings of Christianity.* Ed. F. J. F. Jackson and Kirsopp Lake. London: Macmillan and Co., 1926.

Ross, J. M. "The Ending of the Apocalypse," *Studies in the New Testament Language and Text.* Ed. J. K. Elliott. Leiden: E. J. Brill, 1976, 339-44.

——————. "The Rejected Words in Luke 9," *The Expository Times*, 84:3 (December, 1972), 85-88.

——————. "Some Unnoticed Points in the Text of the New Testament," *Novum Testamentum*, 25 (1983) 59-72.

Royse, James R. "Scribal Habits in the Transmission of New Testament Texts," *The Critical Study of Sacred Texts.* Berkeley: Graduate Theological Union, 1979, 139-61.

——————. "von Soden's Accuracy," *Journal of Theological Studies*, 30:1 (April, 1979), 166-71.

——————. "The Treatment of Scribal Leaps in Metzger's *Textual Commentary*," *New Testament Studies*, 29 (1983), 539-551.

Ruger, von Hans Peter. "Miszellen: ΝΑΖΑΡΕΘ/ΝΑΖΑΡΑ ΝΑΖΑΡΗΝΟΣ/ ΝΑΖΩΡΑΙΝΟΣ," *Zeitschrift für die neutestamentliche Wissenschaft und die Kunde der alten Kirche*, 72 Band (1981 HEFT 3/4), 257-263.

Sagnard, F. M. M. "Holy Scripture in the Early Fathers of the Church," *Studia Evangelica.* Ed. F. L. Cross and others. Berlin: Adakemie-Verlag, 1959.

Salmon, George. "Notes on the Concluding Verses of St. Mark's Gospel," *A Historical Introduction to the Study of the Books of the New Testament.* 3rd. ed. London: John Murray, 1888, 159-64.

——————. *Some Thoughts on the Textual Criticism of the New Testament.* London: John Murray, 1897.

Salvoni, Fausto. "Textual Authority for John 7:53-8:11," *Restoration Quarterly*, 4:1 (1960), 11-15.

Sanday, William. *The Gospels in the Second Century.* London: Macmillan and Co., 1876.

Sanders, E. P. *The Tendencies of the Synoptic Tradition.* Cambridge: At the University Press, 1969.

Sanders, Henry A. The Beatty Papyrus of Revelation and Hoskier's Edition," *Journal of Biblical Literature*, 53 (December, 1934), 371-80.

——————. "An Early Papyrus Fragment of the Gospel of Matthew in the Michigan Collection," *Harvard Theological Review*, 19 (1916), 225-26.

——————. "The Egyptian Text of the Gospels and Acts," *Harvard Theological Review*, 26 (1933), 77-98.

——————. *Facsimile of the Washington Manuscript of the Four Gospels.* Ann Arbor: University of Michigan, 1912.

——————. *The New Manuscripts in the Freer Collection, Part 1, The Washington Manuscript of the Four Gospels.* New York: the Macmillan Co., 1912.

——————. "Recent Text Studies in the New Testament," *Anglican Theological Review*, 16 (October, 1932), 266-82.

——————. *A Third-Century Papyrus Codex of the Epistles of Paul.* Ann Arbor: The University of Michigan Press, 1939.

Sandys, John Edward. "Greek Scholarship in the Second Century," *A History of Classical Scholarship*, Vol. I, 104-44, 309-33.

Saunders, E. W. "Studies in Doctrinal Influences on the Byzantine Text of the Gospels," *Journal of Biblical Literature*, 71 (June, 1952), 85-92.

——————. *Textual Criticism of a Medieval Manuscript of the Four Gospels*, n. p.: Duke University, 1943.

Schaff, Philip. *A Companion to the Greek Testament and the English Version*. New York: Harper and Brothers, 1889.

——————. *Ante-Nicene Christianity*. Vol. 2. of *History of the Christian Church*. Grand Rapids: Wm. B. Eerdmans Publishing Co., 1950.

Schmid, Josef. *Studien zur Geschichte des griechischen Apokalypse Textes*, 2 vol. München: Karl Zink, 1955-1956.

Scott, Julius. "Textual Variants of the 'Apostolic Decree' and Their Setting in the Early Church," *The Living and Active Word of God: Studies in Honor of Samuel J. Schultz*. Ed. by Morris Inch and Ronald Youngblood.

Scrivener, Frederick Henry A. *Adversaria Critica Sacra*. Cambridge: At the University Press, 1893.

——————. *Bezae Codex Cantabrigiensis . . . Edited with a Critical Introduction, Annotations, and Facsimiles*. Cambridge: Deighton, Bell, and Co., 1864.

——————. *An Exact Transcript of the Codex Augiensis*. Cambridge: Deighton, Bell, and Co., 1859.

——————. *A Full Collation of the Codex Sinaiticus with the Received Text of the New Testament*. London: Bell & Daldy, 1861.

——————. *The New Testament in the Original Greek According to the Text Followed in the Authorized Version, Together with the Variations Adopted in the Revised Version*, Cambridge: The University Press, 1902.

——————. *A Plain Introduction to the Criticism of the New Testament*. 4th ed. Ed. Edward Miller. 2 vols. London: n. n., 1894.

——————. *Six Lectures on the Text of the New Testament and the Ancient Manuscripts Which Contain It*. Cambridge: George Bell and Sons, 1875.

Shelley, Bruce, "Scripture, Tradition and Authority in the Second Century," *Bulletin of the Evangelical Theological Soceity*, 6 (May, 1963), 57-63.

Sibinga, J. Smit. "Text and Literary Art in Mark 3:1-6," *Studies in New Testament Language and Text*. Ed. J. K. Elliott. Leiden: E. J. Brill, 1976, 357-65.

Simcox, William Henry. *The Writers of the New Testament, Their Style and Characteristics*. Winona Lake: Alpha Publications, reprint 1980.

Sitterly, Charles F. *Praxis in Manuscripts of the Greek Testament*. New York: Eaton and Mains, 1898.

——————. "Text and Manuscripts of the New Testament," *International Standard Bible Encyclopedia*. V, 2950-57.

Skeat, T. C. "The Provenance of the Codex Alexandrinus," *Journal of Theological Studies*, 6 (October, 1955), 233-35.

——————. *The Use of Dictation in Ancient Book Production*. Londres, s. d.: n. n., 1957.

——————. and H. J. M. Milne. *The Codex Sinaiticus and the Codex Alexandrinus*. London: n. n., 1955.

Slomp, Jan. "Are the Words, 'Son of God' in Mark 1:1 Original?" *The Bible Translator*, 28:1 (January, 1977), 143-50.

Smalley, Beryl. *The Study of the Bible in the Middle Ages*. Oxford: Basil Blackwell, 1952.

Smith, W. B. "The Pauline Manuscripts F and G," *American Journal of Theology*, 7 (1903), 452-82, 662-88.

Smothers, E. R. (S. J.). "Chrysostom and Symeon (Acts 15:14)," *Harvard Theological Review*, 46:4 (October, 1953), 203-15.

——————. "Papyrus Bodmer II: An Early Codex of St. John," *Theological Studies*, 18:3 (September, 1957), 434-41.

——————. "Two Readings in Papyrus Bodmer II," *Harvard Theological Review*, 51 (July, 1958), 109-22.

Snodgrass, Klyne. "Western Non-Interpolations," *Journal of Biblical Literature*, 91:3 (September, 1972), 369-79.

Soden, Hermann Freiherr von. *Die Schriften des Neuen Testaments in ihrer ältesten erreichbaren Textgestalt*, I. Teil, *Untersuchungen*, i. Abteilung, *Die Textzeugen*, Berlin, 1902, 704 pp.; ii. Abteilung, *Die Textformen*, B. *Der Apostolos mit Apokalypse*, 1910, pp. 1521-2203. Göttingen: Vandenhoeck und Ruprecht, 1911-1913.

Soulen, Richard N. *Handbook of Biblical Criticism*. Atlanta: John Knox Press, 1976.

Souter, Alexander. *Novum Testamentum Graece*. London: Oxonii, 1953.

——————. "Progress in the Textual Criticism of the Gospels Since Westcott and Hort," *Mansfield College Essays*. London: Hodder and Stoughton, 1909.

——————. *The Text and Canon of the New Testament*. Revised by C. S. C. Williams. n. p.: Gerald Duckworth and Company, 1954.

Stephenson, A. A. (S. J.). "St. Cyril of Jerusalem and the Alexandrian Heritage," *Theological Studies*, 15:4 (December, 1954), 573-93.

Stewart, John William. "Doctrinal Influence Upon the New Testament Text of Clement of Alexandria." Ph.D. dissertation, Duke University, 1966.

Stoldt, Hans-Herbert. *History and Criticism of the Marcan Hypothesis*. Trans. and ed. by D. L. Niewyk. Macon: Mercer University Press, 1980, esp. 11-23, 263-280.

Stone, Robert Conrad. *The Language of the Latin Text of Codex Bezae*, with an index verborum. Urbana: The University of Illinois Press, 1946.

——————. "Some Remarks on the Provenience of the Codex Bezae," *Classical Studies in Honor of William Abbott Oldfather*. Urbana: The University of Illinois Press, 1943.

Streeter, Burnett Hillman. "The Caesarean Text of the Gospels," *Journal of Theological Studies*, 26 (1925), 373-80.

——————. "The Caesarean Text of Matthew and Luke," *Harvard Theological Review*, 28 (1935), 321-35.

——————. "The Chester Papyrus and the Caesarean Text," *Journal of Theological Studies*, 40 (1939), 36-55.

_____. "The Early Ancestry of the Textus Receptus of the Gospels," *Journal of Theological Studies*, 38 (July, 1937), 225-29.

_____. *The Four Gospels: A Study of Origins Treating of Manuscript Tradition, Sources, Authorship and Date*. London: Macmillan and Co., Ltd., 1924, revised 1930.

_____. "Origen, ℵ and the Caesarean Text," *Journal of Theological Studies*, 36 (April, 1935), 178-80.

_____. "The Washington Manuscript and the Caesarean Text of the Gospels, *Journal of Theological Studies*, 27 (1926), 144-47.

_____. "The Washington Manuscript of the Gospels," *Harvard Theological Review*, 19 (1926), 165-72.

Strugnell, J. "A Plea for Conjectural Emendation in the New Testament, with a Coda on I Cor. 4:6," *Catholic Biblical Quarterly*, 36:4 (1974), 543-58.

Studies in the History and Text of the New Testament in Honor of Kenneth Willis Clark, Ed. Boyd L. Daniels and M. Jacob Suggs, *Studies and Documents*, 29. Salt Lake City: University of Utah Press, 1967.

Stunt, Timothy C. F. "Some Unpublished Letters of S. P. Tregelles Relating to the Codex Sinaiticus," *The Evangelical Quarterly*, 48:1 (January-March, 1976), 15-26.

Suggs, M. Jack. "Eusebius and the Gospel Text," *Harvard Theological Review*, 50:4 (October, 1957), 307-10.

_____. "Eusebius' Text of John in the 'Writings against Marcellus,'" *Journal of Biblical Literature*, 75 (June, 1956), 137-42.

_____. "The Eusebian Text of Matthew," *Novum Testamentum*, I (1956), 233-45.

_____. "The Use of Patristic Evidence in Search for a Primitive New Testament Text," *New Testament Studies*, 4:2 (January, 1958), 139-46.

Swanson, Reuben J. *The Horizontal Line Synopsis of the Gospels, Greek Edition, Vol. I Matthew*. Dillsboro, North Carolina: Western North Carolina Press, Inc. 1982.

Swete, Henry Barclay. "The History and Present State of New Testament Textual Criticism," *Essays on Some Biblical Questions of the Day*. London: Macmillan and Co., 1909, 508-39.

_____. "New Testament Greek in the Light of Modern Discovery," *Essays on Some Biblical Questions of the Day*. London: Macmillan and Co., 1909, 462-505.

Tarelli, C. "The Byzantine Text and the Lectionaries," *Journal of Theological Studies*, 43 (1942), 181-83.

_____. "The Chester Beatty Papyrus and the Caesarean Text," *Journal of Theological Studies*, 40 (January, 1939), 46-55.

_____. "The Chester Beatty Papyrus and the Western and Byzantine Texts," *Journal of Theological Studies*, 41 (1940), 253-60.

_____. "Erasmus' Manuscripts of the Gospels," *Journal of Theological Studies*, 44 (1943), 155-62.

_____. "Erasmus' Manuscripts of the Gospels," *Journal of Theological Studies*, 58 (July-October, 1947), 207-08.

_____. "Historical Greek Grammar and Textual Criticism, "*Journal of Theological Studies*, 38 (1937), 238-42.

_____. "Omissions, Additions, and Conflations in the Chester Beatty Papyrus," *Journal of Theological Studies*, 40 (October, 1939), 382-87.

_____. "Some Further Linguistic Aspects of the Chester Beatty Papyrus of the Gospels," *Journal of Theological Studies*, 43 (1941), 19-25.

_____. "Some Linguistic Aspects of the Chester Beatty Papyrus of the Gospels," *Journal of Theological Studies*, 39 (1938), 254-59.

Tasker, R. V. G. "The Chester Beatty Papyrus and the Caesarean Text of John," *Harvard Theological Review*, 30 (July, 1937), 157-64.

_____. "The Chester Beatty Papyrus and the Caesarean Text of Luke," *Harvard Theological Review*, 29 (1936), 345-42.

_____. *The Greek New Testament Being the Text Translated in the New English Bible 1961 Edited with Introduction and Appendix with Textual Notes.* London: Oxford University Press, 1964.

_____. "An Introduction to the Manuscripts of the New Testament," *Harvard Theological Review*, 41:2 (April, 1948), 71-81.

_____. "The Nature of the Text of the Chester Beatty Papyrus in Acts," *Journal of Theological Studies*, 38 (1937), 383-94.

_____. "The Quotations from the Synoptic Gospels in Origen's Exhortation to Martyrdom," *Journal of Theological Studies*, 36 (January, 1935), 60-64.

_____. "The Readings of the Chester Beatty Papyrus in the Gospel of St. John," *Journal of Theological Studies*, 36 (October, 1935), 387-91.

_____. "The Text of the Fourth Gospel Used by Origen in His Commentary on John," *Journal of Theological Studies*, 37 (April, 1936), 146-55.

_____. "The Text of St. Matthew Used by Origen in His Commentary on St. Matthew," *Journal of Theological Studies*, 38 (1937), 60-64.

_____. "The Text Used by Eusebius in Demonstratio Evangelica in Quoting from Matthew and Luke," *Harvard Theological Review*, 28 (1935), 61-67.

Taylor, R. O. P. *The Groundwork of the Gospels.* Oxford: Basil Blackwell, 1946.

Taylor, Richard A. "Queen Anne Resurrected? A Review Article," *Journal of the Evangelical Theological Society*, 20:4 (December, 1977), 377-81.

Taylor, Vincent. *The Text of the New Testament, A Short Introduction.* New York: St. Martin's Press, 1961.

Teeple, Howard M. "The Greek Article with Personal Names in the Synoptic Gospels, "*New Testament Studies*, 19 (1972-73), 302-17.

_____. and Walker F. Allyn. "Notes on the Plates in Papyrus Bodmer II," *Journal of Biblical Literature*, 78 (1959), 148-52.

Telfer, W. "The Fourth Century Greek Fathers as Exegetes," *Harvard Theological Review*, 50 (April, 1957), 91.

Tenny, Merrill C. *New Testament Survey.* Grand Rapids: Wm. B. Eerdmans Publishing Co., 1961.

_____. "The Quotations from Luke in Tertullian," *Harvard Studies in Classical Philosophy*, 56-57 (1947), 257-260.

Tertullian Adversus Marcion, Books IV-V. Ed. and trans. by Ernest Evans. Oxford: Clarendon Press, 1972. (Appendix 21, 643-46).

Testuz, Michel. *Papyrus Bodmer VII-IX. VII: L'Epitre de Jude, VIII: Les deux Epitres de Pierre, IX: Les Psaumes 33 et 34.* Geneva: Bibliotheca Bodmeriana, 1959.

Thompson, D. A. "The Controversy Concerning the Last Twelve Verses of Mark," *Bible League Quarterly*, 285 (April-June, 1971).

──────────. "Corrupting the Word of God," *Bible League Quarterly*, 285 (April-June, 1971), 37-44.

──────────. "The Downgrade in Many Modern English Translations of Scripture," *Bible League Quarterly*, 289 (April-June, 1972); 290 (July-September, 1972); 291 (October-December, 1972); 292 (January-March, 1973).

Thompson Edward M. *An Introduction to Greek and Latin Palaeography.* Oxford: Clarendon Press, 1912.

Thomson, Robert W. "The Text of the Syriac Athanasian Corpus," *Biblical and Patristic Studies.* Ed. J. Neville Birdsall and Robert W. Thomson. Freiburg: Herder, 1963.

Thoyts, Emma Elizabeth. *How to Decipher and Study Old Documents, Being a Guide to the Reading of Ancient Manuscripts.* Chicago: Ares Publishers, Inc., 1974.

Thrall, Margaret E. "II Corinthians 1:12: ΑΓΙΟΘΗΤΙ? or ΑΠΛΟΘΗΤΙ?" *Studies in New Testament Language and Text.* Ed. J. K. Elliott. Leiden: E. J. Brill, 1976, 366-72.

──────────. "'Putting on' or 'Stripping off' in 2 Corinthians 5:3," *New Testament Textual Criticism, Its Significance for Exegesis: Essays in Honour of Bruce M. Metzger.* Ed. Eldon Jay Epp and Gordon D. Fee. Oxford: Clarendon Press, 1981

Tischendorf, Constantine von. *Novum Testamentum Graece.* Editio octava critica maior. 3 Vols. Lipsae: Giesecke and Devrient, 1869.

──────────. *When Were Our Gospels Written? With a Narrative of the Discovery of the Sinaitic Manuscript.* New York: American Tract Society, 1896.

Tov, Emanuel. "Criteria for Evaluating Textual Readings: The Limitations of Textual Rules," *Harvard Theological Review*, 75 (1982) 429-448.

──────────. *The Text-Critical Use of the Septuagint in Biblical Research. Jerusalem Biblical Studies* 3. Simor. 1981.

Tregelles, Samuel Prideaux. *An Account of the Printed Text of the Greek New Testament with Remarks on Its Revision upon Critical Principal Together with a Collation of Critical Texts of Griesbach, Scholz, Lachmann and Tisch., with That in Common Use.* London: Samuel Bagster and Sons, 1854.

Trevor, John C. "Illustrated History of the Biblical Text," *The Interpreter's Bible*, 12. New York: Abingdon-Cokesbury, 1957.

Trites, Allison A. "The Woman Taken in Adultery," *Bibliotheca Sacra*, 131:522 (April, 1974), 137-146.

Turner, C. H. "Historical Introduction to the Textual Criticism of the New Testament, *Journal of Theological Studies*, 10 (1909), 13-28, 161-82, 354-74; 11 (1910), 1-27, 180-210.

_____. "Marcan Usage: Notes Critical and Exegetical on the Second Gospel," *Journal of Theological Studies*, 25 (1923), 377-86; 26 (1924), 12-20, 26 (1925), 145-56; 26 (1925), 225-40; 26 (1925), 337-46; 27 (1926), 58-62; 28 (1927), 9-30; 28 (1927), 349-62; 28 (1927), 9-30; 28 (1927), 349-62; 28 (1927), 145-58; 28 (1927) 349-62.

Turner, E. G. *Greek Manuscripts of the Ancient World*. Oxford: n. n., 1971.

_____. *Greek Papyri, An Introduction*. Princeton: Princeton University Press, 1968.

_____. *The Typology of the Early Codex*. University of Pennsylvania Press, 1977.

Turner, Nigel. *A Grammar of the New Testament Greek*, by J. H. Moulton, Vol IV *Style*, by N. Turner. Edinburgh: T & T Clark, 1976.

_____. "The Literary Character of the New Testament," *New Testament Studies*, 20:2 (January, 1974), 107-14.

_____. "The Transmission of the Text, (B) New Testament," *A Companion to the Bible*. 2nd ed. Ed. H. H. Rowley. Edinburgh: T & T Clark, 1963.

Turyn, A. *The Byzantine Manuscript Tradition of the Tragedies of Euripedes. Illinois Studies in Language and Literature*, 43. Urbana: University of Illinois Press, 1967.

Twilley L. D. *The Origin and Transmission of the New Testament*. Edinburgh: Tweeddale Court, 1957.

Unger, M. F. "The Papyri and the Critical Evaluation of the New Testament," *Bibliotheca Sacra*, 117 (January-March, 1960), 19-22.

Vaccari, Alberto. "The Hesychian Recension of the Septuagint," *Studies in the Septuagint—Origins, Recensions and Interpretations*. Ed. S. Jellicoe. New York: KTAV, 1974, 336-42.

Vaganay, Leo. *An Introduction to the Textual Criticism of the New Testament*. Trans. B. V. Miller. St. Louis, Missouri: B. Herder Book Co., 1937.

Valentine-Richards, Alfred V. "The History and the Present State of New Testament Textual Criticism," *Cambridge B: Essays on Some Biblical Questions of the Day, by Members of the University of Cambridge*. Ed. Henry Barclay Swete. London: Macmillan and Co., Ltd., 1905.

Valk, M. van der. *Researches on the Text and Scholia of the Iliad. Part I* (1963), *Part II* (1964). Leiden: E. J. Brill.

Vincent, M. R. *A History of the Textual Criticism of the New Testament*. New York: Macmillan Co., 1899.

Vogels, H. J. *Handbuch der Textkritik des Neuen Testaments*. Zweite Auflage, Bohn: Hanstein, 1955.

_____. *Novum Testamentum Graece et Latine*. Editio Quarta. Friburgi: Herder, 1955.

Voobus, Arthur. "Completion of the Vestus Syra Project," *Biblical Research*, 7 (1962), 49-56.

_____. "A Critical Apparatus for the Vestus Syra," *Journal of Biblical Literature*, 2 (1951), 123-28.

_____. *Early Versions of the New Testament, Manuscript Studies*. Stockholm: Estonian Theological Society in Exile, 1954.

_____. "Emergence of the Synodican in the West Syrian Tradition," *Journal of Theological Studies*, 19: Part 1, (April, 1968), 225-28.

_____. *Investigations into the Text of the New Testament Used by Rabbula of Edessa*. Pinneberg: n. n., 1947.

_____. "A New Approach to the Problem of the Shorter and Longer Text in Luke," *New Testament Studies*, 15:4 (July, 1969), 457-63.

_____. "The Old Syriac Version in a New Light, and Urgent Tasks in Textual Criticism of the New Testament," *Apophoreta Tartuensia*. Stockholm: Societas Literarum Estonica in Svecia, 1949.

_____. "Oldest Traces of the Peshitta," *Le Museon*, 63. Louvain: n. n., 1950.

_____. *Researches on the Circulation of the Peshitta in the Middle of the Fifth Century*. Pinneberg: Baltic University, 1948.

Voss, David O. "Is von Soden's K^r a Distinct Type of Text?" *Journal of Biblical Literature*, 57 (1938), 311-18.

Waard, J. De. *A Comparative Study of the Old Testament Text in the Dead Sea Scrolls and in the New Testament*. Grand Rapids: Wm. B. Eerdmans, 1966.

Walker, John Hazeldon. "A Pre-Marcan Dating for the Didache: Further Thoughts of a Liturgist," *Studia Biblica 1978, III: Papers on Paul and Pauline Literature*. Sixth International Congress on Biblical Studies, Oxford, 3-7 April 1978, Ed. by E. A. Livingstone.

Wallace-Hadrill, D. S. "An Analysis of Some Quotations from the First Gospel in Eusebius' *Demonstratio Evangelica*," *Journal of Theological Studies*, I (1950), 168-75.

_____. *Christian Antioch: A Study of Early Christian Thought in the East*. Cambridge. 1982.

_____. "Eusebius and the Gospel Text of Caesarea," *Harvard Theological Review*, 49:2 (April, 1956), 105-14.

Walter, Peter. *The Text of the Septuagint, Its Corruptions and Their Emendation*. Ed. D. W. Gooding. Cambridge: University Press, 1973.

Warfield, B. B. *An Introduction to the Textual Criticism of the New Testament*. London: Hodder and Stoughton, 1887.

Wenham, John W. "How Many Cock-Crowings? The Problem of Harmonistic Text-variants," *New Testament Studies*, 25 (July, 1979), 523-525.

_____. "Why Do You Ask Me About the Good? A Study of the Relation Between Text and Source Criticism," *New Testament Studies*, 28:1 (January, 1982), 116-25.

West, M. L. *Textual Criticism and Editorial Technique Applicable to Greek and Latin Texts*. Stuttgart: B. G. Teubner, 1973.

West, Paige L. "Investigation of the Text of Papyrus Bodmer XV, Chapters Ten Through Fifteen." Unpublished Th.M. thesis, Dallas Theological Seminary, 1964.

Westcott, B. F. "Clement of Alexandria," *Dictionary of Christian Biography*. 4 vols. Ed. William Smith and Henry Wall. Boston: Little, Brown and Co., 1877.

_____. *Introduction to the Studies of the Gospels*. Boston: Gould and Lincoln, 1867.

_____. and Fenton J. Anthony Hort. *The New Testament in the Original Greek*. London: Macmillan and Co., 1895.

_____ and _____. *The New Testament in the Original Greek*. Vol. 2 *Introduction and Appendix* by the editors. New York: Harper and Bros., 1882.

Wettstein, Jacobus. *Novum Testamentum Graecum*. 2 Vols. Graz Austria: Akademische Druk: Verlagsanstalt. 1752-1962.

Wevers, John Wm. "Text History and Text Criticisms of the Septuagint," *Supplements to Vestus Testamentum*, 29. Leiden: E. J. Brill, 1978, 392-402.

Whitney, S. W. *The Revisers' Greek Text*. 2 Vols. Boston: Silver, Burdett & Co., 1892.

Wieand, D. J. "John 5:2 and the Pool of Bethesda," *New Testament Studies*, 12 (October-July, 1964-66), 392-404.

Wikgren, A. P. "Biblical and Early Christian Papyri," *Text, Canon, and Principal Versions of the Bible*. Grand Rapids: Baker Book House, 1956, 17-18.

_____. "Chicago Studies in the Greek Lectionary of the New Testament," *Biblical and Patristic Studies*. Ed. J. Neville Birdsall and Robert W. Thomson. Frieburg: Herder, 1963.

_____. (ed.) *Early Christian Origins*. Chicago: Quadrangle Books, 1961.

_____. "The Lectionary Text of John 8:1-11," *Journal of Biblical Literature*, 53 (December, 1934), 188-98.

_____. "New Testament Greek Lectionaries," *The Text, Canon, and Principal Versions of the Bible*. Grand Rapids: Baker Book House, 1956, p. 19.

_____. "The Problem in Acts 16:12," *New Testament Textual Criticism, Its Significance for Exegesis: Essays in Honour of Bruce M. Metzger*. Ed. Eldon Jay Epp and Gordon D. Fee. Oxford: Clarendon Press, 1981

_____. "Textual Criticism and the New Testament Canon (signale dans), *Journal of Biblical Literature*, 76 (1957), xxxviii.

_____. "The Use of the Versions in New Testament Criticism," *Journal of Biblical Literature*, 67 (June, 1948), 135-42.

Wilcox, Max. "Luke and the Bezan Text of Acts," *Bibliotheca Emphemeridum Theologium Lovaniensium*, 48 (1977). *Les Acts des Apotres*. Ed. J. Duculot, SA. Gembloux, Belgique: Leuven University Press, 447-55.

_____. *The Semitisms of Acts*. Oxford: Clarendon Press, 1965.

Wilhelm-Hooijbergh, Ann E. "In 2 Tim. 1:17 the Greek and Latin Texts may have a Different Meaning," *Studia Biblica 1978, III: Papers on Paul and Pauline Literature*. Sixth International Congress on Biblical Studies, Oxford, 3-7 April 1978. Ed. by E. A. Livingstone.

Williams, Charles Stephen Conway. *Alterations to the Text of the Synoptic Gospels and Acts*. Oxford: Basil Blackwell, 1951.

_____. "P46 and the Textual Tradition of Romans," *Expository Times*, 61 (1949-50), 125-26.

_____. "Syrianisms in the Washington Text of Mark," *Journal of Theological Studies*, 42 (1941), 177.

_____. "Text of the New Testament," *Dictionary of the Bible*. Ed.

James Hastings. Revised edition edited by F. C. Grant and H. H. Rowley. New York: Charles Scribner's Sons, 1963.

Willis, G. G. "Some Interesting Readings of the Book of Mulling," *Studia Evangelica*. Ed. Kurt Aland. IV *Textual Criticism*. Berlin: Akademie-Verlag, 1959.

Wilson, Robert McL. "Philippians in Fayyumic," *Text and Interpretation*, Ed. Ernest Best and Robert McL. Wilson. Cambridge: Cambridge University Press, 1979, 245-50.

Wisse, Frederick. "The Claremont Profile Method for the Classification of Byzantine New Testament Manuscripts: A Study in Method." Ph.D. dissertation, Claremont Graduate School, 1968.

—————————. *The Profile Method for Classifying and Evaluating Manuscript Evidence. Studies and Documents*, 44. Ed. by Irving A. Sparks, Grand Rapids: William B. Eerdmans, 1982.

—————————. and Paul R. McReynolds. "Family E and the Profile Method," *Biblica*, 51 (1970), 67-75.

Wood, H. G. *Amicitiae Corolla, (A volume of Essays Presented to James Rendel Harris);* London: University of London Press, 1932.

Wright, Leon. *Alterations of the Words of Jesus as Quoted in the Literature of the Second Century.* Cambridge: Harvard University Press, 1952.

Wurthwein, Ernst. *The Text of the Old Testament.* Grand Rapids: Wm. B Eerdmans Publishing Co., 1979.

Yoder, James D. *Concordance to the Distinctive Greek Text of Codex Bezae.* Grand Rapids: Wm. B. Eerdmans Publishing Co., 1961.

—————————. "Semitism in Codex Bezae," *Journal of Biblical Literature*, 78 (December, 1959), 317-21.

Youtie, Herbert C. "The Papyrologist: Artificer of Fact," *Greek Roman, and Byzantine Studies*, 4:4 (Winter, 1963), Cambridge: University Press 19-32.

Zuntz, Gunther. *The Ancestry of the Harklean New Testament.* London: Oxford University Press, n. d.

—————————. "The Byzantine Text in New Testament Criticism," *Journal of Theological Studies*, 43 (1942), 25-30.

—————————. *An Inquiry into the Transmission of the Plays of Euripides.* Cambridge: University Press, 1965.

—————————. "A Textual Criticism of Some Passages of the Acts of the Apostles," *Classic et Mediaev*, 3 (1940), 20-46.

—————————. *The Text of the Epistles.* (Schweich Lectures 1946) London: Oxford University Press, 1953.

Zwemer, S. M. "The Last Twelve Verses of the Gospel of Mark," *Evangelical Quarterly*, 17:1 (January, 1945), 13-23.

Indices to the Bibliography

This index lists subjects which are, for the most part, readily identified in the title(s) of the books and articles listed after the individual author's name in the bibliography. Most of these subjects, along with many others, will also be found discussed in the *Introductions* and *Handbooks* to textual criticism. For further reading and research, consult indexes in these works and particularly the works by authors listed in this index under the heading *Bibliographies on N.T.T.C.*

Bezae, see Codex D

Bible Reading in the Early Church
Harnack

Bible Study in the Middle Ages
Smalley

Bibliographies on N.T.T.C.
Duplacy
Klijn
Mattill
Metzger
Richards

Bodmer Papyri, see $P^{66\ 72\ 73\ 74\ 75}$
Filson
Kilpatrick
Testuz

Bohairic Version
Hoskier
Husselmann

Book of Mulling, Readings in
Willis

Book Production, Ancient
Diringer
Kenyon
Moulton
Skeat

Burgon, John W.
Hills
Pickering

Byzantine MSS
Granstrom
Wisse

Byzantine Text
Lake, K. and S.
Lattey
Kilpatrick
Saunders
Streeter
Tarelli
Zuntz

Byzantine Text, Defense of
Borland
Buchanan
Bruggen
Burgon
Fuller
Hills
Hodges
MacLean
Miller
Kilpatrick
Pickering
Scrivener
Thompson

Byzantine Text of Euripedes
Turyn

Caesarean Text
Burkitt
Carder
Colwell
Globe
Hills
Hoskier
Hurtado
Huston
Lake, Blake and New
Metzger
Streeter
Tarelli
Tasker
Wallace-Hadrill

Scripture Index to Bibliography

This is an index of articles and books on text-critical treatment of New Testament passages. For additional comments on these and other texts see *Commentaries on N.T. Text* in the *Subject Index to Bibliography*.

Matthew
1:16	Metzger
5:4,5	Ross
5-7	Peacock
6:9-13	Bandstra
	Bruggen
8:28	Baarda
9:1-8	Reicke
11:25	Klijn
14:22-33	Sibinga
16:2b-3	Hirunuma
19:16,17	Wenham
22:32	Ross
23:14	Ross

Mark
1:1	Globe
	Slomp
1:4	Elliott
1:27	Elliott
1:41	Elliott
3:1-6	Sibinga
5:1	Baarda
5:22	Elliott
6:3	Elliott
6:22	Elliott
6:41	Elliott

8:38	Ross
9:38	Elliott
	Ross
9:44 and 46	Ross
10:2	Elliott
11:24	Elliott
14:24	Emerton
16:9-20	Bruce
	Burgon
	Colwell
	Farmer
	Horst
	Kahle
	Meye
	Salmon
	Thompson
	Zwemer

Luke
1:49	Ross
1:70	Ross
8:26	Baarda
9	Ross
10:42	Baker
	Fee
11:1-4	Bandstra
	Bruggen

22:15-20	Chadwick	15:19	Ross
22:43:44	Duplacy	16:25-27	Hurtado
	Erhman and		
	Plunkett	1 Corinthians	
24:51	Epp	4:6	Strugnell
		10:9	Osburn
John		14:34,35	Ellis
1:3-4	Kilpatrick	15:51	Jones
1:14	Elliott		
1:15	Michaels	2 Corinthians	
1:18	Abbot	1:12	Thrall
	McReynolds	5:3	Thrall
3:25	Ross	5:10	Ross
4:51	Freed		
5:2	Hodges	Galatians	
	Jeremias	4:24-26	Kepple
	Wieand		
5:4	Fee	Ephesians	
	Hodges	1:1	Best
6:56	Ross		Black
7:53-8:11	Hodges		
	Johnson	Phillipians	
	Salvoni	1:11	Ross
	Trites		
	Wikgren	2 Timothy	
8:25	Frank	1:17	Wilhelm-
	Funk		Hooijbergh
8:39	Mees	3:2	Bevenot
10:38	Ross		
12:1	Ross	Hebrews	
		2:9	Elliott
Acts		12:3	Ellingsworth
10:30	Ross		
10:36	Riesenfeld	James	
15:14	Smothers	2	Hodges
16:12	Wikgren		
		1 Peter	
Romans		1:8	Ross
5:1	Moir	2:3	Quinn
9:5	Lattey	5:9	Quinn
	Metzger	5:14	Quinn

Index of Persons
and Subjects in Text

NOTES

NOTES

NOTES

NOTES

NOTES

NOTES

NOTES

NOTES

NOTES

NOTES

NOTES

NOTES